Vaadin 7 Cookbook

Over 90 recipes for creating Rich Internet Applications with the latest version of Vaadin

Jaroslav Holaň

Ondřej Kvasnovský

BIRMINGHAM - MUMBAI

Vaadin 7 Cookbook

First published: April 2013

Production Reference: 1120413

Published by Packt Publishing Ltd.
Livery Place
35 Livery Street
Birmingham B3 2PB, UK.
ISBN 978-1-84951-880-2

www.packtpub.com

Cover Image by Artie Ng (artherng@yahoo.com.au)

Credits

Authors
Jaroslav Holaň
Ondřej Kvasnovský

Reviewers
Martin Cremer
Risto Yrjänä
Jonatan Kronqvist
Michael Vogt

Acquisition Editor
Mary Nadar

Lead Technical Editor
Azharuddin Sheikh

Technical Editors
Veronica Fernandes
Dominic Pereira

Project Coordinators
Anish Ramchandani
Abhijit Suvarna

Proofreaders
Stephen Copestake
Mario Cecere

Indexers
Rekha Nair
Monica Ajmera Mehta

Graphics
Aditi Gajjar
Ronak Dhruv

Production Coordinator
Aparna Bhagat

Cover Work
Aparna Bhagat

About the Authors

Jaroslav Holaň is a skilled and creative Sun Certified Java Programmer. His main focus of interest is on frontend applications. He has experience with web technologies such as Vaadin, GWT, Rich Faces, JSF, and has also created desktop applications in Eclipse SWT and JFace. He has worked on various software projects, ranging from banking systems to mobile applications. He is mainly focused on Java, but is open to other languages and technologies. When he's not programming, he's dealing with magic tricks. You can find him on `http://twitter.com/JaroslavHolan`.

I would like to thank Ondrej, for his excellent cooperation on this book. His enormous enthusiasm was very motivating. I thank him that I could participate in this work. I also thank the Packt Publishing team for their patience and help with the publication of the book. Especially Mary Nadar for her help with the beginning of writing and Anish Ramchandani and Azharuddin Sheikh with the completion of the book. Also, the reviewers' comments were very helpful. Thank you all for your useful advices.

Ondřej Kvasnovský is currently working as a Senior Java Developer in pricing the business for an American company, Vendavo. Ondrej has spent six years in a large international company working mainly for the banking industry in Scandinavia as a Java Programmer, Project Manager, and Manager.

Ondrej's biggest free time interest is working on the Grails plugin for Vaadin (see `http://vaadinongrails.com`) and participation on projects using the Vaadin and Grails frameworks.

He, together with other people, is taking care of the organization of the Java User Group in Ostrava, Czech Republic.

Ondrej can be found on LinkedIn at `http://cz.linkedin.com/in/kvasnovskyondrej`, his public projects on Github can be found at `https://github.com/ondrej-kvasnovsky`, and his blog on `http://ondrej-kvasnovsky.blogspot.com`.

My biggest thanks are for my wife and son. Bara, thank you for providing me so much time for my coding adventures. Miki, thank you for showing me what is really important.

Dear editors and reviewers, you did a great job! Thank you.

About the Reviewers

Martin Cremer is working as a Software Architect for a company in the finance sector. His work focuses on maintaining and developing reference architecture for web-based enterprise applications with Vaadin as well as supporting developers in their daily work.

Born in the eighties, he grew up with the Internet and started exploring its possibilities very early. It was a short step from building static websites to first dynamic web applications. Within about a decade of experience on web development, he worked as a freelance web developer for an agency and later independently, learned application development, studied business information technology and worked as application developer and software architect.

Risto Yrjänä has several years of experience working as a Vaadin Expert at Vaadin. His interests cover UI-design, web technologies, and functional programming.

Jonatan Kronqvist, M.Sc., has been working at Vaadin Ltd, the company behind the Vaadin framework, since 2006. During this time, he has been a Vaadin consultant, a Project Manager, and a core developer of the Vaadin framework. Currently he spends his time focusing on add-ons and tools for easing development with Vaadin.

Before going fulltime on Vaadin, he worked on many different projects ranging from advanced 3D graphics at a CAD software company to leading the development of a popular computer game for children.

I'd like to thank my family and my employer, Vaadin Ltd, for giving me the time needed to make this possible.

Michael Vogt started as a WebObjects developer in the year 2000 at Apple Germany . Since then, he has worked in many different companies and countries, mostly as a freelancer on GWT projects. Currently he works in the services department of Vaadin.

www.PacktPub.com

Support files, eBooks, discount offers and more

You might want to visit www.PacktPub.com for support files and downloads related to your book.

Did you know that Packt offers eBook versions of every book published, with PDF and ePub files available? You can upgrade to the eBook version at www.PacktPub.com and as a print book customer, you are entitled to a discount on the eBook copy. Get in touch with us at service@packtpub.com for more details.

At www.PacktPub.com, you can also read a collection of free technical articles, sign up for a range of free newsletters and receive exclusive discounts and offers on Packt books and eBooks.

http://PacktLib.PacktPub.com

Do you need instant solutions to your IT questions? PacktLib is Packt's online digital book library. Here, you can access, read and search across Packt's entire library of books.

Why Subscribe?

- Fully searchable across every book published by Packt
- Copy and paste, print and bookmark content
- On demand and accessible via web browser

Free Access for Packt account holders

If you have an account with Packt at www.PacktPub.com, you can use this to access PacktLib today and view nine entirely free books. Simply use your login credentials for immediate access.

Table of Contents

Preface

It is really expensive and demanding to develop Rich Internet Applications from scratch. Vaadin is an amazing framework that contains many ready-made components for the creation of user interfaces. Applications created in Vaadin are compatible with all the latest versions of web browsers. Although the screenshots in this book are from Chrome, examples can also run on other browsers such as Firefox Mozilla, Internet Explorer, and Opera.

The *Vaadin 7 Cookbook* contains many practical recipes that we have gathered during the development of Vaadin applications. This book will help you to take your learning experience to the next level by providing you with many solutions to the commonly-faced problems along with explanations. There is even more than that. This book goes beyond the basics and shows you how to build Vaadin applications for real-world scenarios.

The *Vaadin 7 Cookbook* starts with the creation of a project in various tools and languages then moves to components, layouting, events, data binding, and custom widgets. Vaadin, together with Grails, is a powerful tool for the rapid development of RIA applications. This is described in the chapter on how to work with GORM. The quality and stability of the application, testing the Vaadin code, and the data management of Vaadin is also explained in detail.

This book is focused on learning and understanding how to work with Vaadin as well as trying out Vaadin with other technologies such as Grails.

What this book covers

Chapter 1, Creating a Project in Vaadin, shows how to create projects that support three languages—Java, Groovy, and Scala.

Chapter 2, Layouts, is about the practical concepts of layouts in the Vaadin framework. It describes controlling components using the CSS layout, aligning components on the page, creating bookmark-able applications, dragging and dropping between different layouts, and building any layout with `AbsoluteLayout`.

Chapter 3, UI Components, describes how to use server-side components such as `ListSelect`, `Slider`, the very useful `Table` component, and more. We will learn how to visualize data using the Flot chart and Highcharts libraries. We will also describe how to drag-and-drop components.

Chapter 4, Custom Widgets, describes how to create client-side widgets. We will show you how to extend text field widgets from the GWT library. We will learn how to use listeners on the GWT widgets, how to share state between widgets and components, and how to call native JavaScript.

Chapter 5, Events, describes using the events and listeners on the Vaadin components. We will learn how to react on the mouse click and the double click. It also describes using actions that can be grouped in the context menu. We will also learn how to use two different ways to handle server-push events.

Chapter 6, Messages, helps you with the implementation of validation errors, tool tips, component inside a pop-up view, confirmation window, or how to work with progress bars.

Chapter 7, Working with Forms, describes the creation of various forms with different fields. We will learn how to generate fields from a Java bean, how to validate the user's input, and how to filter items using the `ComboBox` component.

Chapter 8, Spring and Grails Integration, helps you with the integration of Spring into a Vaadin application. It also shows how to build Vaadin applications inside the Grails project.

Chapter 9, Data Management, helps us to understand the concept of the Vaadin Data Model that consists of three levels: Property, Item, and Container. It also describes filtering data in the table—using a new function called `Converters`—and storing data in the cookies.

Chapter 10, Architecture and Performance, describes ways and benefits coming from building Vaadin application with the Model View Presenter design pattern. We will see how to improve the performance of Vaadin applications and how to make Vaadin applications visible for search engines.

Chapter 11, Facilitating Development, shows you how to build Vaadin applications with a test-driven approach and how to create tests with TestBench. It also shows tips for tackling widgetset complications in Maven, how to auto-reload changes in code, and how to block uncatchable exceptions in the production mode.

Chapter 12, Fun, describes three fun-oriented recipes. In this chapter, we will put to use everything we have learned in the previous recipes. We will also learn how to use the PlayingCards add-on and also learn to alert the user before closing the web page.

What you need for this book

Vaadin 7: `https://vaadin.com/download`

One of these IDEs:

- Eclipse IDE for Java EE Developers: `http://www.eclipse.org/downloads`
- IntelliJ IDEA Ultimate Edition: `http://www.jetbrains.com/idea/download/index.html`

Any web browser, for example:

- Chrome: `www.google.com/chrome`
- Firefox: `http://www.mozilla.org/en-US/firefox/new`

The Java programming language:

- Java 7, but it can also work in Java 6: `http://www.oracle.com/technetwork/java/javase/downloads`
- In some recipes, these languages are also used:
  - Groovy: `http://groovy.codehaus.org`
  - Scala: `http://www.scala-lang.org`

Other technologies used in some recipes:

- Groovy/Grails Tool Suite: `http://www.springsource.org/downloads/sts-ggts`
- Gradle: `http://www.gradle.org/downloads`
- Maven 3: `http://maven.apache.org`
- Grails 2.1.0: `http://grails.org/download`
- The TestBench plugin in Firefox: `https://vaadin.com/directory#addon/vaadin-testbench`

Who this book is for

This book is for developers who want to create Rich Internet Applications with Vaadin.

Both newcomers to Vaadin and those who have some experience with it will find recipes to expand their working knowledge of Vaadin.

Conventions

In this book, you will find a number of styles of text that distinguish between different kinds of information. Here are some examples of these styles, and an explanation of their meaning.

Code words in text, database table names, folder names, filenames, file extensions, pathnames, dummy URLs, user input, and Twitter handles are shown as follows: "Now we can try to change the code inside the `HellovaadinUI` class, so the application prints out the name of the system user."

A block of code is set as follows:

```
<?xml version="1.0" encoding="UTF-8"?>
<web-app xmlns:xsi="http://www.w3.org/2001/XMLSchema-instance"
xmlns="http://java.sun.com/xml/ns/javaee" xmlns:web="http://java.sun.
com/xml/ns/javaee/web-app_2_5.xsd" xsi:schemaLocation="http://java.
sun.com/xml/ns/javaee http://java.sun.com/xml/ns/javaee/web-app_2_5.
xsd" id="WebApp_ID" version="2.5">
    <display-name>Vaadin Web Application</display-name>
    <context-param>
        <description>Vaadin production mode</description>
        <param-name>productionMode</param-name>
        <param-value>false</param-value>
    </context-param>
    <servlet>
     <servlet-name>Vaadin Application Servlet</servlet-name>
     <servlet-class>com.vaadin.server.VaadinServlet</servlet-class>
     <init-param>
        <description>Vaadin UI to display</description>
        <param-name>UI</param-name>
        <param-value>app.MyVaadinUI</param-value>
     </init-param>
    </servlet>
    <servlet-mapping>
      <servlet-name>Vaadin Application Servlet</servlet-name>
      <url-pattern>/*</url-pattern>
    </servlet-mapping>
</web-app>
```

New terms and **important words** are shown in bold. Words that you see on the screen, in menus or dialog boxes for example, appear in the text like this: "There should be a few Vaadin wizards listed. Choose **Vaadin 7 Project** and click on the **Next** button."

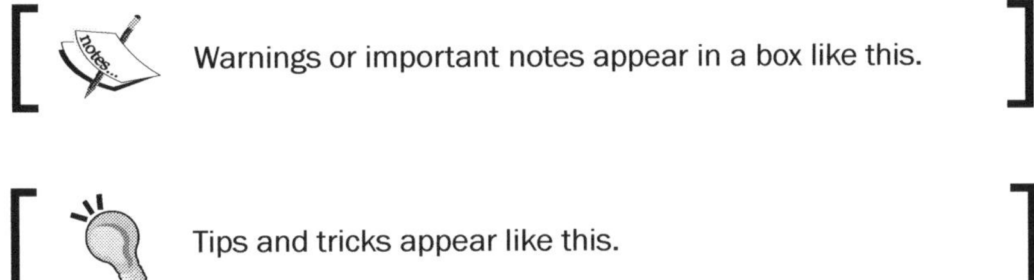

[Warnings or important notes appear in a box like this.]

[Tips and tricks appear like this.]

Reader feedback

Feedback from our readers is always welcome. Let us know what you think about this book—what you liked or may have disliked. Reader feedback is important for us to develop titles that you really get the most out of.

To send us general feedback, simply send an e-mail to `feedback@packtpub.com`, and mention the book title via the subject of your message.

If there is a topic that you have expertise in and you are interested in either writing or contributing to a book, see our author guide on `www.packtpub.com/authors`.

Customer support

Now that you are the proud owner of a Packt book, we have a number of things to help you to get the most from your purchase.

Downloading the example code

You can download the example code files for all Packt books you have purchased from your account at `http://www.packtpub.com`. If you purchased this book elsewhere, you can visit `http://www.packtpub.com/support` and register to have the files e-mailed directly to you.

Errata

Although we have taken every care to ensure the accuracy of our content, mistakes do happen. If you find a mistake in one of our books—maybe a mistake in the text or the code—we would be grateful if you would report this to us. By doing so, you can save other readers from frustration and help us improve subsequent versions of this book. If you find any errata, please report them by visiting `http://www.packtpub.com/submit-errata`, selecting your book, clicking on the **errata submission form** link, and entering the details of your errata. Once your errata are verified, your submission will be accepted and the errata will be uploaded on our website, or added to any list of existing errata, under the Errata section of that title. Any existing errata can be viewed by selecting your title from `http://www.packtpub.com/support`.

Piracy

Piracy of copyright material on the Internet is an ongoing problem across all media. At Packt, we take the protection of our copyright and licenses very seriously. If you come across any illegal copies of our works, in any form, on the Internet, please provide us with the location address or website name immediately so that we can pursue a remedy.

Please contact us at `copyright@packtpub.com` with a link to the suspected pirated material.

We appreciate your help in protecting our authors, and our ability to bring you valuable content.

Questions

You can contact us at `questions@packtpub.com` if you are having a problem with any aspect of the book, and we will do our best to address it.

1

Creating a Project in Vaadin

In this chapter, we will cover:

- Creating a project in Eclipse IDE
- Generating a Vaadin project in Maven archetype
- Building a Vaadin application with Gradle
- Using Vaadin with Scala
- Running Vaadin on Grails

Introduction

Before we start coding, we need a project. Vaadin projects can be created in many ways using several tools and languages.

In this chapter, we will show how to make projects that support three languages: Java, Groovy, and Scala.

First, we will make a simple Java project in Eclipse. Then, we will continue in a more sophisticated way and make a Vaadin application by using Maven and Gradle. Maven is a tool providing a better build process and it uses XML for the description of project, definition of dependencies, plugins, and so on. While Gradle is the next generation of build tools. Gradle combines both Maven and Ant, taking the best from both tools. Maybe the most exciting thing about Gradle is that it is uses Groovy instead of XML.

After we know how to make the project from Maven archetype, we will make the same project in IntelliJ IDEA.

Scala is a programming language that integrates features of object-oriented and functional languages. The server-side part of Vaadin runs on JVM and therefore we can write Vaadin applications in Scala language.

Grails is a web application framework that takes advantage of the Groovy language. Grails follows the *convention over configuration* principle. When we make a new Grails project, we automatically get a persistent model, service, controller and view layers, environments, and localization. We will have a look at how to create a new Grails project and how to use Vaadin instead of a Grails view layer.

Creating a project in Eclipse IDE

In this recipe, we are going to create a new Vaadin project in the Eclipse IDE.

Getting ready

Download and install the latest version from the Eclipse download page (specifically **Eclipse IDE for Java EE Developers**), `http://www.eclipse.org/downloads`.

There is an Eclipse extension for Vaadin, which helps us with the creation of Vaadin projects, widget set compilation, and so on. The instructions on how to install the extension are at `http://vaadin.com/eclipse`.

How to do it...

Carry out the following steps in order to create a new project in Eclipse IDE:

1. Open the **New Project** window and search for `vaadin`.

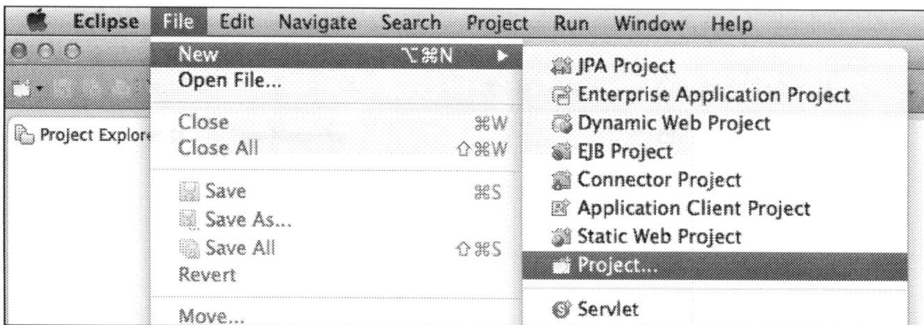

2. There should be a few Vaadin wizards listed. Choose **Vaadin 7 Project** and click on the **Next** button.

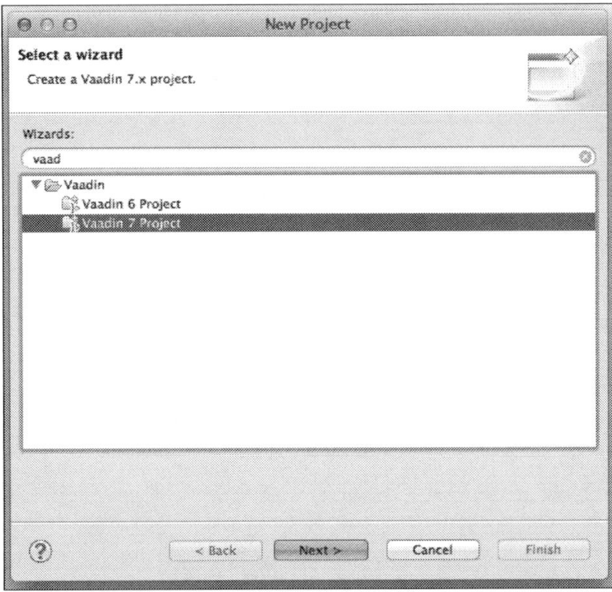

3. Fill in the name of the project. Select **Apache Tomcat v7.0** as **Target runtime** and click on the **Finish** button.

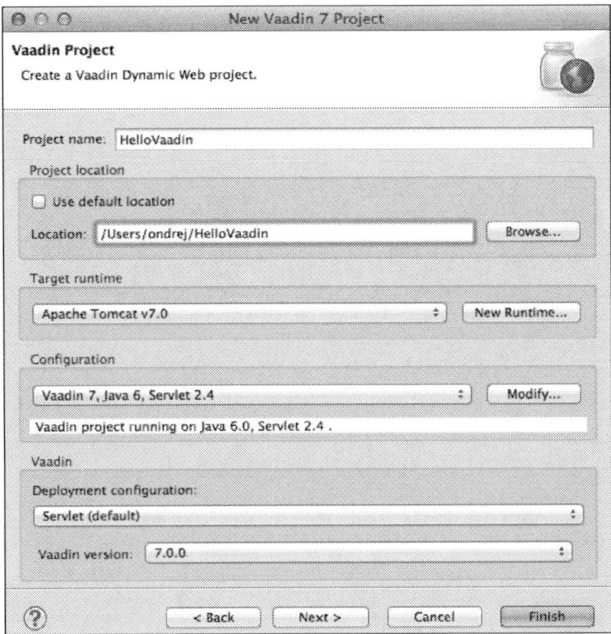

4. Eclipse makes a `Hello world` application for us. All the application code has been placed in the `HellovaadinUI` class. Now we can run the project. Right-click on the name of the project, go to **Run As**, and then click on **Run on Server**. Choose **Apache Tomcat v7.0** to run our application and confirm the dialog window.

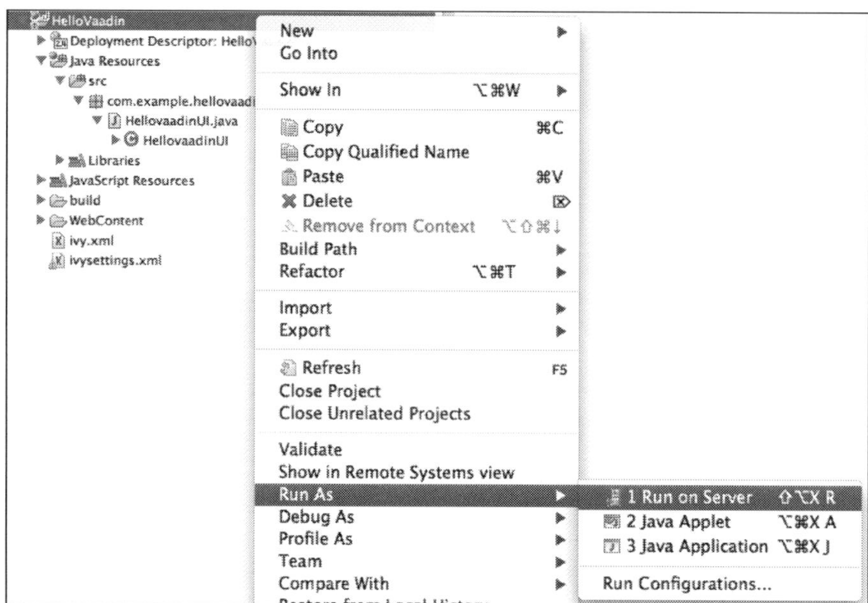

5. The application appears in the Eclipse's **Internal Web Browser** or we can open the started application in our favorite browser: `http://localhost:8080/HelloVaadin`.

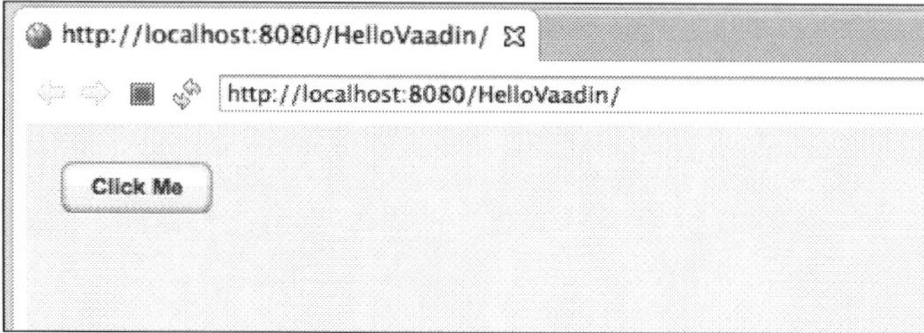

How it works...

Let's have a look at what has been generated by Eclipse.

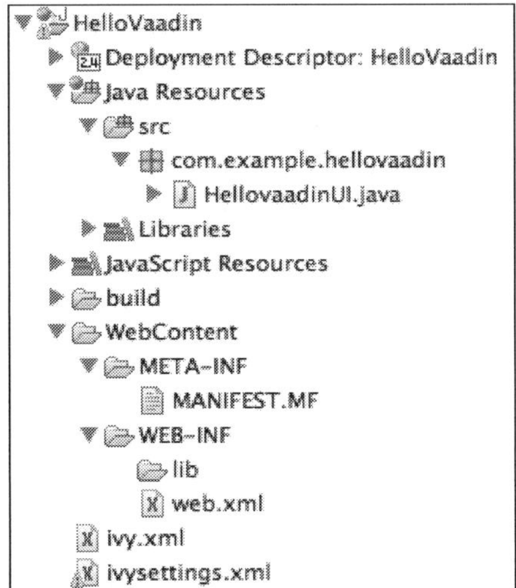

The following table explains the content of the important directories:

Directory / Project Item	Description
`Deployment Descriptor`	Is not a real directory but it offers a user-friendly way to edit the `web.xml` file.
`Java Resources/src`	Contains the entire project's Java source code.
`WebContent`	Contains deployment descriptor file `web.xml`. We can also place here static resources such as images, CSS, or JavaScript files. In this folder we can make a `VAADIN` directory for the new themes.
`build`	Is used to store compiled classes.

> `web.xml` must contain the definition of the UI class, servlet, and URL mapping. It must be located inside the `WEB-INF` folder.

There's more...

Now we can try to change the code inside the `HellovaadinUI` class, so the application prints out the name of the system user.

```
String user = System.getProperty("user.name");
Label label = new Label("Hello Vaadin user: " + user);
layout.addComponent(label);
```

Notice we can see the changes in code without restarting the application server. The project is recompiled after we save a file and changes are visible in the browser right away.

We need to add the `?restartApplication` parameter into the URL when running a Vaadin application with the `@PreserveOnRefresh` annotation on our UI class.

Generating a Vaadin project in Maven archetype

Maven makes the build process really easy. Let's see how easy it is to make a new Vaadin project using Maven. We will use the latest version, Maven 3, which can be downloaded from `http://maven.apache.org/download.html`.

We are going to use the command line in this recipe. We will make the project in the command prompt and then we can import the Maven project into whatever IDE that supports Maven (Eclipse, IntelliJ IDEA, and so on).

Using Maven archetypes is quite handy and a quick way to create a new project. Let's try to make a new Vaadin project using the `vaadin-archetype-application` archetype.

For those who are new to Maven, please learn the basics from the following web page:

`http://maven.apache.org/guides/getting-started/maven-in-five-minutes.html`

How to do it...

Carry out the following steps in order to create a new project in Maven:

1. Open the command prompt and check whether Maven is installed properly. The version of Maven should be displayed. If not, then search the Web for how to install Maven 3 on your operating system.

   ```
   $ mvn --version
   ```

```
Apache Maven 3.0.4
Maven home: /usr/share/maven
```

2. Decide where to put your project and run the following command. It will create a new folder called `vaadin-in-maven-arch` with a sample Vaadin project using the Maven file structure.

```
mvn archetype:generate \
 -DarchetypeGroupId=com.vaadin \
 -DarchetypeArtifactId=vaadin-archetype-application \
 -DarchetypeVersion=LATEST \
 -Dpackaging=war \
 -DgroupId=app \
 -DartifactId=vaadin-in-maven-arch \
 -Dversion=1.0
```

3. Maven asks for confirmation of whether to create the project. Type `y` into the console. Maven will show its `BUILD SUCCESS` message after the project is created.

```
Confirm properties configuration:
groupId: app
artifactId: vaadin-in-maven-arch
version: 1.0
package: app
 Y: : y
```

4. Run the `package` Maven target in order to pack the application as a WAR file and compile the widget set. Run the following command in the root of the project.

```
mvn package
```

5. We are done and we can run our new web application. Go to the root of the project where `pom.xml` file is located and run the following command.

```
mvn jetty:start
```

The application will be running on `http://localhost:8080`.

We are using Jetty, which is open source and a commercially usable web server. Jetty is great for development because it starts really fast.

How it works...

We have made a new Vaadin application from the Maven archetype and all the content needed for running the application was generated for us.

Let's have a look at the folder structure in the project.

Directory / Project Item	Description
pom.xml	Is a Maven configuration file. POM stands for Project Object Model.
src/main/java	Contains the entire project's Java source code.
src/main/webapp/WEB-INF	Contains web.xml, the deployment descriptor.
src/main/webapp/VAADIN	Contains a compiled widget set and can contain new Vaadin themes.
target	Used to place the output from compilation.

Maven archetype could be described as a project template. We can create our own archetypes by running the following command inside the Maven project:

mvn archetype:generate

There's more...

We can configure auto-redeploys in Jetty. The scanning interval can be set to, for example, 2 seconds. After we recompile the code, Jetty redeploys the application so we don't have to stop and start the application server after each change in the code. The following change needs to be made in the pom.xml file:

```
<scanIntervalSeconds>2</scanIntervalSeconds>
```

More about the Jetty plugin can be found on the following link:

http://docs.codehaus.org/display/JETTY/Maven+Jetty+Plugin

Building a Vaadin application with Gradle

Gradle is the next generation of builds tools. It helps with building, publishing, deploying, and actually any other task which should be automated.

Gradle build scripts are written in Groovy, which makes this build tool really straightforward and easy to use. In this recipe, we are going to use the Groovy language.

We will use the Gradle plugin for Vaadin, which makes the development of Vaadin applications in Groovy really luxurious.

Getting ready

Let's install Gradle before we start from `http://gradle.org/installation`.

Create a new directory where we will place the new project:

```
mkdir vaadin-in-gradle
```

How to do it...

Carry out the following steps in order to create a new project in Gradle:

1. Create a file `build.gradle` in the project root. It is going to be just one line that is necessary for running the project.

   ```
   apply from: 'http://plugins.jasoft.fi/vaadin.plugin'
   ```

2. Run the `createVaadinProject` target and fill in the name of the application and package. Alternatively, just press the *Enter* key twice and let the plugin create the default application inside the default package.

   ```
   gradle createVaadinProject
   ```

3. Run target `vaadinRun`, which starts up the embedded Jetty web server, and the application will be deployed.

   ```
   gradle vaadinRun
   ```

   The URL of the web server is printed out in the console as follows:

   ```
   :themes
   :compileJava
   :processResources UP-TO-DATE
   :classes
   :widgetset
   :vaadinRun
   Application running on http://0.0.0.0:8080 (debugger on 8000)
   > Building > :vaadinRun
   ```

How it works...

Gradle is following the *convention over configuration* paradigm and that is why Gradle build scripts are so minimalistic. For example, the default source folder for Groovy files is `src/main/groovy` and we can change it by the following code that we place inside the build script `build.gradle`.

```
sourceSets {
  main {
    groovy {
      srcDirs = ['src/groovy']
    }
  }
}
```

The next valuable thing about Gradle is good documentation:

http://www.gradle.org/docs/current/userguide/userguide_single.html

Let's have a bit more detailed look at what the Gradle plugin for Vaadin did for us.

When we run the `createVaadinProject` target, the plugin creates two files. `MyApplication.groovy` inside `com.example.myapplication` package and `web.xml` in `src/main/webapp/WEB-INF` folder.

Directory / Project Item	Description
`build.gradle`	Gradle build script.
`src/main/groovy`	Contains Groovy source code.
`src/main/webapp/`	Contains `WEB-INF/web.xml`, the deployment descriptor.

The plugin also defines the `vaadinRun` target that starts up the Jetty web server and deploys the application.

There's more...

There are other targets such as `createVaadinTheme`, `devmode`, `widgetset`, and more in the Vaadin plugin. All these, and more information about the plugin configuration, can be found on the GitHub page:

https://github.com/johndevs/gradle-vaadin-plugin

Using Vaadin with Scala

Scala is a multi-paradigm language integrating object-oriented and functional programming. Read more about Scala on `http://www.scala-lang.org`.

Getting ready

Scala installation is quite easy. Just go to `http://www.scala-lang.org/downloads`, download Scala, and set up system variables as follows:

- Linux/Mac

  ```
  SCALA_HOME=/Users/John/Installations/scala
  export SCALA_HOME
  export PATH=$PATH:$SCALA_HOME/bin
  ```

- Windows

  ```
  %SCALA_HOME% = c:\Scala
  %PATH% = %PATH%;%SCALA_HOME%\bin
  ```

We have to maintain our project anyhow and we are going to utilize Gradle.

There is also another way to manage Scala projects. It is called Typesafe and more info is on `http://typesafe.com`.

How to do it...

Carry out the following steps in order to create a new Scala project:

1. Make the project structure so we have folders where we can put our project files.

   ```
   mkdir -p vaadin-in-scala/src/main/{scala/app,webapp/WEB-INF}
   ```

2. Make `build.gradle` in the project root. It is going to be just a few lines that are necessary for running the project.

   ```
   apply plugin: 'war'
   apply plugin: 'jetty'
   apply plugin: 'scala'

   repositories {
     mavenCentral()
   ```

```
}

dependencies {
  scalaTools 'org.scala-lang:scala-compiler:2.10.0'
  scalaTools 'org.scala-lang:scala-library:2.10.0'
  compile 'org.scala-lang:scala-library:2.10.0'
  compile group:'com.vaadin', name:'vaadin-server',
   version:'7.0.4'
  compile group:'com.vaadin', name:'vaadin-client',
   version:'7.0.4'
  compile group:'com.vaadin', name:'vaadin-client-compiled',
   version:'7.0.4'
  compile group:'com.vaadin', name:'vaadin-themes',
   version:'7.0.4'
  compile group:'com.vaadin', name:'vaadin-client-compiler',
   version:'7.0.4'
}
```

3. Create a new Scala class `MyVaadinUI` that we place into the `MyVaadinUI.scala` file in the folder `src/main/scala/app`.

```
package app

import com.vaadin.ui._
import com.vaadin.server.VaadinRequest

class MyVaadinUI extends UI {
  def init(request: VaadinRequest) = {
    val layout = new VerticalLayout()
    layout.setMargin(true)
    setContent(layout)
    layout.addComponent(new Label("Hello Vaadin user."))
    }
}
```

4. Add the `web.xml` file to the `src/main/webapp/WEB-INF` folder.

```
<?xml version="1.0" encoding="UTF-8"?>
<web-app xmlns:xsi="http://www.w3.org/2001/XMLSchema-instance"
xmlns="http://java.sun.com/xml/ns/javaee" xmlns:web="http://java.
sun.com/xml/ns/javaee/web-app_2_5.xsd" xsi:schemaLocation="http://
java.sun.com/xml/ns/javaee http://java.sun.com/xml/ns/javaee/web-
app_2_5.xsd" id="WebApp_ID" version="2.5">
  <display-name>Vaadin Web Application</display-name>
  <context-param>
```

```
    <description>Vaadin production mode</description>
    <param-name>productionMode</param-name>
    <param-value>false</param-value>
  </context-param>
  <servlet>
    <servlet-name>Vaadin Application Servlet</servlet-name>
    <servlet-class>com.vaadin.server.VaadinServlet</servlet-class>
    <init-param>
      <description>Vaadin UI to display</description>
      <param-name>UI</param-name>
      <param-value>app.MyVaadinUI</param-value>
    </init-param>
  </servlet>
  <servlet-mapping>
    <servlet-name>Vaadin Application Servlet</servlet-name>
    <url-pattern>/*</url-pattern>
  </servlet-mapping>
</web-app>
```

5. We are done and we can run the application.

   ```
   gradle jettyRun
   ```

   The following output should be displayed:

   ```
   :compileJava UP-TO-DATE
   :compileScala UP-TO-DATE
   :processResources UP-TO-DATE
   :classes UP-TO-DATE
   > Building > :jettyRun > Running at http://localhost:8080/vaadin-in-scala
   ```

Downloading the example code

You can download the example code files for all Packt books you have purchased from your account at `http://www.packtpub.com`. If you purchased this book elsewhere, you can visit `http://www.packtpub.com/support` and register to have the files e-mailed directly to you.

How it works...

We have made a Gradle project in which we have applied the `scala` plugin. The Scala plugin inside the Gradle build script ensures that all the `.scala` files inside the `src/main/scala` source folder will be compiled. Scala files are compiled to `.class` files that are then deployed on the Jetty web server.

The deployment descriptor (`web.xml` file) defines one servlet. When users access the URL with the `/*` pattern, which is mapped to the Vaadin servlet, `MyVaadinUI` is shown in the browser.

The important thing we need to check is the `init-param` element of the Vaadin servlet. It needs to point exactly to the UI class, which represents our application. The path to the UI class must be the full name of the class together with the package, for example, `app.MyVaadinUI`.

See also

- Scaladin is a Vaadin add-on that makes using Vaadin with the Scala language easier. More information can be found on the Scaladin add-on page at `https://vaadin.com/directory#addon/scaladin`.

Running Vaadin on Grails

Grails is a web application framework, which uses the Groovy language, following the *coding by convention* paradigm. All the information about Grails can be found at the following link:

`http://grails.org`

The Grails plugin called `vaadin` integrates Vaadin into the Grails project. Therefore, we can use Vaadin as a replacement for the Grails view layer. Instead of writing HTML, CSS, and JavaScript, we make Vaadin view in Groovy. More information about the Vaadin integration is available at the following web page:

`http://vaadinongrails.com`

We are going to make a simple Vaadin application that will be running on Grails and written in Groovy.

Getting ready

Install the Eclipse Groovy/Grails Tool Suite (GGTS). download link is available at the Grails pages at `http://grails.org/products/ggts`.

If you are running on Windows, then install GGTS to a folder that does not contain white spaces (for example, `C:\EclipseSTS`).

How to do it...

Carry out the following steps in order to create a new Grails project with Vaadin:

1. Open **File** | **New** | **Grails Project**.

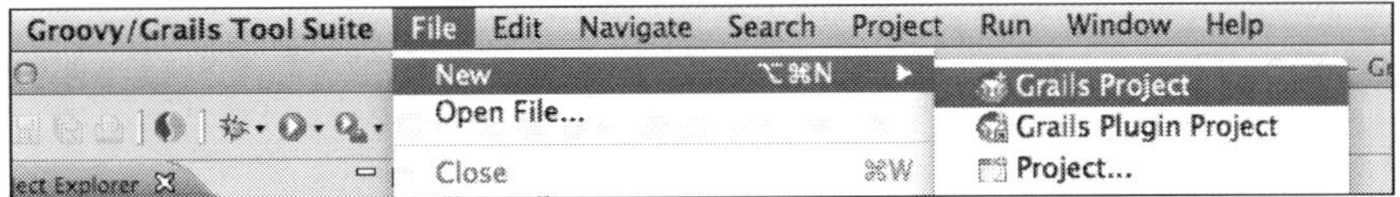

2. Fill in the name of the project and finish the **New Grails Project** wizard.

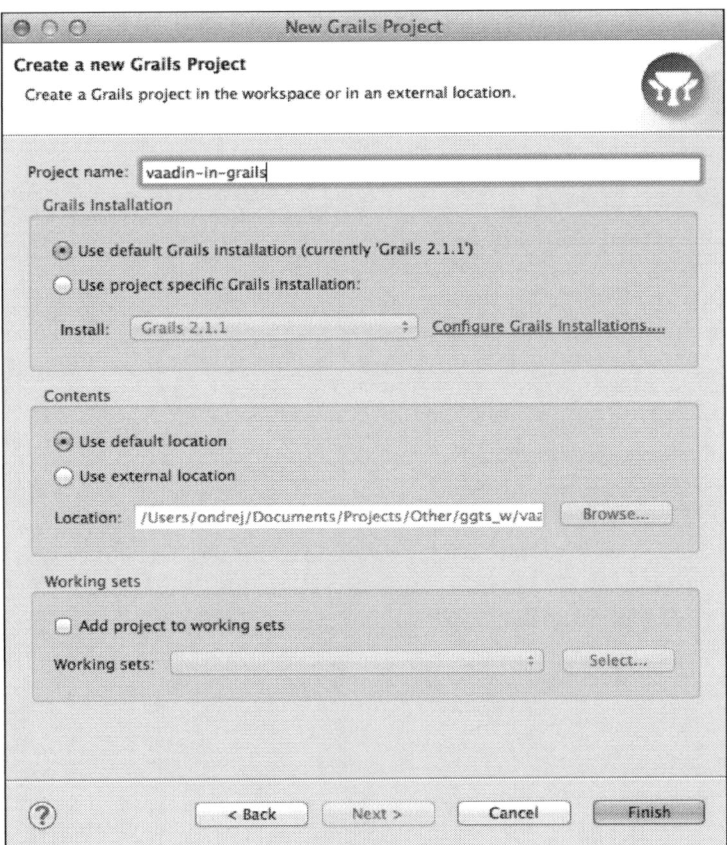

3. Click on the Grails icon, which opens the console that we use for running the Grails command. In this step, we just want to make sure the project is created properly. Run the `run-app` command.

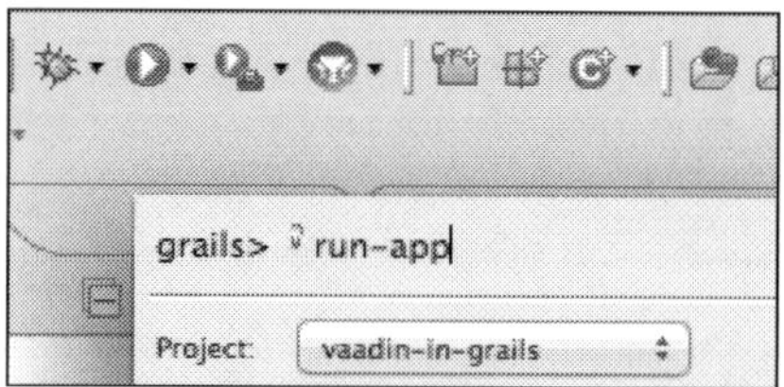

4. The Grails application is opened up in the browser window using `http://localhost:8080/vaadin-in-grails`. It still uses `.gsp` files, which we replace with Vaadin in the next step.

5. Install the Vaadin plugin. Open up the Grails console and run the following command:

```
install-plugin vaadin
```

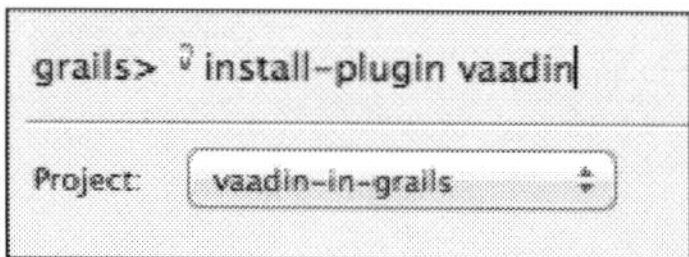

6. Mark the `grails-app/vaadin` folder as the source folder.

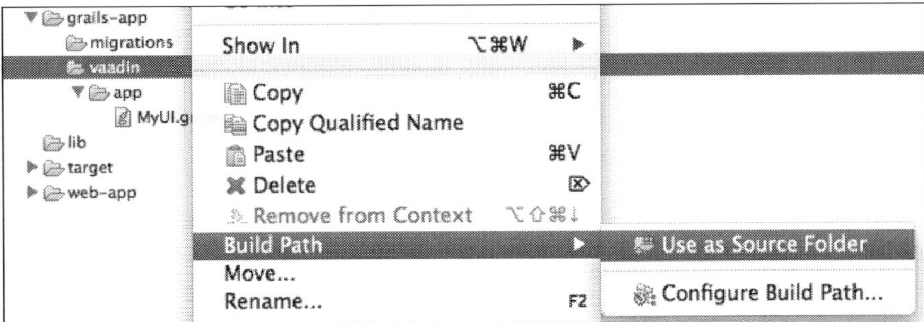

7. Run the application again and open `http://localhost:8080/vaadin-in-grails` in the browser. Vaadin has replaced the Grails view.

How it works...

We have made a Grails project where we have replaced the Grails view layer with a Vaadin framework. The integration between Grails and Vaadin is done by the Grails plugin that is connecting these two frameworks. As you have experienced, the Vaadin plugin is available via the Grails plugin system (`http://grails.org/plugin/vaadin`).

Let's have a close look at what the Vaadin plugin has generated for us.

The `MyUI.groovy` file has been generated inside the `grails-app/vaadin` source folder. `MyUI` represents the Vaadin user interface, which is shown to the user in the browser window.

```
package app

import com.vaadin.ui.UI
import com.vaadin.ui.VerticalLayout
import com.vaadin.server.VaadinRequest
import com.vaadin.ui.Label
import com.vaadin.grails.Grails

class MyUI extends UI {
```

```
    @Override
    protected void init(VaadinRequest vaadinRequest) {
      VerticalLayout layout = new VerticalLayout()
      String homeLabel = Grails.i18n("default.home.label")
      Label label = new Label(homeLabel)
      layout.addComponent(label)
      setContent(layout)
    }
  }
```

We should store all the Vaadin code we create inside the `grails-app/vaadin` source folder.

The Vaadin plugin needs to have information about the location of the `MyUI` class in order to add that information to the `web.xml` deployment descriptor. Therefore, a new file `VaadinConfig.groovy` has been generated inside the `grail-app/conf` folder.

```
vaadin {
  mapping = [ "/*": "app.MyUI" ]
  productionMode = false
}

environments {
  production {
    vaadin {
      productionMode = true
    }
  }
}
```

In `VaadinConfig.groovy`, we can change the path to the UI class. We can also add more UI classes.

```
vaadin {
  mapping = [ "/*": "app.MyUI", "/ui/*": "app.YourUI" ]
```

The last thing which has been done during the plugin installation is the removal of the URL mapping inside the `UrlMappings.groovy` file.

> If we make changes in the code, then the code is recompiled and we don't have to restart the server (just refresh the web page).
>
> Changes on class level (for example, a change of parent class) are not recompiled and we have to restart the application.

See also

- More about Grails can be learned from the manual at `http://grails.org/doc/latest`
- We will explore Grails and Vaadin integration in *Chapter 8, Spring and Grails Integration*

2
Layouts

In this chapter, we will cover:

- Creating an adjustable layout using split panels
- Creating a custom layout
- Controlling components over the CSS layout
- Using CSS layouts for mobile devices
- Binding tabs with a hard URL
- Using Navigator for creating bookmarkable applications with back-forward button support
- Aligning components on a page
- Creating UI collection of components
- Dragging-and-dropping between different layouts
- Building any layout with AbsoluteLayout

Introduction

Layout management in Vaadin is a direct successor of the web-based concept for separation of content and appearance, and of the Java Abstract Windowing Toolkit (AWT) solution for binding the layout and user interface components into objects in programs. Vaadin layout components allow us to position our UI components on the screen in a hierarchical fashion, much as in conventional Java UI toolkits such as AWT, Swing, or SWT (Standard Widget Toolkit). This chapter describes a few of the practical concepts in the Vaadin framework. Layouting is comprehensive and could be published in a separate book. A lot of technical details are described in the Vaadin book on the web page: `https://vaadin.com/book/vaadin7/-/page/layout.html`.

Creating an adjustable layout using split panels

In a more complex layout, it is better to let the user adjust it. If we want to use a more flexible layout, we can use split panels. This recipe is about creating a complex layout with different components, for example, menu, editor, properties view, and **Help** view.

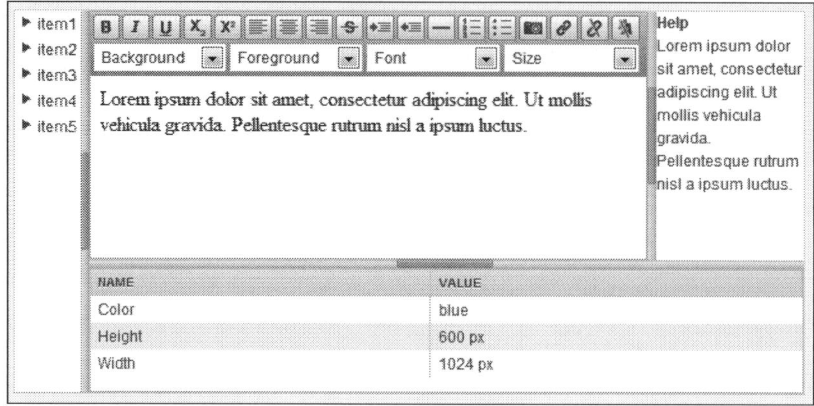

How to do it...

Carry out the following steps to create an adjustable layout:

1. We create a simple Vaadin project with the main UI class called, for example, `Demo`:

   ```
   public class Demo extends UI {…}
   ```

2. Our application will be based on split panels. As a main panel, we use `HorizontaSplitPanel`. This panel is divided into two areas. The first is on the left side, the second is on right the side.

   ```
   public class AdjustableLayout extends HorizontalSplitPanel {…}
   ```

3. In the constructor, we set the properties of this main panel. On the left side we insert the main menu, on the right side we insert the other content. The left area will take 10 percent of the whole panel. And with the `setSizeFull()` method, we set height and width to 100 percent of the window.

   ```
   public AdjustableLayout() {
     setFirstComponent(createMenu());
     setSecondComponent(createContentPanel());
     setSplitPosition(10, Unit.PERCENTAGE);
     setSizeFull();
    }
   ```

4. Now, we can continue with the `createMenu()` method. For our example, we will just create a simple menu based on `Tree`. This menu does not have any special logic. We need it only to fill the space.

```
private Tree createMenu() {
  Tree menu = new Tree();
  for (int i = 1; i < 6; i++) {
    String item = "item" + i;
    String childItem = "subitem" + i;
    menu.addItem(item);
    menu.addItem(childItem);
    menu.setParent(childItem, item);
    menu.setChildrenAllowed(childItem, false);
  }
  return menu;
}
```

5. In the `createContentPanel()` method, we will add other split panels. This time it is `VerticalSplitPanel`. The first area is on the top and the second is on the bottom of the panel. On the top we insert an editor panel and on the bottom we insert a table. For editor panel we set aside 80 percent of the area.

```
private Component createContentPanel(){
  VerticalSplitPanel contentPanel = new VerticalSplitPanel();
  contentPanel.setFirstComponent(createEditorPanel());
  contentPanel.setSecondComponent(createTable());
  contentPanel.setSplitPosition(80, Unit.PERCENTAGE);
  return contentPanel;
}
```

6. For the editor panel, we again use `HorizontalSplitPanel`. On the left side we insert a rich text area and on the right side we insert a label. Editor takes 80 percent of the panel. When we work with raw HTML code in a web application, it's important to be very sure that the HTML is safe and no malicious code is injected here. For this reason, we will use the `SafeHtml` interface. An object that implements this interface encapsulates HTML that is guaranteed to be safe to use (with respect to potential cross-site scripting vulnerabilities) in an HTML context.

```
private Component createEditorPanel() {
  SafeHtml safeHtml = SafeHtmlUtils.fromSafeConstant(
                                   "<b>Help</b> <br />" + LIPSUM);
  HorizontalSplitPanel editorPanel =
                                   new HorizontalSplitPanel();
  RichTextArea editor = new RichTextArea();
  editor.setSizeFull();
  editor.setValue(LIPSUM);
  editorPanel.setFirstComponent(editor);
```

```
    editorPanel.setSecondComponent(
      new Label(safeHtml.asString(), ContentMode.HTML));
      editorPanel.setSplitPosition(80, Unit.PERCENTAGE);
      return editorPanel;
  }
```

7. Now we need some text for the rich text and label area. We create a constant lipsum which contains a simple string of some words called Lorem Ipsum, for example, generated from `http://www.lipsum.com/`.

   ```
   private static final String LIPSUM = "Lorem ipsum dolor …";
   ```

8. We will fill the bottom of the panel with a table. In a lot of cases it can be the table of properties. The size of the table is set to full. It means that this component takes the whole area.

   ```
   private Table createTable() {
     Table table = new Table();
     table.addContainerProperty("Name", String.class, null);
     table.addContainerProperty("Value", String.class, null);
     table.addItem(new Object[] { "Color", "blue" }, null);
     table.addItem(new Object[] { "Height", "600 px" }, null);
     table.addItem(new Object[] { "Width", "1024 px" }, null);
     table.setSizeFull();
     return table;
    }
   ```

9. Now we can use our layout in the root application. We add an instance of `AdjustableLayout` to the `init()` method.

   ```
   public class Demo extends UI {
     @Override
     public void init(VaadinRequest request) {
       setContent(new AdjustableLayout());
     }
   }
   ```

How it works...

Users can adjust the layout by dragging the bar with the mouse. To disable changing the bar position, we can use the `setLocked(true)` method. With the `setSplitPosition(float position)` method, we can programmatically set the bar position. When we don't set any unit, previous unit will be used. `SplitPanel` only supports pixel or percent from the enumeration unit in the interface. This value position means how big an area the first component takes of the panel. The second area takes the rest. If we want to define primarily the size of the second area, we set the reverse parameter to `true`.

For example, take a look at the following line of code:

```
setSplitPosition(30, Unit.Pixels, true);
```

This means that second area takes 30 pixels and first takes the rest.

For setting the size, we can also use the method that takes a string, for example:

```
setWidth("25%");
```

See also

- For more information about the Application Program Interface (API) of the `VerticalSplitPanel` class, visit `https://vaadin.com/api/7.0.0/com/vaadin/ui/VerticalSplitPanel.html`
- For more information about the API of the `HorizontalSplitPanel` class visit `https://vaadin.com/api/7.0.0/com/vaadin/ui/HorizontalSplitPanel.html`
- The Developer's Guide about `SafeHtml` is available at `https://developers.google.com/web-toolkit/doc/latest/DevGuideSecuritySafeHtml`

Creating a custom layout

When we work on a complex web application, we need to cooperate with more people in the team. UX or graphic designers design layouts and for them it is more natural to design layouts using HTML and CSS. In such cases, we can use **Custom layout** that is described in the HTML template.

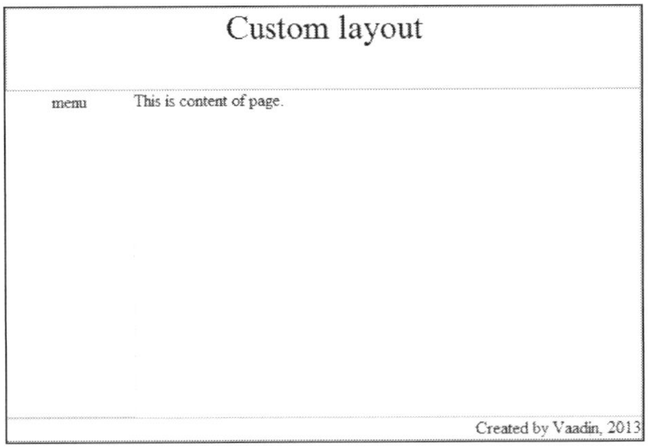

Custom layout

menu This is content of page.

Created by Vaadin, 2013

How to do it...

Carry out the following steps to create a custom layout:

1. Create a project with the main UI class, Demo.

   ```
   public class Demo extends UI {…}
   ```

2. First, we'll create an HTML template. Vaadin separates the appearance of the user interface from its logic using themes. Themes can include Sass or CSS style sheets, custom HTML layouts, and any necessary graphics. We'll call our template mylayout.html and place it under the folder layouts. In the WebContent folder we create this path of folders:

   ```
   WebContent/VAADIN/themes/mytheme/layouts
   ```

3. Next, we define our layout. By setting the location attribute in the <div> element, we mark our specific areas. These elements will be replaced by Vaadin components. On the top we will put a header. We will create one menu on the left side. We will leave the central area for some content page. At the end we will insert a page footer, for example, for a status line. The Attribute class is used for CSS styling.

   ```
   <div location="header" class="header"></div>
   <div location="menu" class="menu"></div>
   <div location="content" class="content"></div>
   <div location="footer" class="footer"></div>
   ```

4. In the next step, we create our CSS style for this layout. Under the folder mytheme we create a file styles.css.

   ```
   WebContent/VAADIN/themes/mytheme/styles.css
   ```

5. In this file, we can say how to align a component in each area, what color and size will be used, and other properties.

   ```
   .header,.menu,.footer {
     border: thin;
     border-style: solid;
     border-color: LightGrey;
   }

   .header {
     text-align: center;
     font-size: 32px;
     height: 75px;
   }
   ```

```
.menu {
  height: 300px;
  width: 20%;
  text-align: center;
  float: left;
}

.content {
  text-align: left;
}

.footer {
  text-align: right;
  clear: both;
}
```

6. Now we will create a simple Vaadin project with a main UI class called `Demo`. We will add the annotation `mytheme`, which means that we use this theme in our application. In the `init()` method, we will set `CustomLayout` as a content. Each component is added by the `addComponent()` method, where the second parameter is the location in the HTML template.

```
@Theme("mytheme")
public class Demo extends UI {
  @Override
  public void init(VaadinRequest request) {
    CustomLayout layout = new CustomLayout("mylayout");
    setContent(layout);

    Label header = new Label("Custom layout");
    header.addStyleName("header");
    layout.addComponent(header, "header");

    Label menu = new Label("menu");
    layout.addComponent(menu, "menu");

    Label content = new Label("This is content of page.");
    layout.addComponent(content, "content");

    Label footer = new Label("Created by Vaadin, 2013");
    layout.addComponent(footer, "footer");
  }
}
```

How it works...

Layout is described in the HTML template file. A template includes the `<div>` elements with a `location` attribute that defines the location identifier. The client-side engine of Vaadin will replace the contents of the location elements with the components. The components are bound to the location elements by the location identifier given to the `addComponent()` method. The template file is separate from the source code. It's placed under the `WebContent/VAADIN/themes/<nameTheme>/layouts` folder. We can set the style of the layout with the CSS file placed in `WebContent/VAADIN/themes/<nameTheme>/styles.css`.

Controlling components over the CSS layout

In some cases, we need to control the CSS style of components programmatically. For example, when we want to create a cloud of the most searched terms or tags in our application, we need to change the size of each tag according to the number of searches. We'll use the CSS layout in that case. Our tag cloud will look like the following screenshot:

How to do it...

Carry out the following steps to create a cloud of tags using the `CssLayout` class:

1. Create an application with the main UI class called, for example, `Demo`.

   ```
   public class Demo extends UI {…}
   ```

2. We need our own label with the `fontSize` variable. We create a `TagLabel` class that extends `Label`.

   ```
   public class TagLabel extends Label {…}
   ```

3. Next we add the `fontSize` attribute and the appropriate `get` method.

   ```
   private int fontSize;

   public int getFontSize() {
     return fontSize;
   }
   ```

4. In the constructor we call the parent's constructor by `super(text)` and pass the value of `fontSize`. If we want to wrap labels on the line, we have to set the `size` to `Undefined`, because the size of `Label` is naturally set to `100` percent and it won't allow wrapping label on the line.

   ```
   public TagLabel(String text, int fontSize) {
     super(text);
     this.fontSize = fontSize;
     setSizeUndefined();
   }
   ```

5. Now we create our `TagCloud` class that extends `CssLayout`.

   ```
   public class TagCloud extends CssLayout {…}
   ```

6. Main functionality is in the `getCss()` method. We override and modify it according to our needs. We control only instances of the `TagLabel` class. Here we create a different CSS style for each `TagLabel`. We set `font-size` and `line-height` according to the `fontSize` variable. We also add style `display: inline-block` which we need for wrapping the component on the line.

   ```
   @Override
   protected String getCss(Component c) {
     String css = null;
     if (c instanceof TagLabel) {
       TagLabel tag = (TagLabel)c;
       css = "font-size: " + tag.getFontSize() + "px;";
       css += "line-height: " + tag.getFontSize() + "px;";
       css += "display: inline-block;";
       css += "margin: 3px;";
     }
     return css;
   };
   ```

7. Now we can use `TagCloud` in our application in the main UI class. For creating `TagLabel`, we need two arrays. The first is for the names and the second is for the font size. We set the `width` to `150` pixels in this layout.

   ```
   @Override
   public void init(WrappedRequest request) {
     String names[] =
     {"HTML", "Java","Vaadin", "GWT", "CSS", "Javascript"};
     int fontSizes[] = {12,20,32,24,17,19};

     TagCloud tagCloud = new TagCloud();
     for (int i=0; i<names.length; i++){
       tagCloud.addComponent(new TagLabel(names[i],fontSizes[i]));
     }
   ```

```
        tagCloud.setWidth(150, Unit.PIXELS);
        setContent(tagCloud);
    }
```

That's all. We can run the server and open the application in the web browser.

How it works...

Each component inside the layout is controlled by the `getCss()` method. Here we set the style for the `TagLabel` objects. Only `font-size` and `line-height` are changed. The values of these properties are stored in the `fontSize` array that is created in the main UI class.

See also

- The API of the `CssLayout` class is available at `https://vaadin.com/api/7.0.0/com/vaadin/ui/CssLayout.html`
- Detailed information about `CssLayout` is on the Vaadin web page at `https://vaadin.com/book/vaadin7/-/page/layout.csslayout.html`

Using CSS layouts for mobile devices

Another nice feature of the CSS layout is that components are wrapped when they reach the width of the layout. This feature can be used to create layouts for small displays, for example, mobile phones or some tablets. We will create a simple layout with a header, two menus, and content in the middle of them.

As we can see in the following screenshot, if the user opens our application on a wide screen, components are displayed side by side. Except the header that takes up the whole width of the page.

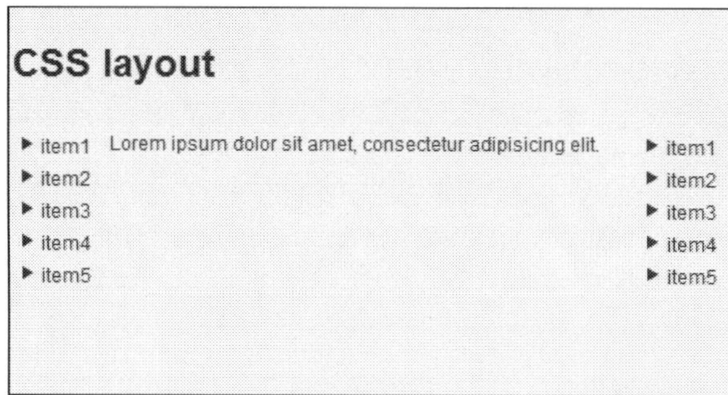

If the user opens our application on a narrow screen, for example, on a mobile device, then all components will be aligned into the one column.

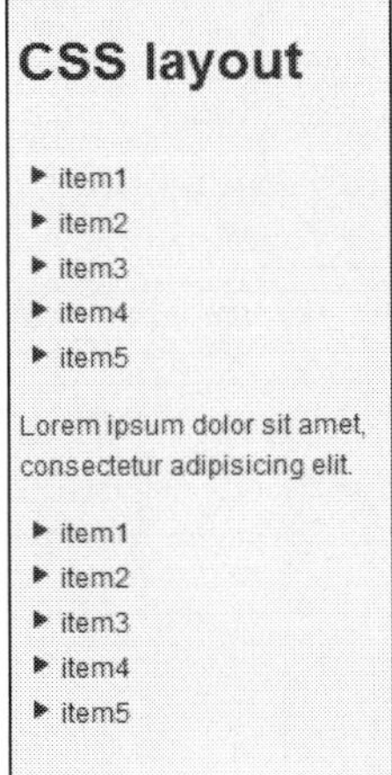

How to do it...

Carry out the following steps to create an application with a flexible layout for mobile devices:

1. Create a project with the main UI class called, for example, `Demo`.

   ```
   public class Demo extends UI {…}
   ```

2. We create a `MobileLayout` class that extends `CssLayout`.

   ```
   public class MobileLayout extends CssLayout {…}
   ```

3. At first we create a constant with Lorem Ipsum text.

   ```
   private static final String LIPSUM =
     "Lorem ipsum dolor sit amet, consectetur adipisicing elit.";
   ```

4. The key functionality is in the constructor. Here we create all the sections of the layout. On the top of the page we put the header. On the left and right sides we insert menus. In the middle will be the content of the page.

   ```
   public MobileLayout() {
     Label header =
     new Label("<h1>CSS layout</h1>", ContentMode.HTML);
     addComponent(header);

     addComponent(createMenu());

     Label content = new Label(LIPSUM);
   ```

```
  content.setWidth(70, Unit.PERCENTAGE);
  addComponent(content);

  addComponent(createMenu());
}
```

5. For a better look, we set a margin around all components. We also align them vertically upwards. As in the previous recipe, we can do it by overriding the `getCss()` method.

```
@Override
protected String getCss(Component c) {
  return "margin: 5px; vertical-align: top;";
}
```

6. Implementation of the `createMenu()` method is the same as in the *Creating an adjustable layout using split panels* recipe of this chapter.

```
private Tree createMenu() {...}
```

7. That's all. Now we can use or create `MobileLayout` in the main UI class called `Demo`.

```
public class Demo extends UI {
  @Override
  protected void init(VaadinRequest request) {
    setContent(new MobileLayout());
  }
}
```

We can run the server and open the application in the web browser.

How it works...

All the components in the `CssLayout` class are inserted horizontally and wrapped when they reach the width of the layout. Except the header that takes up the whole width of the page, because `Label` has a default setting of `100` percent width.

`CssLayout` has a very simple Document Object Model (DOM) structure. It's the fastest of the layout components.

See also

- The *Controlling components over the CSS layout* recipe

Binding tabs with a hard URL

If we have an application that works with bigger UI groups, it's nice to separate them with tabs. For example, we want to show different screens for our **Contractors**, **Customers**, **Employees**, and **Help** pages. The following screenshot shows the initial page of our application. We can see that the **Home** screen corresponds to the URL.

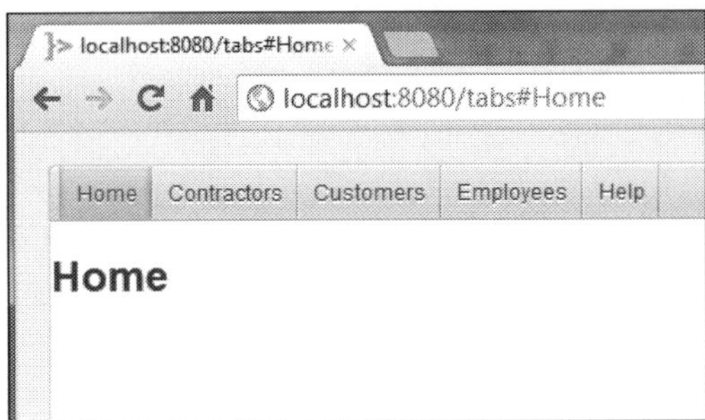

And if the user clicks on another tab, the URL has changed.

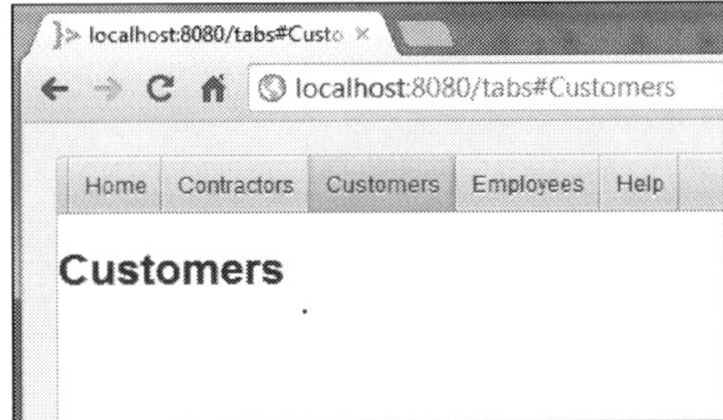

How to do it...

Carry out the following steps to create tabs bound with the URL:

1. Create a project with the main UI class called, for example, `Demo`.

   ```
   public class Demo extends UI {…}
   ```

2. We create a `TabsURL` class that extends `TabSheet`.

   ```
   public class TabsURL extends TabSheet{…}
   ```

3. Now we create an array of UI group names.

   ```
   private static final String tabNames[] =
     {"Home", "Contractors", "Customers", "Employees", "Help"};
   ```

4. We use these names for creating tabs. We insert the `createTabs()` method into our `TabsURL` class. Each tab contains a vertical layout with a big label according to the tab's name.

```
private void createTabs(String tabNames[]){
  for (String tabName : tabNames) {
    VerticalLayout layout = new VerticalLayout();
    layout.setCaption(tabName);
       layout.addComponent(
          new Label("<h1>" + tabName + "</h1>", ContentMode.HTML));
    layout.setHeight(400, Unit.PIXELS);
    addComponent(layout);
  }
}
```

5. We insert a calling method into the constructor.

```
public TabsURL() {
  createTabs(tabNames);

}
```

6. We need two mechanisms. The first will change the URL according to the selected tab. The second will select the tab according to the URL. For the first one, we add the `SelectedTabChangeListener()` listener. In this listener, we get the name of the selected tab. And we use this name for setting the URL fragment. We add the following listener into the `TabsURL` constructor:

```
public TabsURL() {
  createTabs(tabNames);
  addSelectedTabChangeListener(new SelectedTabChangeListener(){
    @Override
    public void selectedTabChange(SelectedTabChangeEvent event)
    {String selectedTabName =
                 event.getTabSheet().getSelectedTab().
getCaption();
       UI.getCurrent().getPage().setUriFragment(selectedTabName);
    }
  });
}
```

7. Next, we need a method that selects the tab according to the URL. We create another `selectTab()` method in our `TabsURL` class. It must be public because we will call it from the root class. From the page, we get the URL fragment. If the returned fragment has a null value, it means that no string after the # character in the URL has been set. In that case, we select the first tab. If the fragment has been set, we change it to lower-case, because we don't need a case-sensitive URL now. Then, using the iterator we go through all the tabs in `TabSheet` and check if the fragment equals the tab's name. If no match is found, we select the first tab.

```
public void selectTab(){
    String fragment= UI.getCurrent().getPage().getUriFragment();
    if (fragment == null) {
      setSelectedTab(0);
      return;
    }
    Iterator<Component> iterator = getComponentIterator();
    while (iterator.hasNext()){
      Component tab = iterator.next();
      String name = tab.getCaption().toLowerCase();
      if (fragment.toLowerCase().equals(name)){
      setSelectedTab(tab);
      return;
    }
  }
  setSelectedTab(0);
}
```

8. Now let's return to our root class called `TabRoot`. In the `init()` method, we create an object of the `TabsURL` class and set this object as a content of the application. After that we can call the `selectTab()` method. It ensures that the appropriate tab is selected at the initialization application. For selecting tabs after each changing of the URL, we add `FragmentChangedListener()`.

```
@Override
public void init(WrappedRequest request) {
  final TabsURL tabsURL = new TabsURL();
  setContent(tabsURL);
  tabsURL.selectTab();

getPage().addUriFragmentChangedListener(
                              new UriFragmentChangedListener() {
    @Override
    public void uriFragmentChanged(
                                UriFragmentChangedEvent event) {
      tabsURL.selectTab();
    }
  });
}
```

How it works...

In this example, we write and read browser fragment changes. `Fragment` is the string after the # character in the URI. Writing is performed by the `setFragment(String fragment)` method. Reading is performed by `FragmentChangedListener` that is added to the `init()` method in the root class. When the user clicks on a tab in the `TabSheet` layout, the URI fragment is changed according to the selected tab's name. When the URI is changed, a tab is selected according to the fragment string. If the fragment does not match with any tab's name, the first tab is selected.

There's more...

Using the caption as an identifier can cause failures in some circumstances (for example, i18n). In this recipe we used a simple identifier, but when we want to use a complicated identifier we have to convert it to the correct URI fragment.

For example we can use the method that replaces all whitespaces with dash:

```
private String convertNameToFragment(String name) {
  return name.replaceAll("\\s","-");
}
```

In our case, we can use it as follows:

1. Update in the `TabsURL()` constructor.

   ```
   UUI.getCurrent().getPage().setUriFragment(
     convertNameToFragment(selectedTabName));
   ```

2. Update in the `selectTab()` method.

   ```
   String name = convertNameToFrament(
     tab.getCaption().toLowerCase());
   ```

3. And also insert some spaces in the tab names.

   ```
   tabNames[] = {"Home", "Contractors", "New customers",
     "Employees", "Quick help"};
   ```

See also

- Vaadin 7 comes with a new set of APIs to aid navigation within our application. The main concepts Navigator and View are described in the following recipe. Other recipes describing the work with the listeners are in *Chapter 5, Events*.
- The API of the `TabSheet` class is available at `https://vaadin.com/api/7.0.0/com/vaadin/ui/TabSheet.html`.

Using Navigator for creating bookmarkable applications with back-forward button support

Vaadin 7 has introduced a new capability for easy creation of bookmarkable applications with back and forward button support: the Navigator.

We will see how to use the `Navigator` class and what is needed to get it working. `Navigator` works with views, layouts that implement the `View` interface.

We are going to make an application with two views. We will be able to navigate between these two views with the back and forward buttons or make a bookmark.

The first view will be the welcome view, which we map to an empty URL fragment, so it becomes accessible at `http://localhost:8080 address`.

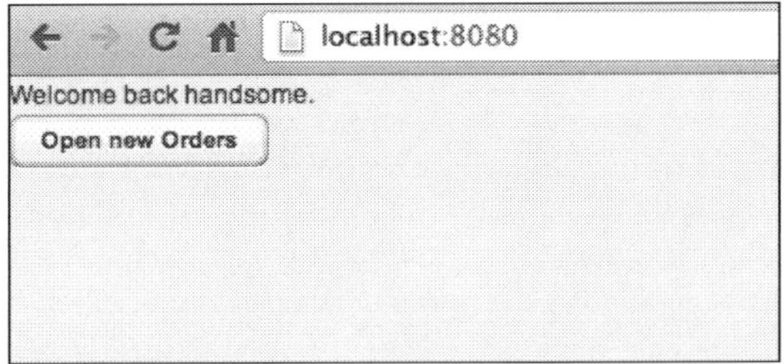

When a user clicks on the **Open new Orders** button, the orders view is displayed with the orders URL fragment.

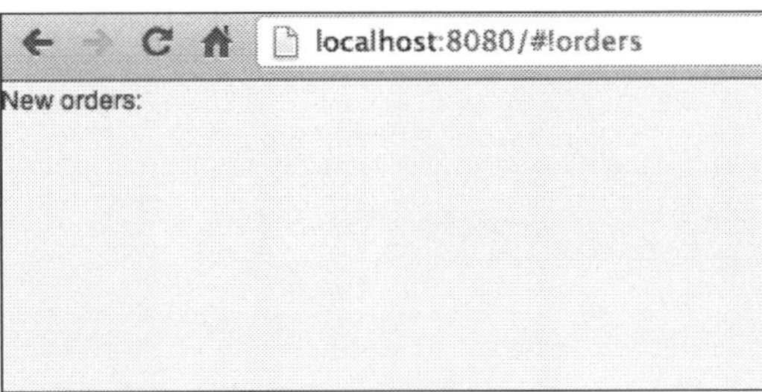

How to do it...

Carry out the following steps to learn how to work with `Views` in Vaadin 7:

1. Create a new Vaadin project with the main UI class called, for example, `MyVaadinUI`.
2. Create the welcome view that will show a flattering label with the greeting **Welcome back handsome**.

```
public class WelcomeView extends VerticalLayout implements View {

  public static final String VIEW_NAME = "";

  public WelcomeView() {
    Label lblWelcome = new Label("Welcome back handsome.");
    addComponent(lblWelcome);

    Button btnOrders = new Button("Open new Orders");
    btnOrders.addClickListener(new Button.ClickListener() {
      @Override
      public void buttonClick(Button.ClickEvent clickEvent) {
        UI ui = UI.getCurrent();
        Navigator navigator = ui.getNavigator();
        navigator.navigateTo(OrdersView.VIEW_NAME);
      }
    });
    addComponent(btnOrders);
  }

  @Override
  public void enter(ViewChangeListener.ViewChangeEvent event){
  }
}
```

3. Create a new view for orders and also, place there a label, which indicates we are browsing the orders.

```
public class OrdersView extends VerticalLayout implements View {

  public static final String VIEW_NAME = "orders";

  public OrdersView() {
    Label lblOrders = new Label("New orders: ");
    addComponent(lblOrders);
  }
```

```
    @Override
    public void enter(ViewChangeListener.ViewChangeEvent event) {
      // for example: load / reload data from database
    }
  }
```

4. Create a new UI class and set up the navigator.

```
public class MyVaadinUI extends UI {

  @Override
  protected void init(VaadinRequest request) {
    Navigator navigator = new Navigator(this, this);

    navigator.addView(WelcomeView.VIEW_NAME, new WelcomeView());
    navigator.addView(OrdersView.VIEW_NAME, OrdersView.class);

    navigator.navigateTo(WelcomeView.VIEW_NAME);
  }
}
```

5. Run the application and click on the **Open new Orders** button. Orders view appears and when we click on the back button in the browser, we will be returned to the welcome view.

How it works...

We have made a new instance of `Navigator` in the `init` method. Then we have added two views into the navigator and we have commanded the navigator to navigate to `WelcomeView`.

The first view has been added as a new instance of the `WelcomeView` class. That way, we ensure there will be only one instance of the `WelcomeView` class created for all navigation events.

```
navigator.addView(WelcomeView.VIEW_NAME, new WelcomeView());
```

The second view has been initialized via the `OrdersView` class. Setting a class instead of an instance is the opposite approach to setting an instance of a view to the navigator. Because when we add a class as a view to the navigator, a new instance of the view class is created for each navigation event.

```
navigator.addView(OrdersView.VIEW_NAME, OrdersView.class);
```

Both Welcome and Orders views are created as layouts that implement the `View` interface and contain a static field `VIEW_NAME` that defines the name of the view that is going to be set as a fragment into the URI.

When a view is being opened, the `enter` method is called. For example, we could fetch data from the database in the `enter` method, instead of fetching data in the constructor. The reasoning why we don't touch the database in a constructor is that, when we have tied I/O operations with the constructor, the class will become difficult to test.

There's more...

We can pass additional parameters into the view. We just extend the link with additional parameters, for example, `http://localhost:8080/#!order/detail/1`.

Then we get the parameters in the `enter` method. The parameters variable contains `detail/1` string from the previous example.

```
public void enter(ViewChangeListener.ViewChangeEvent event) {
  String parameters = event.getParameters();
  addComponent(new Label(parameters));
```

Aligning components on a page

Aligning components is easy in Vaadin. We can align them on the left, on the right, on the top, on the bottom, and also center them vertically or horizontally. In this recipe, we will create a demo application in which we can see how aligning works. We will create three buttons in three different positions, as we can see in the following screenshot:

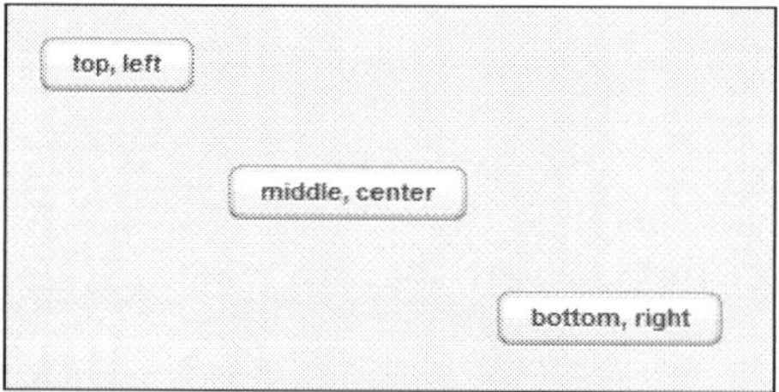

How to do it...

Carry out the following steps to create and learn how alignment works in Vaadin.

1. We create a Vaadin project with the main UI class named `Demo`.

   ```
   public class Demo extends UI {…}
   ```

2. We create a class called `AligningDemo` that is based on the `VerticalLayout`.

   ```
   public class AligningDemo extends VerticalLayout {…}
   ```

3. In the constructor, we create and add all three buttons. The first button is placed on the top left side. We'll do it by the `setComponentAlignment()` method. As a parameter, we use predefined alignments from the `Alignment` class.

   ```
   public AligningDemo() {
     Button leftButton = new Button("top, left");
     addComponent(leftButton);
     setComponentAlignment(leftButton, Alignment.TOP_LEFT);
   ```

4. The next button is centered in the middle of the page.

   ```
     Button centerButton = new Button("middle, center");
     addComponent(centerButton);
     setComponentAlignment(centerButton, Alignment.MIDDLE_CENTER);
   ```

5. And the last button is aligned at the bottom on the right.

   ```
     Button rightButton = new Button("bottom, right");
     addComponent(rightButton);
     setComponentAlignment(rightButton,
       Alignment.BOTTOM_RIGHT);
   ```

6. For a better view, we enable layout margins on all four sides of the layout and we stretch the layout to fill the screen.

   ```
     setMargin(true);
     setSizeFull();
   }
   ```

7. That's all. Now we can use our `AligningDemo` class in the root class.

   ```
   public class Demo extends UI {
     @Override
     public void init(VaadinRequest request) {
       setContent(new AligningDemo());
     }
   }
   ```

How it works...

We can set the alignment of the component inside a specific layout with the `setComponentAlignment()` method. The method takes the component contained in the layout to be formatted as its parameters, and also takes the horizontal and vertical alignment. The easiest way to set alignments is to use the constants defined in the `Alignment` class.

See also

- Additional information about aligning in the layout is described on the Vaadin web page at `https://vaadin.com/book/vaadin7/-/page/layout.settings.html#layout.settings.alignment`
- API of the `Alignment` class, available at `https://vaadin.com/api/7.0.0/com/vaadin/ui/Alignment.html`

Creating UI collections of components

Imagine that we need to create an editor for the UI design. What is it usually composed of? It's usually composed of the toolbar, editor, and a collection of components. In this recipe, we will create a UI collection of components. When we work with many components, it is good to group them by types. For grouping, we use the `Accordion` layout.

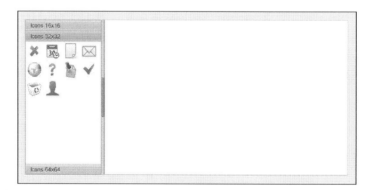

How to do it...

Carry out the following steps to create a UI collection of components:

1. Let's create a new project and name the main UI class as `Demo`.

   ```
   public class Demo extends UI{…}
   ```

2. We begin with the creation of a `ComponentCollection` class that extends the `Accordion` layout.

   ```
   public class ComponentCollection extends Accordion {…}
   ```

3. For our example, we use icons from the internal Vaadin theme `Runo` because they are easily accessible using the `ThemeResource` class. They are divided into three groups by size. So we create two array variables.

   ```
   private String[] sizes = { "16", "32", "64" };
   private String[] icons = {
   ```

```
"cancel.png", "calendar.png", "document.png",
"email.png", "globe.png", "help.png",
"note.png", "ok.png", "trash.png", "user.png" };
```

4. Now we need a method that creates tabs. Each tab represents one collection of UI components. And components are represented by icons. We call the `createTabs()` method and pass the `sizes[]` parameters.

   ```
   private void createTabs(String sizes[]) {…}
   ```

5. Each group needs its own layout. We use `CssLayout` that allows us to wrap components in the line. Groups will have a name according to the size of icons inside. We insert this code in the `createTabs()` method.

   ```
   for (String size : sizes) {
     CssLayout layout = new CssLayout(){
       @Override
       protected String getCss(Component c) {
         return "display: inline-block;";
       }
     };
     layout.setCaption("Icons " + size + "x" + size);
     addComponent(layout);

   }
   ```

6. In the next step after the `addComponent(layout)` method, we go through an array of icons and create images from the theme resource `Runo`. Our `createTabs()` method is done.

   ```
     for (String icon : icons) {
       Resource imageResource =
         new ThemeResource("../runo/icons/" + size + "/" + icon);
       Image image = new  Image(null, imageResource);
       layout.addComponent(image);
     }
   ```

7. We will call this method from the constructor. And also we need to fill the whole space by our layout so that we add two methods to the constructor.

   ```
   public ComponentCollection() {
     setSizeFull();
     createTabs(sizes);
   }
   ```

8. Now we return to our root class `Demo`. The base layout for our application will be `HorizontalSplitPanel`. On its left area we insert our collection of components.

```
public class Demo extends UI {
  @Override
  public void init(VaadinRequest request) {
    HorizontalSplitPanel horSplitPanel =
                                   new HorizontalSplitPanel();
     horSplitPanel.setSplitPosition(20, Unit.PERCENTAGE);
    horSplitPanel.setFirstComponent(
                                   new ComponentCollection());
    setContent(horSplitPanel);
  }
}
```

How it works...

It's an example of layout for a simple UI designer. For grouping components, we used the `Accordion` layout that has separate tabs. We can put a collection of components on the left side and an editor on the right side. By the splitter in the middle, we can adjust the width of the area as we wish.

There's more...

If we want components to be able to be dragged, we can easily wrap each component by `DragAndDropWrapper`. We can update the code inside the `createTabs()` method:

```
for (String icon : icons) {
  Resource imageResource =
   new ThemeResource("../runo/icons/" + size + "/" + icon);
   Image image = new Image(null, imageResource);

  DragAndDropWrapper imageWrap = new DragAndDropWrapper(image);
  imageWrap.setDragStartMode(DragStartMode.COMPONENT);
  imageWrap.setSizeUndefined();

  layout.addComponent(imageWrap);
}
```

For dropping components, we can create a layout according to the *Dragging-and-dropping between different layouts* recipe and put this layout as a second component into the `SplitPanel` class in the root `Demo` class. We can also use `AbsoluteLayout` as an editor for components.

See also

- The API of the `Accordion` layout is available at `https://vaadin.com/api/7.0.0/com/vaadin/ui/Accordion.html`

Dragging-and-dropping between different layouts

Each layout has a different wrap behavior. If we want to try this behavior for ourselves, we will have to create a simple demo. In this demo, we can drag-and-drop components between the four different layouts. We can also change the size of each layout by moving the separator and watch how components are wrapped. If the line cannot be wrapped, a scroll bar appears.

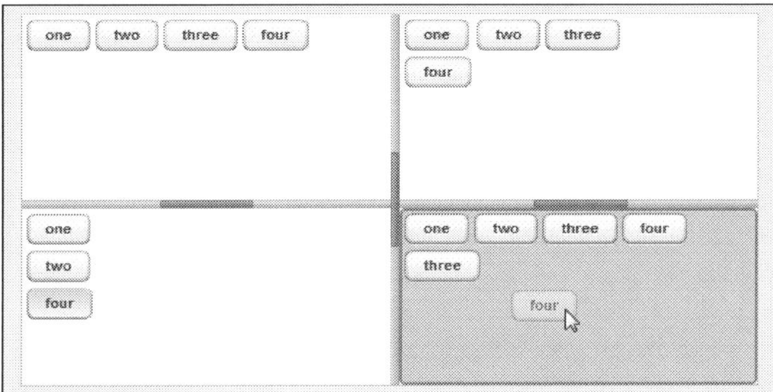

How to do it...

Carry out the following steps to create a drag and drop panel:

1. We create project with the root `Demo` class.

   ```
   public class Demo extends UI {…}
   ```

2. All four layouts will be inserted into the `DragndropPanel` class that extends `HorizontalSplitPanel`.

   ```
   public class DragndropPanel extends HorizontalSplitPanel {…}
   ```

3. Now let's insert the `createLayout()` method. In this method we add buttons to the layout that is taken over the `AbstractLayout` parameter. Next we wrap this layout by the `DragAndDropWrapper` class and set `DropHandler`. Here we implement two methods. First is `getAcceptCriterion()` that accepts all components and second is the `drop()` method in which we add the dropped component into the layout.

   ```
   private Component createLayout(final AbstractLayout layout) {
       layout.addComponent(createButton("one"));
   ```

```
    layout.addComponent(createButton("two"));
    layout.addComponent(createButton("three"));
    layout.addComponent(createButton("four"));
    DragAndDropWrapper dndLayout =
    new DragAndDropWrapper(layout);
    dndLayout.setSizeFull();
    dndLayout.setDropHandler(new DropHandler() {
      @Override
      public AcceptCriterion getAcceptCriterion() {
        return AcceptAll.get();
      }
      @Override
      public void drop(DragAndDropEvent event) {
        WrapperTransferable t =
        (WrapperTransferable) event.getTransferable();
        layout.addComponent(t.getSourceComponent());
      }
    });
    return dndLayout;
  }
```

4. Buttons are created in a different method because we also need to wrap them by `DragAndDropWrapper`.

```
private Component createButton(String name) {
  Button button = new Button(name);
  DragAndDropWrapper buttonWrap =
  new DragAndDropWrapper(button);
  buttonWrap.setDragStartMode(DragStartMode.COMPONENT);
  buttonWrap.setSizeUndefined();
  return buttonWrap;
}
```

5. Now we continue with a constructor. Here we create two `VerticalSplitPanels`. We insert the first on the left side of `HorizontalSplitPanel` and the second on the right side. Now we have four parts of `SplitPanel`, where we insert `HorizontalLayout`, `VerticalLayout`, `GridLayout`, and `CssLayout`.

```
public DragndropPanel() {
  VerticalSplitPanel leftSplitPanel =
  new VerticalSplitPanel();
  leftSplitPanel.setSizeFull();
  leftSplitPanel.setFirstComponent(
    createLayout(new HorizontalLayout()));
  leftSplitPanel.setSecondComponent(
    createLayout(new VerticalLayout()));
```

```
    VerticalSplitPanel rightSplitPanel =
    new VerticalSplitPanel();
    rightSplitPanel.setSizeFull();
    rightSplitPanel.setFirstComponent(
    createLayout(new GridLayout(3, 3)));
    rightSplitPanel.setSecondComponent(
    createLayout(new CssLayout() {
      @Override
      protected String getCss(Component c) {
        return "display: inline-block;";
      }
    }));
    setFirstComponent(leftSplitPanel);
    setSecondComponent(rightSplitPanel);
    setSizeFull();
  }
```

6. Now our `DragndropPanel` constructor is done. We can use it in the main UI `Demo` class in the `init()` method.

```
public class Demo extends UI {
  @Override
  public void init(VaadinRequest request) {
    setContent(new DragndropPanel());
  }
}
```

How it works...

In Vaadin, we can drag-and-drop components simply by wrapping them inside `DragAndDropWrapper`. We can enable dragging by calling the `setDragStartMode(DragStartMode mode)` method. For dropping a component, we have to define an accepted criterion on the target component and drop the component by the `drop(DragAndDropEvent event)` method.

See also

- More information about drag-and-drop is described on the Vaadin web page at `https://vaadin.com/book/vaadin7/-/page/advanced.dragndrop.html`

Building any layout with AbsoluteLayout

If the basic layouts offered by Vaadin limit us, and we want to create some other special crazy layout, we can use `AbsoluteLayout`. There are no limits in this layout. We can insert components into any place we want. In this recipe, we will create a demo of a custom layout, **Circle layout**. There are also some reasons not to use `AbsoluteLayout`. They are described in the *There's more...* section at the end of this recipe.

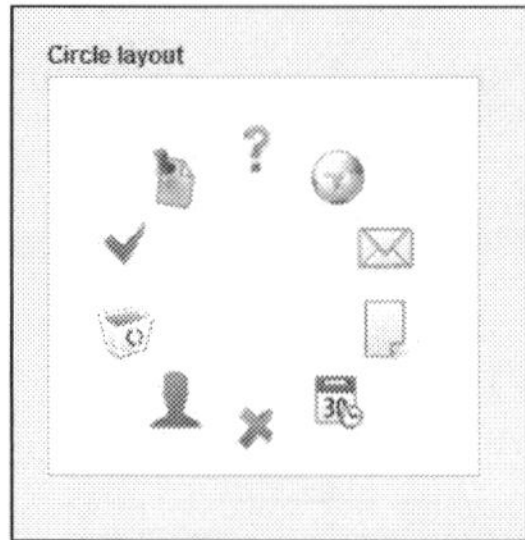

How to do it...

Carry out the following steps to create a custom layout using the `AbsoluteLayout` class:

1. We create a project with the main UI class called `Demo`.

   ```
   public class Demo extends UI {…}
   ```

2. We will create a class called `CircleLayoutDemo` that extends `AbsoluteLayout`.

   ```
   public class CircleLayoutDemo extends AbsoluteLayout {...}
   ```

3. Let's use icons from the `Runo` theme. So we create an array of icon names.

   ```
     private String[] icons = {
     "cancel.png", "calendar.png", "document.png",
     "email.png", "globe.png", "help.png",
     "note.png", "ok.png", "trash.png", "user.png" };
   ```

4. In the constructor, we add some mathematical variables to calculate the circle. If we change the `radius` variable, `CircleLayout` automatically changes size.

   ```
   public CircleLayoutDemo() {
     double step = 360.0 / icons.length;
     int radius = 70;
     int i = 0;
     int xMargin = 20;
     int yMargin = 20;

   }
   ```

5. Now let's create images according the names in the array icons. In the `AbsoluteLayout` class, components are placed with horizontal and vertical coordinates relative to an edge of the layout area. The distance from the top edge is defined by the `xMargin` variable and the distance from the left edge is defined by the `yMargin` variable. So we calculate the x and y coordinates and we use them in the `addComponent()` method.

   ```
   for (String icon : icons) {
     Resource imageResource =
       new ThemeResource("../runo/icons/32/" + icon);
     Image image = new Image(null, imageResource);
     double degrees = Math.toRadians(i * step);
     int x = (int) (Math.cos(degrees) * radius)
     + xMargin + radius;
     int y = (int) (Math.sin(degrees) * radius)
     + yMargin + radius;
     addComponent(image, "left: "+ y + "px; top: "+ x + "px;");
     i++;

   }
   ```

6. In the last part of the code in the constructor, we compute and set the width and height of the layout.

   ```
     setWidth((xMargin * 4) + (radius * 2), Unit.PIXELS);
     setHeight((yMargin * 4) + (radius * 2), Unit.PIXELS);
   }
   ```

7. In the root `Demo` class, we can simply add our `CircleLayoutDemo` class.

   ```
   public class Demo extends UI {
     @Override
     public void init(VaadinRequest request) {
       setContent(new CircleLayoutDemo());
     }
   }
   ```

How it works...

`AbsoluteLayout` allows placing components in arbitrary positions in the layout area. The positions are specified in the `addComponent()` method with horizontal and vertical coordinates relative to an edge of the layout area. The positions can include a third depth dimension, and the z-index, which specifies which components are displayed in front and which are behind other components.

There's more...

In web development in general, `AbsoluteLayout` is the last resort. In some cases we can use it for special layouts as mentioned with `CicrleLayout` or we can use it for animation. But there are lots of reasons not to use it. For example, if the font sizes change, the content increases and decreases. If the size of the page is changed, the components aren't wrapped. It's recommended that if we want to do special layouts without the constraints and help from the Vaadin layouting system, we should use `CssLayout`. `CssLayout` allows strong control over styling of the components contained inside the layout.

See also

- More information about `AbsoluteLayout` is described on the Vaadin web page at `https://vaadin.com/book/vaadin7/-/page/layout.absolutelayout.html`
- API of the `AbsoluteLayout` class is available at `https://vaadin.com/api/7.0.0/com/vaadin/ui/AbsoluteLayout.html`
- API of the `CssLayout` class is available at `https://vaadin.com/api/7.0.0/com/vaadin/ui/CssLayout.html`

3
UI Components

In this chapter, we will cover:

- Viewing details of items in ListSelect
- Inserting a button to remove a table row
- Creating a line chart with Flot
- Creating a pie chart with Highcharts
- Drag-and-drop from the desktop
- Using DateField with Joda-Time DateTime
- Zooming with the slider
- Restricting buttons in Rich text area
- Styling components with CSS

Introduction

Vaadin provides a comprehensive set of User Interface components. UI components are configurable, reusable elements that make up the user interface. We will show some of them.

Vaadin gives many alternatives for selecting one or more items from a list, using drop-down and regular lists, radio button and checkbox groups, tables, trees, and so on. We will learn how to use the `ListSelect` component and we will also briefly mention differences in some other selection components. A very important component is a `Table`. In this book, it is used in various examples. In this chapter, we will learn how to generate an additional column in the `Table`.

We will show how to visualize data by using Flot chart and Highcharts libraries. Both chart libraries are written in JavaScript, which runs in the client browser. We will show how to integrate them with Vaadin server-side code.

Drag-and-drop is a very useful and practical feature. Users can simply grab an object with the mouse and drag it to a different location. It is possible to create drag-and-drop components for every component in Vaadin. We will use this feature for our custom file uploader.

The Joda-Time library provides better classes for work with dates in Java. We will show how to display a `DateTime` type inside a Vaadin form.

Next, we will describe the `Slider` component. It's a very useful component when we need to select a value between a minimum and maximum range.

Vaadin 7 comes with built-in support for **SASS** (**Syntactically Awesome Stylesheets**), which is an extension of **CSS3**. Finally, we will learn how to use **CSS** styles to restrict buttons in the `RichTextArea` and how to the change the style of components.

Viewing details of items in ListSelect

In this recipe, we will show the use of a `ListSelect` component. It's a list box that shows the selectable items in a vertical list. If the number of items exceeds the height of the component, a scrollbar is shown. We will use it for viewing details of contacts in a list as shown in the following screenshot. We'll create it as a custom component.

Our Contact viewer is based on the `HorizontalSplitPanel` that contains two components and lays them horizontally. On the left side, we will have list of full names and on the right side we will have details about the selected user. We will learn how to add items to the `ListSelect` component using the `Container` and how to work with the listener.

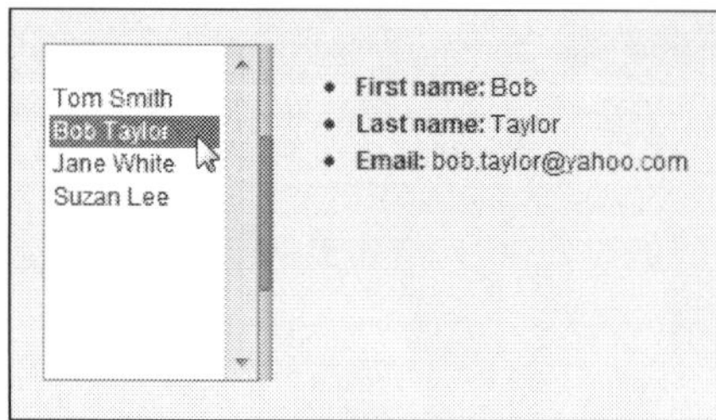

How to do it...

Carry out the following steps for viewing the details of items in the list:

1. We create a Vaadin project with the main UI class called `Demo`.

```
public class Demo extends UI {
```

2. First, we need a bean called `Contact`. We create a simple bean with first name, last name, and e-mail. We also create a method that returns the full name. This name will be shown in the UI list. We add appropriate constructor and getter methods as follows:

```
public class Contact {

  private String firstName;
  private String lastName;
  private String email;

public Contact(String firstName, String lastName,
  String email) {
    this.firstName = firstName;
    this.lastName = lastName;
    this.email = email;
  }

  public String getFullName() {
    return firstName + " " + lastName;
  }
  <insert getters and setter>
  …
}
```

3. Now we create our custom component called `ContactViewer`.

```
public class ContactViewer extends CustomComponent {…}
```

4. The constructor will have one parameter, `BeanItemContainer<Contact> contacts`. Through this parameter, we pass the container of contacts. In the constructor, we create the main horizontal split panel that has to be the final object because we will use it from the inner class `ValueChangeListener`. We use this panel as a compositions root in our custom component.

```
public ContactViewer(BeanItemContainer<Contact> contacts) {

  final HorizontalSplitPanel panel =
                        new HorizontalSplitPanel();
  setCompositionRoot(panel);
  …
```

5. Then we create our main component `contactSelect` that is an instance of the `SelectList` class. We stretch this component over the entire area by the `setSizeFull()` method and we set it to the immediate mode, which means that changes in this component are fired immediately. Item captions will be read from the property specified with the `setItemCaptionPropertyId(Object propertyId)` method. In our case, we use the `fullName` property that returns the first name and last name of `Contact`.

```
final ListSelect contactSelect = new ListSelect();
contactSelect.setSizeFull();
contactSelect.setImmediate(true);
contactSelect.setContainerDataSource(contacts);
contactSelect.setItemCaptionPropertyId("fullName");
...
```

6. In the `contactSelect` object, we add a listener for changes in the selected item. After each change, we update the second component in the panel with the details of the selected contact. At the end of the constructor, we set the `contactSelect` object as a first component in the main split panel.

```
  contactSelect.addValueChangeListener(
    new ValueChangeListener() {
      @Override
      public void valueChange(ValueChangeEvent event) {
        Contact contact =
        (Contact) event.getProperty().getValue();
          panel.setSecondComponent
          (createInfoLabel(contact));
        contactSelect.focus();
      }
    });
  panel.setFirstComponent(contactSelect);
}
```

7. Next, we add a method that creates our info label for viewing details of the selected contact. It's a simple `Label` with safe HTML code. The `SafeHtml` class has been already described in the *Creating an adjustable layout using split panels* recipe in *Chapter 2, Layouts*.

```
private Label createInfoLabel(Contact contact) {
  String info = "";
  if (contact != null) {
    info = "<ul>";
    info += String.format("<li><b>First name:
      </b> %s </li>",
    contact.getFirstName());
    info += String.format("<li><b>Last name:
      </b> %s </li>",
```

```
      contact.getLastName());
      info += String.format("<li><b>Email: </b> %s </li>",
      contact.getEmail());
      info += "</ul>";
    }
    SafeHtml safeHtml =
      SafeHtmlUtils.fromSafeConstant(info);
    return new Label(safeHtml.asString(),
      ContentMode.HTML);
    }
```

8. Now we can use our `ContactViewer` component in the main UI class `Demo`. Here we insert a method that creates a contact container with some dummy data.

```
public class Demo extends UI {

  @Override
  protected void init(VaadinRequest request) {
    ContactViewer contactViewer =
            new ContactViewer(createContactContainer());
    setContent(contactViewer);
  }

  private BeanItemContainer<Contact>
    createContactContainer(){
    BeanItemContainer<Contact> contacts =
          w BeanItemContainer<>(Contact.class);
    contacts.addItem(
      new Contact("Tom", "Smith",
      "tom.smith@gmail.com"));
    contacts.addItem(
      new Contact("Bob", "Taylor",
      "bob.taylor@yahoo.com"));
    contacts.addItem(
      new Contact("Jane", "White",
      "jane.white@gmail.com"));
    contacts.addItem(
      new Contact("Suzan", "Lee", "suzan.lee@aol.com"));
    return contacts;
  }

}
```

The application is ready now. We can run the server and show it in the web browser.

How it works...

The ListSelect component used in this recipe is a list box that shows selected and selectable items in a vertical list. A user can select an item by using the mouse or by using the up and down arrow keys. After selecting an item, ValueChangeEvent is caught in the ValueChangeListener. In this event, an info label with detailed information about the contact is created and added to the right side of the split panel.

There's more...

Vaadin gives many alternatives for selecting one or more items from a list: using drop-down and regular lists, radio button and checkbox groups, tables, trees, and so on. The core library includes the following selection components, all based on the AbstractSelect class. Here are some of them with shortened generated HTML code:

- ComboBox: It is a text field with a drop-down list. Users can filter the displayed items and add new ones. It's very similar to the Select component that is deprecated in Vaadin 7. In HTML, it's represented by the element <input>. Lists of items are added as a small pop up created by divs and table elements.

```
<input type="text">
<div class="popupContent">
  <table>
    <tr>
      <td class="gwt-MenuItem"><span>first
      item</span></td>
    </tr>
  </table>
</div>
```

- NativeSelect: It is a good alternative to ComboBox if we want to use a simple select component without extra generated HTML code. This component is without features such as filtering and adding new items. In HTML, it's a <select> element with a default size of 1 item.

```
<select size="1">
  <option value="1">first item</option>
  <option value="2">second item</option>
</select>
```

- ListSelect: It is a vertical list box with items. Users can use single or multiple selection modes. In HTML, it is represented by the element <select> with a default size of 10 items.

```
<select size="10">
  <option value="1">first item</option>
  <option value="2">second item</option>
</select>
```

- `OptionGroup`: It is one class for two components known as radio button and checkbox. If we set it as a multi-select `setMultiSelect(true)`, it will be a checkbox component.

```
<span>
  <input type="checkbox" id="gwt-uid-1">
  <label for="gwt-uid-1">first item</label>
</span>
```

  If we set it as a single-select `setMultiSelect(false)`, it will be a radio button. It's the default value.

```
<span>
  <input type="radio" id="gwt-uid-1">
  <label for="gwt-uid-1">first item</label>
</span>
```

See also

- More information about selecting items is described on the Vaadin web page at `https://vaadin.com/book/vaadin7/-/page/components.selecting.html`

Inserting a button to remove a table row

When we are working with tables, we can use a useful feature for generating columns. In Vaadin, a table is created according to the `Container` that is used as a data source. If we use the `BeanItemContainer` class, then for each field in the container bean one column is generated. So, if we want to add an other column, we can generate it using the `Table.addGeneratedColumn()` method. This generated column exists only in the `Table`, not as a property in the underlying `Container`. We will use it for generating buttons that remove a current row, as shown in the following screenshot:

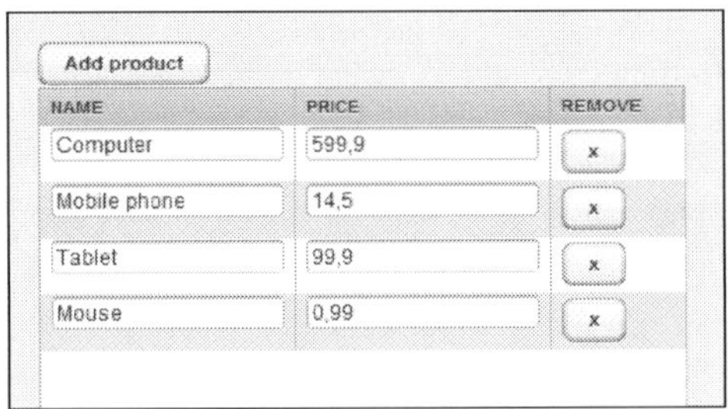

How to do it...

Carry out the following steps to learn how to insert a new column in the table:

1. We create a Vaadin project with the main UI class called `Demo` as follows:

   ```
   public class Demo extends UI {…}
   ```

2. Our table will be a list of some products with prices. Therefore, we start with bean `Product`. This bean consists of name and price. We create an appropriate constructor and we also insert getter and setter methods for these variables. We do this as follows:

   ```
   public class Product {

     private String name;
     private double price;

     public Product(String name, double price) {
       this.name = name;
       this.price = price;
     }

     <insert getter and setter methods for name and price>
   }
   ```

3. Now we create our custom component called `PriceList`.

   ```
   public class PriceList extends CustomComponent {…}
   ```

4. All items will be stored in the container that will be used as a data source of the table. We will use it from the constructor and employ two methods; therefore it will be a global variable. More information about using containers is described in the *Binding a container to a component* recipe in *Chapter 9, Data Management*.

   ```
     private BeanItemContainer<Product> container;
   ```

5. The constructor will have one parameter: `BeanItemContainer<Product> container`. Through this parameter, we pass the container of `Product` to the table. Next, we create `VerticalLayout` that is used as the main layout for our custom component. We insert a button and table into this layout. The button will be used for adding new items to the container.

   ```
   public PriceList(BeanItemContainer<Product> container) {
     this.container = container;
     Table table = createTable();
     table.setContainerDataSource(container);
   ```

```
    VerticalLayout layout = new VerticalLayout();
    layout.addComponent(createAddProductButton());
    layout.addComponent(table);
    setCompositionRoot(layout);
  }
```

6. Next we insert a method that creates the **Add product** button. It is a simple button with caption **Add product** and with one `ClickListener`. On the click event, a new instance of the `Product` class will be added to our container.

```
private Button createAddProductButton() {
  Button addProductButton = new Button("Add product");
  addProductButton.addClickListener
  (new ClickListener() {
    public void buttonClick(ClickEvent event) {
      container.addItem(new Product("", 0));
    }
  });
  return addProductButton;
}
```

7. The table is created in a separate method. As a data source, we set our global container. We want to edit items directly in the table row. So we do it by the `setEditable(true)` method. If the table is editable, an editor of type `Field` is created for each table cell.

```
private Table createTable(){
  Table table = new Table();
  table.setContainerDataSource(container);
  table.setEditable(true);
  ...
```

8. Next we add our generated column named `Remove`. We create an implementation of the `ColumnGenerator` interface. In this interface, there is only one method called `generateCell()`. This method is called by `Table` when a cell in a generated column needs to be generated. In the body of the method, we create a button with caption **x** and we add a listener in which we remove the item (row in table) with current `itemId`.

```
    table.addGeneratedColumn("Remove",
      new Table.ColumnGenerator() {

        public Object generateCell(

          Table source,final Object itemId,Object
          columnId){
            Button removeButton = new Button("x");
```

```
            removeButton.addClickListener
            (new ClickListener(){
              public void buttonClick(ClickEvent event) {
                table.removeItem(itemId);
              }
          });
          return removeButton;
        }
      });

      return table;
    }
```

9. That is all. Now we can use our created custom component in the main UI class called `Demo`. Here we insert a method that creates a container of `Product` with some dummy data.

```
public class Demo extends UI {

  @Override
  protected void init(VaadinRequest request) {
    PriceList priceList =
              new PriceList(createProductContainer());
    setContent(priceList);
  }

  private BeanItemContainer<Product>
  createProductContainer(){
    BeanItemContainer<Product> container =
        new BeanItemContainer<Product>(Product.class);
    container.addItem(new Product("Computer", 599.90));
    container.addItem(new Product("Mobile phone", 14.5));
    container.addItem(new Product("Tablet", 99.90));
    container.addItem(new Product("Mouse", 0.99));
    return container;
  }

}
```

The application is done. We can run the server and show it in the web browser.

How it works...

We have made a simple custom component that consists of a table and buttons. Columns in a `Table` are generated according to fields in the container bean. One button is used for adding new items to the container. Other buttons are placed into the generated column.

Generating the new column is performed by the `Table.addGeneratedColumn()` method. A generated column exists only in the `Table`. `Table` will not listen to value change events from properties overridden by the generated columns. If the content of our generated column depends on properties that are not directly visible in the table, we have to attach a value change listener to update the content on all depended properties. Otherwise, our UI might not get updated as expected.

Also note that the `getVisibleColumns()` method will return the generated columns, while `getContainerPropertyIds()` will not.

Our generated buttons are used for removing items from the container. Each item is visually represented as a row in the table. So, if the user clicks on the button with caption **x**, one row is removed.

As a data source, we used the instance of the `BeanItemContainer` class, which is a container for JavaBeans. The properties of the container are determined automatically by inspecting the used JavaBean class. Only beans of the same type can be added to the container. In our example, it's `Product` type.

See also

- More information about using containers is described in the *Binding a container to a component* recipe in *Chapter 9, Data Management*

Creating a line chart with Flot

Flot is a JavaScript library for building charts. In this recipe, we will show how to integrate the Java server-side Vaadin code with the Flot JavaScript library.

We will make a line chart, which can be seen in the following screenshot:

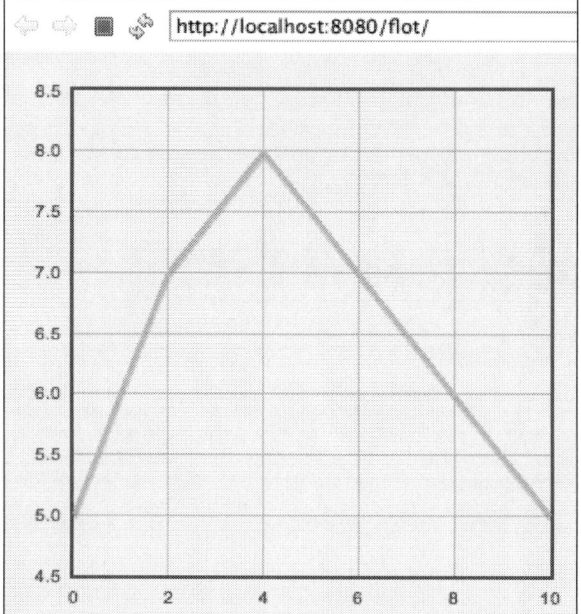

More information about Flot can be found at `http://www.flotcharts.org`.

How to do it...

Carry out the following steps in order to create a line chart with the Flot library:

1. Create a `FlotChartState` class that extends `JavaScriptComponentState`. This class will be used as a transport box between Java and JavaScript. Therefore, we set data in our Java server-code and we get it in JavaScript later on.

```
package com.packtpub.vaadin;
import com.vaadin.shared.ui.JavaScriptComponentState;
import org.json.JSONArray;

public class FlotChartState extends JavaScriptComponentState {

  private JSONArray data;

  public JSONArray getData() {
    return data;
  }

  public void setData(JSONArray data) {
    this.data = data;
  }
}
```

2. Create a `FlotChart` class that will represent the Vaadin component that is able to communicate with the Flot JavaScript. We also need to link this component with JavaScript files. Therefore, we add the `@JavaScript` annotation to the `FlotChart` class. The files inside the `@JavaScript` annotation will be loaded by the client together with this component.

```
package com.packtpub.vaadin;
import com.vaadin.annotations.JavaScript;
import com.vaadin.ui.AbstractJavaScriptComponent;
import org.json.JSONArray;
import org.json.JSONException;

@JavaScript({"https://ajax.googleapis.com/ajax/libs/
  jquery/1.7.2/jquery.min.js","jquery.flot.js",
  "flot_connector.js" })
public class FlotChart extends AbstractJavaScriptComponent {

  @Override
  public FlotChartState getState() {
    return (FlotChartState) super.getState();
  }

  public void setData(String source) {
    JSONArray data;
    try {
      data = new JSONArray(source);
      getState().setData(data);
    } catch (JSONException e) {
      e.printStackTrace();
    }
  }
}
```

3. We are referring to the `jquery.flot.js` file that should be located in our project, as in the following screenshot. Let's create a new source folder called `resources` with directory `com`. Place the `jquery.flot.js` file into this folder. The `jquery.flot.js` file can be downloaded from the Flot home page at `http://www.flotcharts.org`.

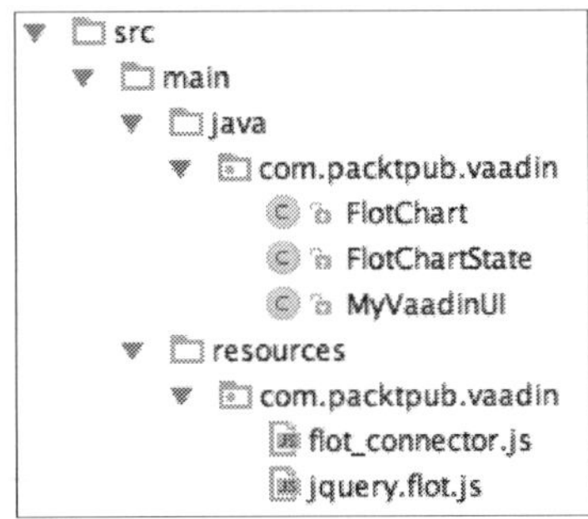

4. Now we will implement the content of the `init` method in the `UI` class as follows:

```
protected void init(VaadinRequest request) {
  VerticalLayout layout = new VerticalLayout();
  layout.setMargin(true);
  setContent(layout);

  FlotChart flot = new FlotChart();
  flot.setWidth("300px");
  flot.setHeight("300px");

  String data =
  "[" +
      "[" +
          "[0, 5]," +
          "[2, 7]," +
          "[4, 8]," +
          "[10, 5]" +
      "]" +
  "]";

  flot.setData(data);
  layout.addComponent(flot);
}
```

5. We are about to send JSON data to the JavaScript chart. Therefore, we need to make a connection between Java and JavaScript. Create a new file named `flot_connector.js` and put the following code into it:

```
window.com_packtpub_vaadin_FlotChart = function() {
  var element = $(this.getElement());

  this.onStateChange = function() {
    $.plot(element, this.getState().data);
  }
}
```

Run the project and the line chart appears in the browser.

How it works...

Inside the `@JavaScript` annotation, we have referenced three JavaScript files:

- `jquery.min.js`: This is a jQuery library, which is required by the Flot library, because Flot is built with jQuery

- `jquery.flot.js`: This is the chart Flot library
- `flot_connector.js`: This is the connector between Vaadin server-side Java code and the JavaScript client-side Flot library

The `FlotChart` class represents the chart at the server side. This chart uses the `FlotChartState` class for exchanging the data between Java server-side code and JavaScript client-side code. The data format for values that are shown in the chart is **JSON** (**JavaScript Object Notation**).

We have made a simple JSON array and passed it to `FlotChart`. The JSON data was passed to the JavaScript connector `flot_connector.js` and rendered to the Vaadin element.

There's more...

We can add chart options to the line chart we have made. We could simply enhance the `FlotChartState` class as follows:

1. Add a new field `options` into the `FlotChartState` class, together with getter and setter.

   ```
   private JSONObject options;
   ```

2. Then add a new method named `setOptions` in the `FlotChart` class as follows:

   ```
   public void setOptions(String options) {
     try {
       JSONObject root = new JSONObject(options);
         getState().setOptions(root);
     } catch (JSONException e) {
       e.printStackTrace();
     }
   }
   ```

   The new method simply takes the JSON string, parses it to `JSONObject`, and sets it to the chart state.

   The configuration of the chart could be the following. Let's change the background of the line chart.

   ```
   String options =
           "{" +
               "grid:{"          +
                   "backgroundColor:{" +
                       "colors:["+
                         "\"#fef\"," +
                         "\"#eee\""+
                       "]"+
   ```

```
                    "}"+
                "}"+
            "}";
flot.setOptions(options);
```

3. The last step is to change `flot_connector.js` so it handles the `options` field from the state.

```
this.onStateChange = function() {
  var state = this.getState();
  var options = state.options;
  var data = state.data;
  $.plot(element, data, options);
}
```

4. Now let's have a look what we have made. Start up the application and open it in the Internet browser.

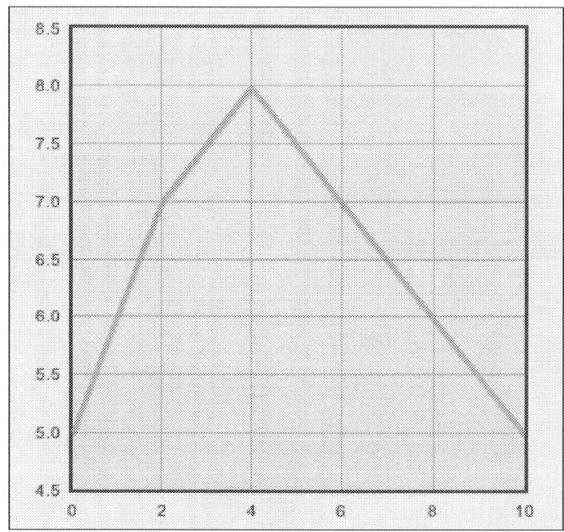

Creating a pie chart with Highcharts

We will make a pie chart in this recipe. We will create Java server-side code that interacts with the Highcharts JavaScript library. More information about Highcharts can be found at `http://www.highcharts.com`.

The pie chart will display three answers for the question "Why Don't I Have a Girlfriend?".

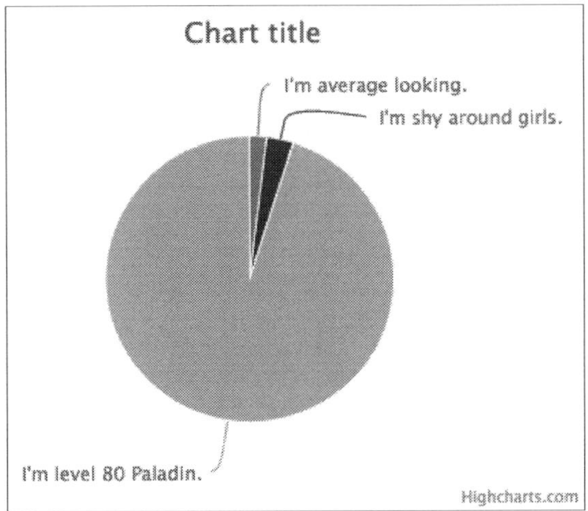

Getting ready

Download the Highcharts JavaScript library from `http://www.highcharts.com/download`.

How to do it...

Carry out the following steps to create a pie chart using Highcharts:

1. Create a class named `HighchartsState` that extends `JavaScriptComponentState`. This class will be used as a transport box between Java and JavaScript.

```
package com.packtpub.vaadin;

import com.vaadin.shared.ui.JavaScriptComponentState;
import org.json.JSONObject;

public class HighchartsState extends JavaScriptComponentState {

  private JSONObject data;

  public JSONObject getData() {
    return data;
  }

  public void setData(JSONObject data) {
    this.data = data;
  }
}
```

2. Create a `Highcharts` class that will represent a Vaadin component that is able to communicate with JavaScript. We need to link this component with JavaScript files. We will do this by using the `@JavaScript` annotation from Vaadin as follows:

```
@JavaScript({
  "https://ajax.googleapis.com/ajax/libs/jquery/1.7.2/
  jquery.min.js",
  "http://code.highcharts.com/highcharts.js",
  "highcharts_connector.js" })
public class Highcharts extends
  AbstractJavaScriptComponent {

  @Override
  public HighchartsState getState() {
    return (HighchartsState) super.getState();
  }

  public void setData(String jsonData) {
    try {
      JSONObject data = new JSONObject(jsonData);
      getState().setData(data);
    } catch (JSONException e) {
      e.printStackTrace();
    }
  }
}
```

3. Now we should add the code that displays the chart into the `init` method of the `HighchartsUI` class. We make JSON data as a pure string and set it to the Highcharts component.

```
public class MyVaadinUI extends UI {

  @Override
  protected void init(VaadinRequest request) {
    VerticalLayout layout = new VerticalLayout();
            layout.setMargin(true);
            setContent(layout);

    String jsonData =
    "{" +
      "chart : " +
      "{renderTo : 'chart',}, " +
      "series : " +
      "[ " +
        "{" +
```

```
                "type : 'pie', " +
                "data : " +
                "[ " +
                  "[ 'I'm average looking.', 2 ], " +
                  "[ 'I'm shy around girls.', 3 ], " +
                  "[ 'I'm level 80 Paladin.', 95 ] " +
                "] " +
              "} " +
            "] " +
        "}";
        Highcharts highchartsPie = new Highcharts();

        highchartsPie.setData(jsonData);
        highchartsPie.setId("chart");
        highchartsPie.setWidth("400px");
        highchartsPie.setHeight("300px");

        layout.addComponent(highchartsPie);
    }
}
```

4. We are about to send JSON data to the JavaScript chart. Therefore, we need to make a connection between Java and JavaScript. Make a new source folder named `resources` and create a `com.packtpub.vaadin` package in it. Create a new file named `highcharts_connector.js` and put the the following code into it:

```
window.com_packtpub_vaadin_Highcharts = function() {

  this.onStateChange = function() {
    var chart = new Highcharts.Chart
    (this.getState().data);
  }
}
```

Run the application and the pie chart appears in the browser.

How it works...

First, we create JSON data that we want to send to JavaScript. Then, we set the JSON data to the instance of the `Highcharts` class. This propagates the data to JavaScript via `HighchartsState`.

We have also set `Id` to `chart` on the `highchartPie` variable. This marks the HTML element so the chart library knows where to render the chart (`renderTo : 'chart'`).

Inside the `@JavaScript` annotation, we have defined all the JavaScript libraries that need to be downloaded before the Highcharts can be used. We have added links to the libraries from the web, `http://code.highcharts.com/highcharts.js` for example. We should download the libraries and put them into the project folder, so the downloading does not depend on external websites.

```
@JavaScript({ "jquery.min.js", "highcharts.js",
  "highcharts_connector.js" })
```

The way we have passed the JSON data into the Highcharts chart can be used for all the charts contained in the Highcharts library.

See also

- We do not have to implement all the charts by ourselves. Vaadin Charts is a paid add-on that uses the Highcharts library and contains many ready-made charts. More information about this add-on can be found at `https://vaadin.com/add-ons/charts`.

Drag-and-drop from the desktop

Drag-and-drop is a very useful and practical feature. Users can simply grab an object with the mouse and drag it to a different location. It's very common that users can drag-and-drop objects inside the application. But we will create something much more interesting. We will create an application that allows us to grab an object on the desktop (a file, image, or document) and drop it to the Vaadin application. And there's more. This object will be uploaded to the server. We'll call it `DragAndDropUploader`.

We will learn how to create a drag-and-drop component for every component in Vaadin and how to upload files to the server. The list of the uploaded files will be shown in the table, as we can see in the following screenshot:

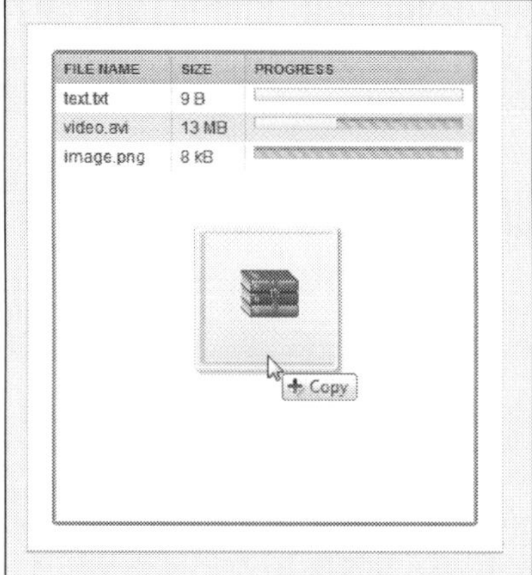

How to do it...

Carry out the following steps to create a drag-and-drop uploader:

1. We create a Vaadin project with the main UI class named `Demo`, for example, as follows:

```
public class Demo extends UI {…}
```

2. We create new class `DragAndDropUploader` as follows:

```
public class DragAndDropUploader extends
  VerticalLayout {…}
```

3. First, we need a repository for our uploaded files. We create a folder called `vaadin-repo` on our disk and we write this path to the `REPOSITORY` constant .

```
private static final String REPOSITORY =
               <insert path to Vaadin-repo folder>;
```

4. In the constructor, we create and initialize the table and then we wrap this table by `DragAndDropWrapper`. This wrapper enables creation of the droppable component. We will call that object `dropTable`.

```
  public DragAndDropUploader() {
    final Table table = new Table();
    table.setSizeFull();
    table.addContainerProperty
      ("File name",String.class,null);
    table.addContainerProperty
      ("Size", String.class, null);
    table.addContainerProperty("Progress",
          ProgressIndicator.class, null);
    DragAndDropWrapper dropTable =
          new DragAndDropWrapper(table);
```

5. In `dropTable`, we set `DropHandler`. This handler is used for working with dropped objects on this table. The `getAcceptCriterion()` method returns the `AcceptCriterion` object used to evaluate whether the `Transferable` object will be handed over to the `DropHandler.drop(DragAndDropEvent)` method. If we don't want to add any special restrictive criteria, we can accept all dropped objects by calling the `AcceptAll.get()` method.

```
    dropTable.setDropHandler(new DropHandler() {

      @Override
      public AcceptCriterion getAcceptCriterion() {
        return AcceptAll.get();
    }

    …
```

6. Next we add the implementation of the `drop()` method. In the `setDropHandler()` method, we get the transferred object from the object event. Then, we obtain all transferred files as an array of `Html5File`. For each file, we create a progress indicator that will show us that a big part of the file has already been uploaded. We set a 100 milliseconds polling interval on this indicator. It ensures the server is visited every 100 milliseconds. As an example, it is OK, but on the production system it is better to set a longer interval. Next, we add a new row to the table that consists of three columns: file name, size of file, and progress indicator.

```
@Override
public void drop(DragAndDropEvent event) {

  WrapperTransferable transferred =
  (WrapperTransferable) event.getTransferable();
  Html5File files[] = transferred.getFiles();
  if (files != null) {
    for (final Html5File file : files) {
      ProgressIndicator indicator =
                         new ProgressIndicator();
      indicator.setPollingInterval(100);
      indicator.setSizeFull();
      table.addItem(new Object[] {
        file.getFileName(),
        getSizeAsString (file.getFileSize()),
        indicator}, null;
```

7. Streaming files to the server is provided by the `streamVariable` object. We create this object in the next method. We also add a notification for the unsupported dropped object. At the end in the constructor, we add a `dropTable` component to the layout and set the size of this layout.

```
          StreamVariable streamVariable =
                    createStreamVariable(file, indicator);
                    file.setStreamVariable(streamVariable);
          }
        } else {
          Notification.show(
            "Unsupported object", Type.ERROR_MESSAGE);
        }
      }
    });

    addComponent(dropTable);
    setSizeUndefined();
  }
```

8. Now we add a method for creating the `streamVariable` object. In this method, we have to implement many methods. For example, in the `onProgress()` method, we can update the progress indicator. In the `streamFailed` method, we can inform the user about errors. And a very important method is `streamingFinished()`, because this method will allow us to save the uploaded file on the disk installed on the server. After a successful upload, we set the indicator's value to `1.0` which means that the upload is done.

```
private StreamVariable createStreamVariable
(final Html5File
           file, final ProgressIndicator indicator) {
  final ByteArrayOutputStream outputStream =
        new ByteArrayOutputStream();
  return new StreamVariable() {

    public OutputStream getOutputStream() {
      return outputStream;
    }

    public boolean listenProgress() {
      return true;
    }

    public void onProgress(StreamingProgressEvent
      event) {
      indicator.setValue((float)
      event.getBytesReceived() / file.getFileSize());
    }

    public void streamingStarted(StreamingStartEvent
      event){
    }

    public void streamingFinished
    (StreamingEndEvent event) {
      try {
        FileOutputStream fos = new FileOutputStream(
                  REPOSITORY + file.getFileName());
        outputStream.writeTo(fos);
      } catch (IOException e) {
        Notification.show(
          "Streaming finished failed",
          Type.ERROR_MESSAGE);
      }
      indicator.setValue(new Float(1.0));
    }
```

```
        public void streamingFailed
        (StreamingErrorEvent event) {
          Notification.show(
            "Streaming failed", Type.ERROR_MESSAGE);
        }

        public boolean isInterrupted() {
          return false;
        }
      };
    }
```

9. In the last method, we adapt the number of `long` type to `String`. We use this method for adding units.

```
    private String getSizeAsString(long size) {
      String unit = "B";
      if (size > 1024) {
        size = size / 1024;
        unit = "kB";
      }

      if (size > 1024) {
        size = size / 1024;
        unit = "MB";
      }

      return size + " " + unit;
    }
```

10. Now we add our created `DragAndDropUploader` to the main UI class as follows:

```
public class Demo extends UI {

  @Override
  protected void init(VaadinRequest request) {
    setContent(new DragAndDropUploader());
  }
}
```

The application is now ready. We can run the server and show it in the web browser.

How it works...

Users can easily grab an object from the desktop and drop it to the table in our web application. It works in all web browsers that support HTML 5.

The `DragAndDropWrapper` allows dragging files from outside the browser and dropping them on a component wrapped in the wrapper. In our case, it's the `Table` component. Dropped files are automatically uploaded to the application and they are acquired from the wrapper (the `WrapperTransferable` class) with the `getFiles()` method that returns an array of `Html5File`. Using the `StreamVariable`, we upload those files to the server. `StreamVariable` is a special kind of variable whose value is streamed to an `OutputStream` provided by the `getOutputStream()` method.

If we want to restrict dropping some object into our wrapped component, we can do it by the `getAcceptCriterion()` method of the `DropHandler` interface. A drop handler must define the criterion on the objects that it accepts as suitable to be dropped on the target. We can create *client-side* criteria by extending the `ClientSideCriterion` abstract class or *server-side* criteria by extending `ServerSideCriterion`. If we don't have a lot of users, we can use *server-side* criteria because doing so allows fully programmable logic for accepting drops. However, it causes a lot of requests to the server. More detailed information about accepting drops is on the Vaadin web page at the link mentioned in the following section.

See also

- More information about `ProgressIndicator` and error messages are described in the *Informing about file transfers by a progress bar* recipe in *Chapter 6, Messages*
- Detailed information about drag-and-drop features is on the Vaadin web page `https://vaadin.com/book/vaadin7/-/page/advanced.dragndrop.html`

Using DateField with Joda-Time DateTime

Form creation has been improved in Vaadin 7, so it is easier to handle custom types. In this recipe, we will show how to create a form that handles a bean that contains `DateTime` type from the Joda-Time library.

We will create a simple form for editing a post. The post will be represented by a domain object, which will consist of text and date fields. The text field will be a simple string, as shown in the following screenshot. The date field will be of the `DateTime` type from the Joda-Time framework.

More information about the Joda-Time framework can be found at `http://joda-time.sourceforge.net`.

Getting ready

If you are using the Eclipse project, then go to `http://joda-time.sourceforge.net` and download the Joda-Time library. Copy `joda-time-[version].jar` into the `WebContent/WEB-INF/lib` folder.

In case of Maven, add the dependency to the Joda-Time library in the `pom.xml` file:

```
<dependency>
  <groupId>joda-time</groupId>
  <artifactId>joda-time</artifactId>
  <version>2.2</version>
</dependency>
```

How to do it...

Carry out the following steps in order to make a form with the `DateTime` type:

1. Make a domain object that represents a post.

   ```
   package com.packtpub.vaadin;

   import org.joda.time.DateTime;

   public class Post {

     private String text;
     private DateTime created;
     // generate getter and setter methods
   ```

2. Create and set up an instance of the `Post` class inside the `init` method of our `UI` class.

   ```
   Post post = new Post();
   String label = "I really need that stuff.";
   post.setText(label);
   DateTime created = DateTime.now();
   post.setCreated(created);
   ```

3. Create `BeanItem` to which we pass the instance of the `Post` class and put that instance into the instance of `FieldGroup`.

   ```
   BeanItem<Post> postBean = new BeanItem<Post>(post);
   FieldGroup fieldGroup = new FieldGroup(postBean);
   ```

4. At this moment, we need to define our own `FieldGroupFieldFactory` that will allow us to make a `DateField` with a special converter for the Joda `DateTime` type.

```
public class JodaFieldFactory extends
DefaultFieldGroupFieldFactory {

  @Override
  public <T extends Field> T createField
  (Class<?> type, Class<T> fieldType) {
    T field;
    if (type.isAssignableFrom(DateTime.class)) {
      DateField dateField = new DateField();
      dateField.setConverter(new DateTimeConverter());
      field = (T) dateField;
    } else {
      field = super.createField(type, fieldType);
    }
    return field;
  }
}
```

5. The converter should be able to convert `Date` to `DateTime` and vice versa. It is because `Date` is a type that is used for presentation type of `DateTime` for `DateField`.

```
public class DateTimeConverter implements Converter<Date,
DateTime> {

  @Override
  public DateTime convertToModel
    (Date value, Locale locale)
  throws ConversionException {
    return new DateTime(value);
  }

  @Override
  public Date convertToPresentation(DateTime value,
    Locale locale) throws ConversionException {
    Date date = value.toDate();
    return date;
  }

  @Override
  public Class<DateTime> getModelType() {
    return DateTime.class;
  }
```

```
    @Override
    public Class<Date> getPresentationType() {
      return Date.class;
    }
  }
```

6. Make an instance of `JodaFieldFactory` and set it to the `fieldGroup`.

```
FieldGroupFieldFactory fieldFactory = new
  JodaFieldFactory();
fieldGroup.setFieldFactory(fieldFactory);
```

7. Create `FormLayout` and add the components by using the `buildAndBind` method from the `FieldGroup` class.

```
FormLayout formLayout = new FormLayout();
formLayout.addComponent(fieldGroup.buildAndBind("text"));
formLayout.addComponent(fieldGroup.buildAndBind
  ("created"));
```

8. The last step is to add `formLayout` into the layout and we can then run the application.

```
VerticalLayout layout = new VerticalLayout();
layout.setMargin(true);
setContent(layout);
layout.addComponent(formLayout);
```

How it works...

Forms, as we know from Vaadin 6, are dramatically refactored in Vaadin 7. They now consist of two parts: data binding and layout. The data binding is done by `FieldGroup`, while the layout is done by `FormLayout`. That is why we initially bound the data via `BeamItem` and `FieldGroup`, and then took care of the layout by using `FormLayout`.

We have made our own `FieldGroupFieldFactory`. There we make our Joda-Time date and time fields with a special convertor `DateTimeConverter` assigned. That converter enables the conversion of the presentation type `DateField` to `DateTime` and vice versa.

There's more...

Note that `FieldGroup` is not a UI component and therefore it cannot be added to a Vaadin container. The `buildAndBind` method builds the component by using a factory field and also binds data from the domain object so they appear in the created components.

Zooming with the slider

Another nice component is the slider. We use this component in situations when we want to select a value between minimum and maximum. Users can change a value by sliding a graphical *thumb*. The slider can be in a horizontal or vertical position. Using the slider is very easy in a Vaadin application. We will show it for zooming in on images. The minimum value will be 0 percent and the maximum will be 100 percent.

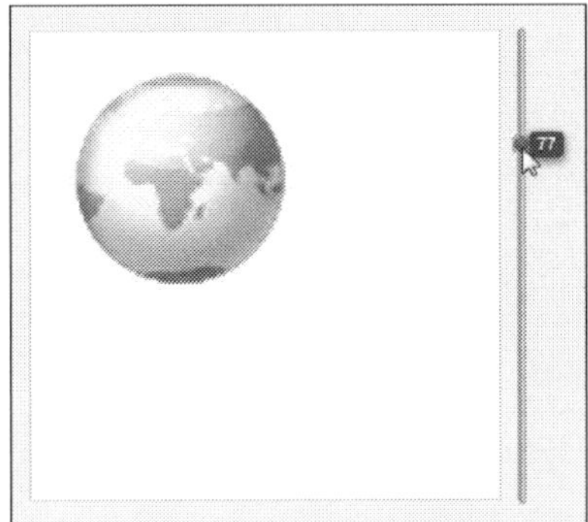

How to do it...

Carry out the following steps to learn how to use the slider component:

1. We create a Vaadin project with the main UI class named `Demo`, for example, as follows:

   ```
   public class Demo extends UI {…}
   ```

2. We create another class named `Zooming` that extends `HorizontalLayout` as follows:

   ```
   public class Zooming extends HorizontalLayout {…}
   ```

3. We add a constant for the default image zoom.

   ```
   private static final int DEFAULT_ZOOM = 60;
   ```

4. Now we create a zoom panel in the constructor. Our zoomed image will be icon `globe.png` from the Runo theme. We add it on the panel that will have a fixed width and height.

   ```
   public Zooming() {
     setSpacing(true);
     setMargin(true);

     Panel zoomPanel = new Panel();
     final Image = new Image("",
   ```

```
        new ThemeResource("../runo/icons/64/globe.png"));
  image.setWidth(DEFAULT_ZOOM, Unit.PERCENTAGE);
  zoomPanel.addComponent(image);
  zoomPanel.setWidth(300, Unit.PIXELS);
  zoomPanel.setHeight(300, Unit.PIXELS);
  ...
```

5. Next, we create the slider. This slider is vertically oriented and takes the full size. We set our default zoom value, because we want to keep the same value on the image and on the slider. Next, we add `ValueChangeListener`. After each change of the slider value, the new width of the image is set in percentage. When we change only one size (width or height) on the HTML image, the second size is adjusted accordingly. The image will still keep its proportions, but it will be bigger or smaller than the original value.

```
    final Slider slider = new Slider();
    slider.setSizeFull();
    slider.setImmediate(true);
    slider.setOrientation(SliderOrientation.VERTICAL);
    slider.setValue((double) DEFAULT_ZOOM);
    slider.addValueChangeListener(
          new Property.ValueChangeListener() {
      @Override
      public void valueChange(ValueChangeEvent event) {
        double value = slider.getValue();
        image.setWidth((float) value, Unit.PERCENTAGE);
      }
    });
    ...
```

6. Now we add a zoom panel and slider to the layout as follows:

```
      addComponent(zoomPanel);
      addComponent(slider);
    }
  }
```

7. At the end, we insert our created `Zooming` component into the main UI class as follows:

```
public class Demo extends UI {
  @Override
  protected void init(VaadinRequest request) {
    setContent(new Zooming());
  }
}
```

The application is now ready. We can run the server and show it in the web browser.

How it works...

Our simple application consists of one panel with an image and one vertical slider. When the user changes the value by the slider, the image size will be changed accordingly. The slider's minimum and maximum values are `0` and `100` by default, so we don't need to change these values because we work with the same range from 0 percent to 100 percent. When we want to set a different range, we can do it in the `Slider(int min, int max)` constructor. Using the `setResolution(int resolution)` method, we can also set the number of digits after the decimal point of the displayed value.

Restricting buttons in Rich text area

Vaadin provides a very useful component called `RichTextArea`. In this area, we can edit formatted text. The content is represented in HTML and it consists of two toolbars. Sometimes users don't need all the functions, for example in a simple web chat. Only basic functions such as bold, italic, and underline are sufficient. In those cases, it's better to use fewer buttons than those set by default. The editor then becomes clearer and easier for users. Sometimes less is more. In this example, we will learn how to do it.

This is the Rich text area with default buttons:

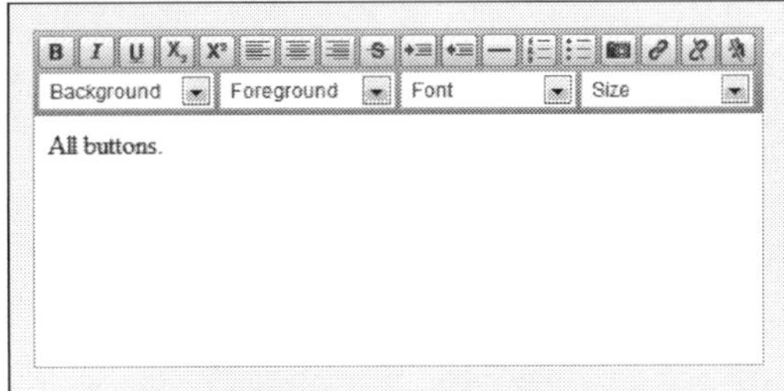

This is our target. We have restricted the number of buttons.

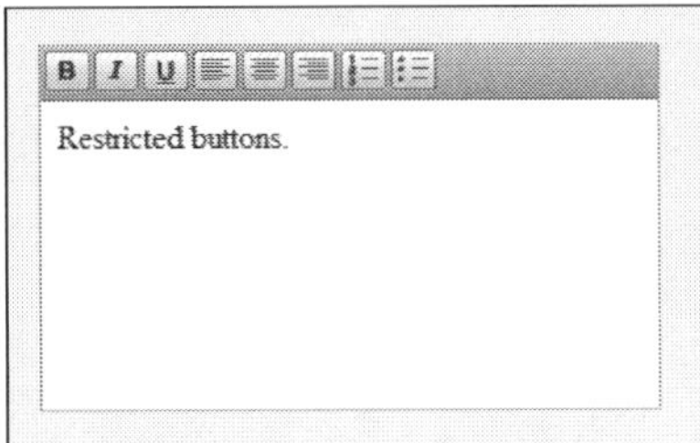

How to do it...

Carry out the following steps to restrict the number of buttons in the Rich text area component:

1. We create a Vaadin project with the main UI class named `Demo` as follows:

   ```
   public class Demo extends UI {…}
   ```

2. In the `init` method, we create an instance of the `RichTextArea` class and we set it as the content of our application. We will create a new SCSS style with a class called simply `my`. If we want to use a style defined in this class, we have to set this name as a style name on the component.

   ```
   public class Demo extends UI {
     @Override
     protected void init(VaadinRequest request) {

       RichTextArea richTextArea = new RichTextArea();
       richTextArea.setStyleName("myRichTextArea");
       setContent(richTextArea);
     }
   }
   ```

3. For restricting buttons, we will create a new theme. If we want to use this theme, we have to specify it by annotation on the main UI class. We can call it `mytheme`.

   ```
   @Theme("mytheme")
   public class Demo extends UI {…}
   ```

4. Now we create a folder called `mytheme` in the following path and we create two SCSS files in this folder. We use SCSS files because Vaadin uses Sass and the recommended structure is to divide our own theme into at least two files. More information about theming is described in the next recipe.

   ```
   WebContent/VAADIN/themes/mytheme/styles.scss
   WebContent/VAADIN/themes/mytheme/mytheme.scss
   ```

5. The main file is `styles.scss`. In this file, we import our style called `mytheme`.

   ```
   @import "mytheme.scss";
   .mytheme {
     @include mytheme;
   }
   ```

6. Next, we create our own style in the `mytheme.scss` file. In the beginning, we need some default style. So we import the Reindeer style on the first line in our SCSS file.

   ```
   @import "../reindeer/reindeer.scss";
   ```

7. Then we mix our style with this default one as follows:

```
@mixin mytheme {
  @include reindeer;
  ...
```

8. On the next line, we restrict the whole bottom toolbar of Rich text area defined only to our CSS `my` class.

```
  .my .gwt-RichTextToolbar-bottom {
    display: none;
  }
  ...
```

9. To restrict specific buttons, we add the following code:

```
  .my .gwt-RichTextToolbar .gwt-ToggleButton
    [title="Toggle Subscript"],
  .my .gwt-RichTextToolbar .gwt-ToggleButton
    [title="Toggle Superscript"],
  .my .gwt-RichTextToolbar .gwt-ToggleButton
    [title="Toggle Strikethrough"],
  .my .gwt-RichTextToolbar .gwt-PushButton
    [title="Indent Right"],
  .my .gwt-RichTextToolbar .gwt-PushButton
    [title="Indent Left"],
  .my .gwt-RichTextToolbar .gwt-PushButton
    [title="Insert Horizontal Rule"],
  .my .gwt-RichTextToolbar .gwt-PushButton
    [title="Insert Image"],
  .my .gwt-RichTextToolbar .gwt-PushButton
    [title="Create Link"],
  .my .gwt-RichTextToolbar .gwt-PushButton
    [title="Remove Link"],
  .my .gwt-RichTextToolbar .gwt-PushButton
    [title="Remove Formatting"]{
  display: none;
}
```

That's all. Now we can run our application and show it in the web browser.

How it works...

An element can be hidden using the `display: none` property. It's completely hidden. There isn't any free space left (after `visibility: hidden`). Web browsers normally download all elements that are hidden using `display: none`. When we hide a button, it does not mean that its related function is disabled. For example, when we hide the button for the *Bold* function, users can still use this style by pressing *Ctrl* + *B*.

There's more...

If we need to restrict other buttons or a toolbar, we can use CSS classes from this list:

- The following screenshot shows the top toolbar. In CSS it's defined by the `.gwt-RichTextToolbar-top` class.

- The following screenshot shows the bottom toolbar. In CSS it's defined by the `.gwt-RichTextToolbar-bottom` class.

- In the following figure, we can find the CSS classes of all buttons used in the Rich text area. Some of them are toggle buttons and others are push buttons.

Styling components with CSS

In this recipe, we will learn how to change the CSS style of components. We'll create a new theme for the `Table`. Vaadin's `Table` has gray stripes by default. We will change it. Our new table will be without static stripes. Instead, we will add a style for a dynamic strip. The yellow strip will appear when the mouse hovers over the row.

The following screenshot shows the default style for tables:

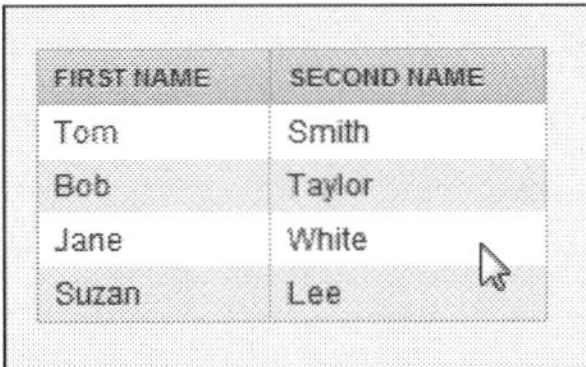

The following screenshot shows our new style for tables:

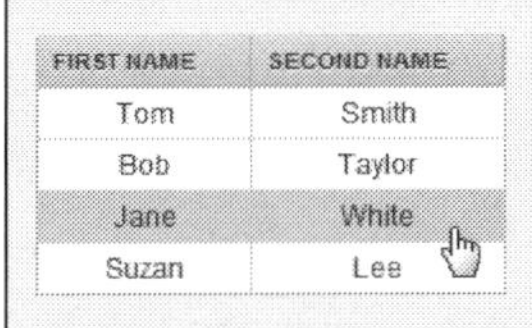

How to do it...

Carry out the following steps to learn how to change the CSS style of components:

1. We create a Vaadin project with the main UI class called `Demo` as follows:

   ```
   public class Demo extends UI {…}
   ```

2. In the main class of the `init()` method, we create a simple `Table` with some rows. In the following steps, we will create our new style called `myTable`. We set this style name to the Table. For a better view, we set the number of visible table rows according to the number of items in the table using the `setPageLength()` method.

   ```
   @Override
     public void init(WrappedRequest request) {

       Table table = new Table();
       table.setStyleName("myTable");
       table.addContainerProperty(
             "First name", String.class, null);
       table.addContainerProperty(
   ```

```
            "Second name", String.class, null);
        table.addItem(new Object[]{"Tom", "Smith"}, 0);
        table.addItem(new Object[]{"Bob", "Taylor"}, 1);
        table.addItem(new Object[]{"Jane", "White"}, 2);
        table.addItem(new Object[]{"Suzan", "Lee"}, 3);
        table.setPageLength(table.size());
        addComponent(table);

    }
```

3. Using the `@Theme` annotation on the UI class, we specify the theme we want to use in our application. So we use the theme called `mytheme`.

```
@Theme("mytheme")
public class Demo extends UI {…}
```

4. Now we create a folder called `mytheme` placed in the following path and we create two SCSS files in this folder. We use SCSS files because Vaadin uses Sass and the recommended structure is to divide our own theme into at least two files.

```
WebContent/VAADIN/themes/mytheme/styles.scss
WebContent/VAADIN/themes/mytheme/mytheme.scss
```

5. The main file is `styles.scss`. In this file we import our style called `mytheme`.

```
@import "mytheme.scss";
.mytheme {
  @include mytheme;
}
```

6. Next, we create our own style in the `mytheme.scss` file. In the beginning, we need a default style. So we import the Reindeer style on the first line in our SCSS file.

```
@import "../reindeer/reindeer.scss";
```

7. Then, we mix our style with this default one as follows.

```
@mixin mytheme {
  @include reindeer;
  …
```

8. At first we set the background color to white on all rows only for our CSS `myTable` class.

```
  .myTable .v-table-row,
  .myTable .v-table-row-odd {
    background: white;
  }
  …
```

9. Then we set a gold background and show the cursor type as pointer on the hovered rows.

```
.myTable .v-table-row:hover,
.myTable .v-table-row-odd:hover {
  background-color: gold;
  cursor: pointer;
}
```

10. Finally, we align text to the center and apply a light gray border around each cell in the content.

```
.myTable .v-table-cell-content {
  text-align: center;
  border-top: 1px solid lightgray;
}
```

The new style is done. Now we can run the server and open our application in the web browser.

How it works...

Vaadin 7 uses Sass for stylesheets. Sass is an extension of **CSS3** that adds nested rules, variables, mixins, selector inheritance, and other features to **CSS**. Sass supports two formats for stylesheets: `.scss` and `.sass`. Vaadin themes are written in **SCSS** (Sassy CSS, `.scss`) which is a superset of **CSS3**. It means that every valid **CSS3** stylesheet is valid **SCSS** as well. We can also use older syntax Sass (`.sass`) that allows a more concise indented format.

Custom themes are placed in the fixed location under the `VAADIN/themes` folder. We need to have a theme folder for each theme we use in our application.

There's more...

Each component in Vaadin has its own CSS style class that we can use to control the appearance of the component. Some components have additional subelements that also allow styling. These classes are listed at the end of chapters about UI components on the Vaadin web. For example, CSS Style rules of `Table` are described at `https://vaadin.com/book/vaadin7/-/page/components.table.html#components.table.css`.

See also

- More information about using and creating themes in Vaadin is available at `https://vaadin.com/book/vaadin7/-/page/themes.html`
- Sass stylesheet language is described at `http://sass-lang.com/`

4
Custom Widgets

In this chapter, we will cover:

- Creating a TextField with counter
- Creating a TextField only for digits
- Creating a chroma-hash password field
- Creating a tri-state checkbox using JavaScript
- Styling widgets
- Speeding up widget set compilation

Introduction

The main benefit of the custom widget is that core implementation is on the client side on the web browser and it does not need communication between server and client. The widget is represented by HTML and JavaScript. We will show how to extend text field widgets from the GWT library. We will create our custom text fields and our tri-state checkbox. We will learn how to use listeners on the GWT widgets, how to share state between widget and component, and how to call native JavaScript. We will also show how to change the CSS style of widget. Compiling a widget set during development can take a long time. In the last recipe, we will describe how to speed up the compilation. All these recipes are made in the Eclipse IDE.

If we want to create a new component, we will need to make three things:

- **A client-side widget**: It will render our component in the web browser using HTML and JavaScript. It uses GWT Java libraries.
- **A connector**: It handles the communication between the widget and the component.
- **A server-side component**: This will be used in our application. It uses Vaadin Java libraries.

Creating a TextField with counter

In some cases, we need to use text fields with limited character length, usually for forms that submit data to database. It is nice to tell the user how many characters remain. For that case, we can create our custom text field with a counter, as shown in the following screenshot. In this recipe, we will show how to do it.

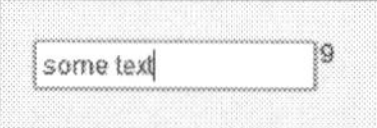

How to do it...

Carry out the following steps to create a `TextField` with a counter:

1. We create a Vaadin project with a main UI class named `Demo` as follows:

   ```
   public class Demo extends UI {…}
   ```

2. The easiest way to create a new component is to use Eclipse IDE. We open the context menu on the project and choose **New | Other...**. A wizard will open. In the wizard, we type `vaadin`. Then we select the item **Vaadin Widget** and click on the **Next** button, as shown in the following screenshot:

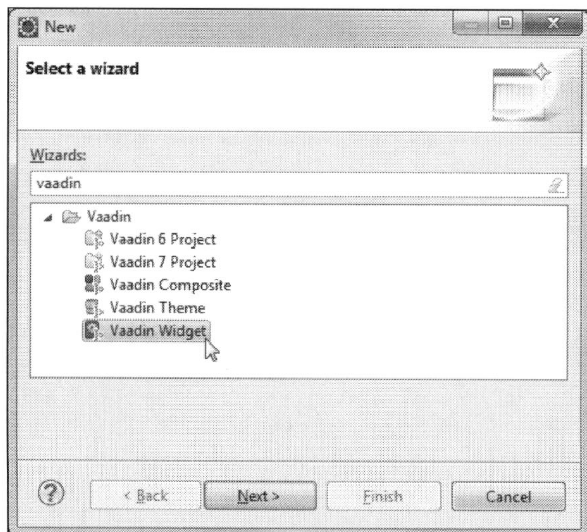

3. On the next page, we set some properties. Package will be `com.packtpub.vaadin.widget`. The name of our new component will be `CountedTextField` and as a superclass we set `com.vaadin.ui.TextField`. After filling in the properties, we click on the **Finish** button, as shown in the following screenshot:

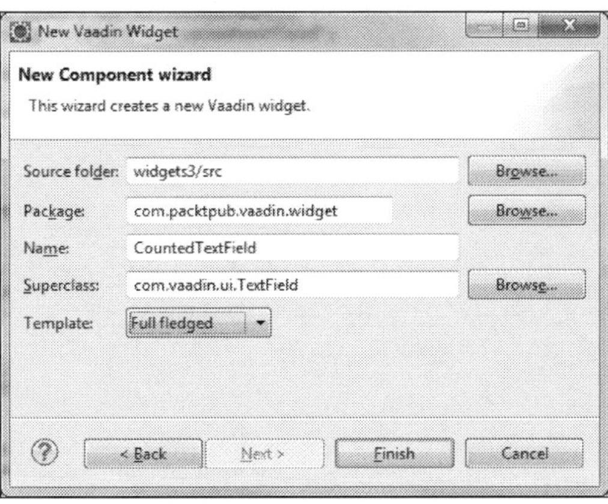

4. Eclipse will generate a skeleton of a simple custom component, as shown in the following screenshot. In our next step, we will edit it by removing and adding some methods.

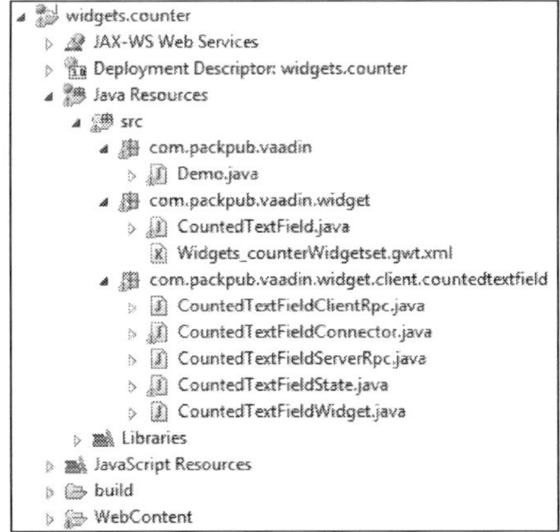

5. We start with editing the class `CountedTextFieldWidget`. This client-side widget will extend `Composite`. The `Composite` is a type of widget that wraps another widget. It hides the wrapped widget's methods.

```
import com.google.gwt.user.client.ui.Composite;

public class CountedTextFieldWidget extends Composite {
  ...
}
```

6. This widget consists of two parts: `TextBox` for user input and `Label` for showing the number of characters in `TextBox`. These two parts will be added to the `HorizontalPanel` because we want to show the label on the right side of the textbox. We create instances of these classes at the beginning of the `CountedTextFieldWidget` class. The generated constant `CLASSNAME` will be used to set default CSS style name of our widget.

```
import com.google.gwt.user.client.ui.TextBox;
import com.google.gwt.user.client.ui.Label;
import com.google.gwt.user.client.ui.HorizontalPanel;
 ...

private TextBox textBox = new TextBox();
private Label countLabel = new Label("0");
private HorizontalPanel panel = new HorizontalPanel();
public static final String
  CLASSNAME="countedtextfield";
```

7. In the constructor, we initialize our main panel because our widget is wrapped by the composite. It is very important to initialize the wrapped widget before calling any `Widget` methods on this object. Otherwise, our widget doesn't appear on the web page. This method may only be called once for a given composite. Then we set the name of our used CSS style and we add the created widgets to the panel.

```
public CountedTextFieldWidget() {
  initWidget(panel);
  setStyleName(CLASSNAME);
  panel.add(textBox);
  panel.add(countLabel);
}
```

8. Next, we add getters and setters. The best way to create an API is to hide the implementation of the internally used widgets. On the outside, we provide only the methods that are necessary for our `CountedTextFieldWidget`. For example, if we want to return text from our widget, we simply add the `getText()` method that hides implementation of the inner `textBox.getText()` method.

```
public String getText() {
  return textBox.getText();
}

public void setText(String text) {
  textBox.setText(text);
}

public void setCount(int count) {
  countLabel.setText("" + count);
}
```

9. At the end, we create a method for adding `KeyUpHandler`. Each `addXxxHandler()` method returns the `HandlerRegistration` interface. This interface contains the `removeHandler()` method that can be used to remove the handler from the widget.

   ```
   public HandlerRegistration addKeyUpHandler(
                              KeyUpHandler handler) {
     return textBox.addKeyUpHandler(handler);
   }
   ```

10. In the `CountedTextFieldState` class, we only rewrite the name of the primary style. We will do it using the non-static block that is executed before any constructor. The `primaryStyleName` string is inherited from the `AbstractFieldState` class. In that class, it's set to `v-textfield`. We remove this style because it conflicts with the default GWT style `gwt-TextBox`.

    ```
    public class CountedTextFieldState extends
      com.vaadin.shared.ui.textfield.AbstractTextFieldState {

      {
        primaryStyleName = null;
      }

    }
    ```

11. Now we continue to edit the `CountedTextFieldConnector` class. We don't need the generated stuff in the constructor. So, we clean the whole constructor and add `KeyUpHandler`. On the `KeyUp` event we update the value of the `countLabel` object. It causes the count of characters to be updated immediately after each key press.

    ```
    public CountedTextFieldConnector() {
      getWidget().addKeyUpHandler(new KeyUpHandler() {

        @Override
        public void onKeyUp(KeyUpEvent event) {
          String text = getWidget().getText();
          getWidget().setCount(text.length());
        }
      });
    }
    ```

12. Next, we edit the overridden method `onStateChanged()`. After each change of state, this method will update the value of `text` and `count` on our created widget. The variable `text` is from the inherited `AbstractTextFieldState` class.

    ```
    @Override
    public void onStateChanged(
                      StateChangeEvent stateChangeEvent) {
    ```

```
    super.onStateChanged(stateChangeEvent);
    final String text = getState().text;
    getWidget().setText(text);
    getWidget().setCount(text.length());
  }
```

13. In the server-side component `CountedTextField`, we can delete the generated stuff except the `getState()` method. Then we insert the overridden getter and setter of the component's `text` value. This value is propagated through the `CountedTextFieldState` component. Sending events from the server to the client works automatically in Vaadin. But the changes on the client side aren't automatically sent to the server-side component. For this purpose, we can use the **Remote Procedure Calls** (**RPC**) mechanism. The link to the Vaadin website about this mechanism is added in the *See also* section at the end of this recipe.

```
public class CountedTextField extends com.vaadin.ui.TextField {

  @Override
  public CountedTextFieldState getState() {
    return (CountedTextFieldState) super.getState();
  }

  @Override
  public String getValue() {
    return getState().text;
  }

  @Override
  public void setValue(String value) {
    getState().text = value;
  }
}
```

14. The last two generated classes `CountedTextFieldClientRpc` and `CountedTextFieldServerRpc` aren't used in our widget. We can delete them.

15. After editing all classes, we need to compile the widget set. We can do this by pressing *Ctrl* + *6* or by clicking on the icon, as shown in the following screenshot:

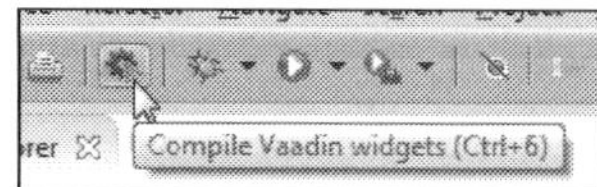

16. We can see the compiling process in the console in the following screenshot:

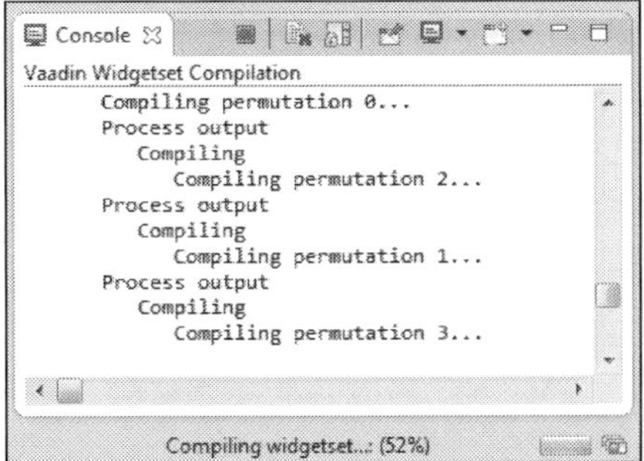

17. Generated files are in the `WebContent/VAADIN/widgetsets` folder.

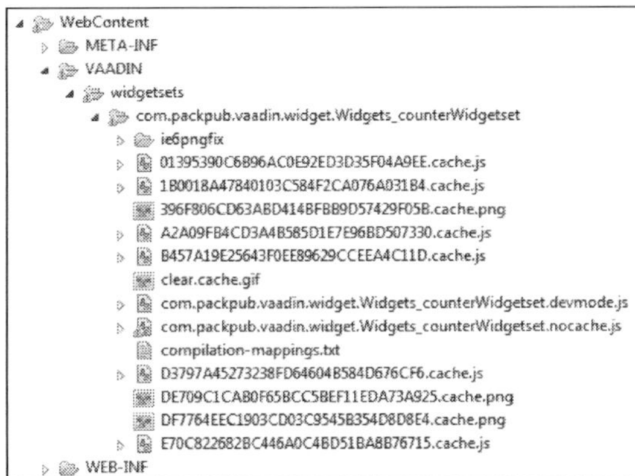

18. Our custom component is created. We can use it in our application as follows:

```
public class Demo extends UI {

  @Override
  protected void init(VaadinRequest request) {
    setContent(new CountedTextField());
  }

}
```

Now we can run the server and open our `Demo` application in a web browser.

How it works...

We created our custom text field with a counter. The counter shows how many characters are in the textbox. If the user enters some text to this field, then the `onKeyUp()` method in the `KeyUpHandler` on the `CountedTextFieldWidget` is called. Inside this method, we set the value of the label counter. It causes the counter to be updated immediately after each keystroke. Because changes on the client side aren't automatically sent to the server-side component, we can use the RPC mechanism that is described on the Vaadin website mentioned in the *See also* section.

There's more...

The Vaadin Plug-in for Eclipse can automatically compile the widget set after every client-side source file. This function is suspended by default. If we want to activate it, we can do it in the project properties in the following way. It can help us because we'll still have the last compiled widget set but it can use a lot of CPU and slow down the computer.

1. We open the context menu on the project.
2. Then we select the last item **Properties**. The properties wizard opens.
3. In menu, we select item **Vaadin.** The properties page for the Vaadin project opens.
4. In the **Widgetsets** frame, we uncheck **Suspend automatic widgetset builds**.

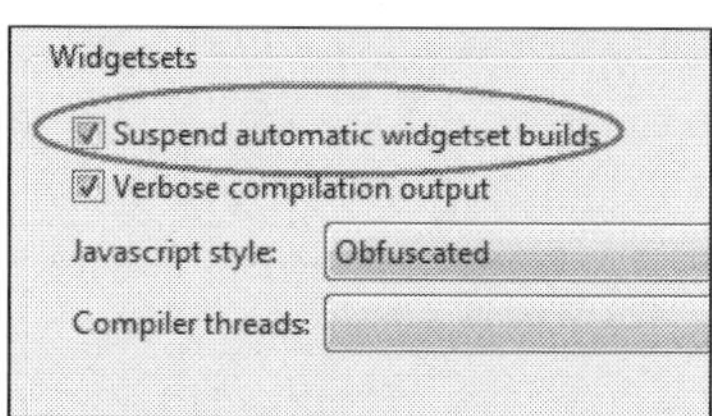

5. At the end we click on the **OK** or the **Apply** button.

See also

- Additional information about creating new widgets is available at the Vaadin website at `https://vaadin.com/book/vaadin7/-/page/part-clientside.html`
- Information about using the RPC mechanism to send event from the client to the server is described here `https://vaadin.com/book/vaadin7/-/page/gwt.rpc.html`

Creating a TextField only for digits

There are two ways to get valid input from the user using a textbox. Validate it after confirmation on the server side or during writing text on the client side. In this recipe, we will create a custom text field that validates the input during pressing keys. It will allow only digit keys.

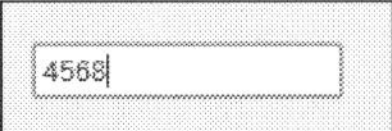

How to do it...

Carry out the following steps to create a text field that accepts only digit keystrokes from zero to nine:

1. We create a Vaadin project with the main UI class named `Demo` as follows:

   ```
   public class Demo extends UI {…}
   ```

2. We open the context menu on the project and choose **New** | **Other…**. A wizard opens. In the wizard, we select **Vaadin Widget** and click on the **Next** button.
3. On the next page we set some properties. Package will be `com.packtpub.vaadin.widget`. The name of our new component will be `IntegerTextField` and we set the superclass to `com.vaadin.ui.TextField`. After filling the properties, we click on the **Finish** button.
4. Eclipse will generate a skeleton of a simple custom component. In the next step we will edit it by removing and adding some methods.
5. We start with editing the `IntegerTextFieldWidget` class. This widget extends `TextBox` from the GWT library. We don't need any special methods. Only set the CSS style in the constructor.

   ```
   import com.google.gwt.user.client.ui.TextBox;

   public class IntegerTextFieldWidget extends TextBox {
     public static final String CLASSNAME =
       "integertextfield";

     public IntegerTextFieldWidget() {
       setStyleName(CLASSNAME);
     }

   }
   ```

6. Our main functionality is in the `IntegerTextFieldConnector` class. Here we need a constructor in which we add a key press handler in our textbox widget. It will check each keystroke. If the pressed key isn't a digit, then this keyboard event will be suppressed.

```
public IntegerTextFieldConnector() {
  getWidget().addKeyPressHandler(new KeyPressHandler() {

    @Override
    public void onKeyPress(KeyPressEvent event) {
      if (!Character.isDigit(event.getCharCode())) {
        getWidget().cancelKey();
      }
    }
  });

}
```

7. Other parts of the code are used, as they were generated. It's these methods: `createWidget()`, `getWidget()`, `getState()` and `onStateChanged()`. For example, in the generated `onStateChange()` method, we can see that the text of our widget is set according to the text in the state. The state is an instance of the `IntegerTextFieldState` class. This method is called if we set text on the state on the server-side component.

```
  @Override
  public void onStateChanged(
             StateChangeEvent stateChangeEvent) {
    super.onStateChanged(stateChangeEvent);
    final String text = getState().text;
   getWidget().setText(text);
  }
```

8. In the generated `IntegerTextFieldState` class, we delete the `public String text` variable because it's in conflict with the `text` variable inherited from the `AbstractTextFieldState` class. In our recipe we use the empty `IntegerTextFieldState` class.

```
public class IntegerTextFieldState extends
  com.vaadin.shared.ui.textfield.AbstractTextFieldState {

}
```

9. Now we can edit the server-side component `IntegerTextField`. Here we delete all the generated stuff. We only need the `getState()` method and we override the getter and setter methods for the variable value. As mentioned in the previous recipe, the changes on the client side aren't automatically sent to the server-side component. For this purpose we can use the RPC mechanism.

```
public class IntegerTextField extends
    com.vaadin.ui.AbstractComponent {

  @Override
  public IntegerTextFieldState getState() {
    return (IntegerTextFieldState) super.getState();
  }

  @Override
  public String getValue(){
    return getState().text;
  }

  @Override
  public void setValue(String value) {
    getState().text = value;
  }
}
```

10. The last two generated classes `IntegerTextFieldClientRpc` and `IntegerTextFieldServerRpc` aren't used in our widget. We can delete them.
11. After editing all classes, we need to compile the widget set. We can do it by pressing *Ctrl* + *6* or by clicking on the icon with a mouse.
12. Now we can use our new component in the topmost class:

```
public class Demo extends UI {

  @Override
  protected void init(VaadinRequest request) {
    setContent(new IntegerTextField());
  }
}
```

That is all. Now we can run the server and open the `Demo` application in a web browser.

How it works...

We created a textbox that allows only digit keystrokes. The keystrokes are checked in the `onKeyPress()` method in the `KeyPressHandler` that is added to the textbox widget. If the key pressed is not a digit, than this key will be suppressed.

See also

- Additional information about creating new components is on the Vaadin website at `https://vaadin.com/book/vaadin7/-/page/part-clientside.html`

Creating a chroma-hash password field

For security reasons, while entering the password, only the placeholders are displayed instead of the characters in the text field. In such a case, it may be easily misspelled. Some applications will block the user after a few bad attempts. To avoid these inconveniences, we use a very useful component chroma-hash password text field. This text field shows us the hash code of the text with colored stripes. When we create a new password, we remember this color combination. Then, when we enter the password, we know whether it's correct before it's sent to the system.

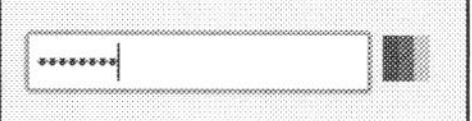

How to do it...

Carry out the following steps to create a password field with chroma-hash stripes:

1. We create a Vaadin project with the main UI class named `Demo` as follows:

   ```
   public class Demo extends UI {…}
   ```

2. We open the context menu on the project and choose **New | Other...**. A wizard opens. In the wizard, we select **Vaadin Widget** and click on the **Next** button.
3. On the next page we set some properties. The package will be `com.packtpub.vaadin.widget`. The name of our new component will be `ChromaHashPasswordField` and we set the superclass to `com.vaadin.ui.PasswordField`. After filling these properties, we click on the **Finish** button.
4. Eclipse will generate a skeleton of a simple custom component. In the next steps we will edit it by removing and adding some methods.

5. We start with editing the `ChromaHashPasswordFieldWidget` class. This widget extends `Composite` from the GWT library.

```
import com.google.gwt.user.client.ui.Composite;

public class ChromaHashPasswordFieldWidget
  extends Composite {…}
```

6. In this class, we initialize three objects: password textbox, color hash stripes that are represented by HTML `div`, and panel. Through the `numberStripes` variable, we can change the number of color stripes.

```
import com.google.gwt.user.client.ui.PasswordTextBox;
import com.google.gwt.user.client.ui.HTML;
import com.google.gwt.user.client.ui.HorizontalPanel;

  private PasswordTextBox textBox = new
    PasswordTextBox();
  private HTML chromaHashStripes = new HTML();
  private HorizontalPanel panel = new HorizontalPanel();
  private int numberStripes = 3;
```

7. In the constructor, we initialize the widget panel and then we add the password textbox and the HTML chroma hash stripes to this panel.

```
  public ChromaHashPasswordFieldWidget() {
    initWidget(panel);
    setStyleName(CLASSNAME);
    panel.add(textBox);
    panel.add(chromaHashStripes);
  }
```

8. Next, we create a method for getting color hash. It creates an array of codes according to the input text. The input text will be split into parts according to the required number of stripes. Then for each part a hash code is created. Using the `intToRGB()` method, we transform the given hash code to the hexadecimal RGB color value. This value will be used in the CSS style in the `updateChromaHashStripes()` method.

```
private String[] getChromaHash(
                String text, int numberStripes) {
  String salt = "du467e4aSdfe";
  text += salt;
  String[] colors = new String[numberStripes];
  int hash;
  int part = text.length() / numberStripes;
  for (int i = 0; i < numberStripes; i++) {
```

```
      hash = text.substring(part * i,
                         (part * i) + part).hashCode();
      colors[i] = "#" + intToRGB(hash);
    }
    return colors;
  }

  public String intToRGB(int i) {
    return Integer.toHexString(((i >> 16) & 0xFF))
        + Integer.toHexString(((i >> 8) & 0xFF))
        + Integer.toHexString((i & 0xFF));
    }
```

9. Our next method `updateChromaHashStripes()` should be declared as public, because it will be called from another object. It updates the `chromaHashStripes` object .

```
    public void updateChromaHashStripes() {
      String[] chromaHash =
               getChromaHash(getText(), numberStripes);
      int height = 18;
      int width = 6;

      String htmlStripes = "<div style=\"margin: 3px;\">";
      for (int i = 0; i < numberStripes; i++) {
        htmlStripes +=
        "<div style=\"background-color: "+ chromaHash[i]
             + "; float: left; height: " + height
             + "px; width: " + width + "px;\"></div>";
      }
      htmlStripes += "</div>";
      chromaHashStripes.setPixelSize(
                        height * 2, width * numberStripes);
      chromaHashStripes.setHTML(htmlStripes);
    }
```

10. Next, we add getters and setters. The best way to create an API is to hide the implementation of the internally used widgets. On the outside, we provide only the methods that are necessary for our widget. We also insert a method for adding `KeyUpHandler`.

```
    public String getText() {
      return textBox.getText();
    }
```

```
public void setText(String text) {
  textBox.setText(text);
}

public HandlerRegistration addKeyUpHandler
  (KeyUpHandler handler) {
  return textBox.addKeyUpHandler(handler);
}
```

11. In the `ChromaHashPasswordFieldConnector` class, we insert a constructor with one `KeyUpHandler`. After each keystroke, chroma hash stripes are updated.

```
public ChromaHashPasswordFieldConnector() {

  getWidget().addKeyUpHandler(new KeyUpHandler() {
    @Override
    public void onKeyUp(KeyUpEvent event) {
      getWidget().updateChromaHashStripes();
    }
  });
}
```

12. In the same class, we update the `onStateChange()` method. In this method, text value of the textbox is updated. We also insert a method that will update chroma hash stripes. This method is called after each change of state in the server-side component.

```
@Override
public void onStateChanged(
            StateChangeEvent stateChangeEvent) {
  super.onStateChanged(stateChangeEvent);
  final String text = getState().text;
  getWidget().setText(text);
  getWidget().updateChromaHashStripes();
}
```

13. In the `ChromaHashPasswordState` class, we only rewrite the name of the primary style. We'll do it using the non-static block that is executed before any constructor. The `primaryStyleName` string is inherited from the `AbstractFieldState` class. In that class, it's set to `v-textfield`. We remove this style because it conflicts with the default GWT style.

```
public class ChromaHashPasswordFieldState extends
  com.vaadin.shared.ui.textfield.AbstractTextFieldState {
  {
    primaryStyleName = null;
  }
}
```

14. The server-side component `ChromaHashPasswordField` is simple. We delete all generated stuff except the `getState()` method and we insert the overridden getter and setter of the value.

```
public class ChromaHashPasswordField extends
  com.vaadin.ui.PasswordField {

  @Override
  public ChromaHashPasswordFieldState getState() {
    return (ChromaHashPasswordFieldState)
      super.getState();
  }

  @Override
  public String getValue() {
    return super.getValue();
  }

  @Override
  public void setValue(String value) {
    getState().text = value;
  }
}
```

15. The last two generated classes `ChromaHashPasswordFieldClientRpc` and `ChromaHashPasswordFieldServerRpc` aren't used in our widget. We can delete them.
16. After editing all classes, we need to compile the widget set. We can do it by pressing *Ctrl* + *6* or clicking on the icon by mouse.
17. Now we use our new component in the main class `Demo`.

```
public class Demo extends UI {

  @Override
  protected void init(VaadinRequest request) {
    setContent(new ChromaHashPasswordField());
  }
}
```

That is all. We can run the server and open the application `Demo` in a web browser.

How it works...

In this recipe, we extended the common password text field. We added chroma-hash stripes that a user can use to check the entered password. The stripes are generated according to the entered text and they are updated immediately after each keystroke. They are represented by the HTML `<div>` elements with their own background color.

Creating a tri-state checkbox using JavaScript

The basic feature of a checkbox is to have two states: checked or unchecked. However, there are situations when we cannot decide the state of the checkbox. For example, if we have a list of checkboxes and one global checkbox for all these checkboxes in the list, and if all checkboxes in the list are checked, then global checkbox is also checked. If all checkboxes are unchecked, the global one is unchecked too. But what if some checkboxes are checked and some of them are unchecked? In that case, we set the global checkbox to an indeterminate state. As shown in the following screenshot, it's visually displayed as a filled square in the checkbox in the Chrome web browser. Unfortunately, it cannot be done through HTML. There are two possibilities: either create a custom icon for this state and then set the CSS style or set this state by calling JavaScript. The second option is better because it allows us to show an element natively using the web browser. In this recipe, we'll create such a tri-state checkbox button.

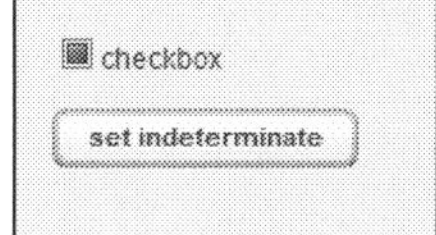

How to do it...

1. We create a Vaadin project with the main UI class named `Demo` as follows:

   ```
   public class Demo extends UI {…}
   ```

2. Open the context menu on the project and choose **New** | **Other...**. A wizard opens. In the wizard, we select **Vaadin Widget** and press the **Next** button.
3. On the next page we set some properties. The package will be `com.packtpub.vaadin.widget`. The name of our new component will be `TriStateCheckbox` and we set the superclass to `com.vaadin.ui.CheckBox`. After filling the properties, we click on the **Finish** button.
4. Eclipse will generate a skeleton of a simple custom component. In the next step, we will edit it by removing and adding some methods as follows.
5. We start with editing the `TriStateCheckboxWidget` class. This widget extends `CheckBox` from the GWT library.

   ```
   import com.google.gwt.dom.client.Element;
   import com.google.gwt.user.client.ui.CheckBox;

   public class TriStateCheckboxWidget extends CheckBox {
   ```

6. Next, we add our main variable `indeterminate` whose type is `boolean`. If the value of this variable is `true` then it means that the checkbox is in the indeterminate state and a filled square will be displayed in the checkbox. The generated constant `CLASSNAME` will be used as a CSS style name of this widget.

   ```
   private boolean indeterminate = false;
   public static final String
     CLASSNAME="tristatecheckbox";
   ```

7. The getter method for the `indeterminate` variable is simple and is as follows:

   ```
   public boolean isIndeterminate() {
     return indeterminate;
   }
   ```

8. Next, we insert a setter in which we pass the given `boolean` value to the internal variable `indeterminate`. Using the `setVisualIndeterminate()` method, we set the value of the HTML element. The checkbox is located as the first descendant of the current element.

   ```
   public void setIndeterminate(boolean indeterminate) {
     this.indeterminate = indeterminate;
     setVisualIndeterminate(
       getElement().getFirstChildElement(),indeterminate);
   }
   ```

9. Now we create method that will call the native JavaScript and set the `indeterminate` state of the given checkbox. If the `indeterminate` value will be `true`, a filled square will be displayed in the checkbox widget.

   ```
   public final native String setVisualIndeterminate(
     Element checkbox, boolean indeterminate) /*-{
     checkbox.indeterminate = indeterminate;
   }-*/;
   ```

10. Using the RPC (Remote Procedure Calls) mechanism, we can send information about changing the checkbox value from the widget on the client side to the component on the server side. This communication will be done through the `valueChanged()` method. We add this method signature to the `TriStateCheckboxServerRpc` interface.

    ```
    public interface TriStateCheckboxServerRpc
      extends ServerRpc {

      void valueChanged(boolean value);

    }
    ```

11. In the `TriStateCheckboxState` class we used the generated `text` field and we add another field called `indeterminate`. Through these fields we will share information about the component's state from the server to the client.

```
public class TriStateCheckboxState extends
  com.vaadin.shared.ui.checkbox.CheckBoxState {

  public String text = "This is TriStateCheckbox";
  public boolean indeterminate = false;

}
```

12. In the `TriStateCheckboxConnector` class, we update the constructor. Here we need only mouse click handler. On the click event we'll call method that will inform server component about change of the checkbox value. It causes that server-side component will keep an updated value.

```
  public TriStateCheckboxConnector() {

    getWidget().addClickHandler(new ClickHandler() {
      @Override
      public void onClick(ClickEvent event) {
        rpc.valueChanged(getWidget().getValue());
      }
    });
  }
```

13. Next we update generated `onStateChanged()` method. This method is called after each `TriStateCheckboxState` change. Here we update three variables of the checkbox. The variables `text` and `indeterminate` are from our `state` and the variable `checked` is from the inherited `CheckBoxState` class.

```
  @Override
  public void onStateChanged(
              StateChangeEvent stateChangeEvent) {
    super.onStateChanged(stateChangeEvent);
    getWidget().setText(getState().text);
    getWidget().setValue(getState().checked);
    getWidget().setIndeterminate
      (getState().indeterminate);
  }
```

14. In the server-side component `TriStateCheckbox`, we'll replace the generated code by our code. First, we add implementation of the `TriStateCheckboxServerRpc` interface. In the implemented `valueChanged()` method we set the boolean `value` of the checkbox and we set the `indeterminate` state to `false`, because if we set a `value`, we know the state of the checkbox and therefore it can't be indeterminate. The `valueChanged()` method is called from the client side widget after the mouse click event in the `TriStateCheckboxConnector` class. The `setValue()` method is inherited from the `AbstractField` class and the `setIndeterminate()` method will be added at the end of this class.

```
public class TriStateCheckbox extends
  com.vaadin.ui.CheckBox {

  private TriStateCheckboxServerRpc rpc =
          new TriStateCheckboxServerRpc() {

    @Override
    public void valueChanged(boolean value) {
      setValue(value);
      setIndeterminate(false);
    }
  };
```

15. In the constructor, we call the method for setting the checkbox's text and we register the created `rpc` object.

```
public TriStateCheckbox(String text) {
  getState().text = text;
  registerRpc(rpc);
}
```

16. The method `getState()` is the same as generated.

```
@Override
public TriStateCheckboxState getState() {
  return (TriStateCheckboxState) super.getState();
}
```

17. Next, we add two methods for setting and getting the information about the indeterminate value of the checkbox. This value is propagated through the inner state. When we change this state, the `onStateChanged()` method in the `TriStateCheckboxConnector` class is called.

```
public void setIndeterminate(boolean indeterminate) {
  getState().indeterminate = indeterminate;
}
```

```
    public boolean isIndeterminate() {
      return getState().indeterminate;
    }
  }
```

18. After editing all classes, we need to compile the widget set. We can do this by pressing *Ctrl* + *6* or by clicking on the icon.

19. Now we can use our created component in the main class `Demo`. It's a simple application with one `TriStateCheckbox` and one `Button`. If the user clicks on the button, the checkbox is set to the indeterminate state.

```
public class Demo extends UI {

  @Override
  protected void init(VaadinRequest request) {
    VerticalLayout layout = new VerticalLayout();
    layout.setSpacing(true);
    layout.setMargin(true);
    setContent(layout);

    final TriStateCheckbox triStateCheckbox =
          new TriStateCheckbox("checkbox");

    Button indeterminateButton =
           new Button("set indeterminate");
    indeterminateButton.addClickListener(
                        new ClickListener() {
      @Override
      public void buttonClick(ClickEvent event) {
        triStateCheckbox.setIndeterminate(
                   !triStateCheckbox.isIndeterminate());
      }
    });

    layout.addComponent(triStateCheckbox);
    layout.addComponent(indeterminateButton);
  }

}
```

Next, we run the server and open the application in the web browser.

How it works...

In this recipe, we extended a simple checkbox. We added a third state called `indeterminate`. When the component is in this state, a filled square is displayed in the middle of the checkbox. We can set the checkbox to this indeterminate state by using the `setIndeterminate(true)` method on the serve-side component called `TriStateCheckbox`. Setting this value causes a change of the inner `TriStateCheckboxState`. This change is detected by the `onStateChanged(StateChangeEvent)` method in the `TriStateCheckboxConnector`. And in this method we set the `indeterminate` value on the client widget, which then uses native JavaScript to set the given value on the HTML element.

Styling widgets

The default CSS style of a custom widget is based on the GWT style. In this recipe, we will show how to change it. As shown in the following screenshot, we will make a simple change. The label of the counter is aligned at the bottom and has a gray color.

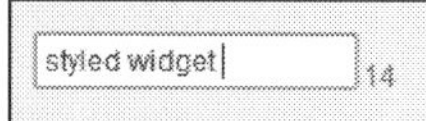

Getting ready

We create a widget text field with a counter as described in the *Creating a TextField with counter* recipe.

How to do it...

Carry out the following steps to learn how to style a widget:

1. In the constructor of the `CountedTextFieldWidget` class, we set the primary CSS style name of each widget because we want to set a new style for a specific widget. The name consists of a base style name plus a general name of the widget separated by a dash.

```
public CountedTextFieldWidget() {
  setStylePrimaryName(CLASSNAME);
  textBox.setStylePrimaryName(CLASSNAME + "-field");
  countLabel.setStylePrimaryName(CLASSNAME + "-label");
  ...
}
```

2. On the same level as the `*.gwt.xml` file, we create the `public/countedtextfield/styles.css` folder with the `styles.css` file.

The folder structure is shown in the following screenshot:

3. In the `styles.css` file, we write the CSS style of our widget.

```
.countedtextfield-label{
  color: gray;
  vertical-align: bottom;
}
```

4. Now we can recompile the widget set, run the server, and show the `Demo` application in the web browser.

How it works...

By default, the class name for each component is `gwt-<classname>`. For example, the `Label` widget has a default style of `gwt-Label`. Using the `setStylePrimaryName (String style)` method removes the default style and replaces it with our style name. Then we can define this new style in the `styles.css` file that is placed on the same level as the `*.gwt.xml` file.

There's more...

We can change each part of our component through CSS. We can also import and use the default CSS styles `Reindeer` or `Runo`.

When we want to change the style of all labels, we can do it by the default CSS class name. In that case, we replace the name `.countedtextfield-label` with `.gwt-Label` in the `styles.css` file. And we don't use the `setStylePrimaryName()` method.

Speeding up widget set compilation

Compiling a widget set takes a few minutes. It is because GWT compiles several versions for different browsers and different i18n languages. For example, if our application supports internationalization with three languages (English, Finish, and Czech) and we compile it to five web browsers (IE8, Gecko, Gecko1_8, Safari, and Opera) then it gives *3 * 5 = 15* permutations. At the time of development, we usually work with only one web browser with an application that uses one language. Therefore, we only need the version compiled for this one browser. In this recipe, we will see how to modify this compilation process and we will show how to speed up compilation by the use of parallel compilation using multiple processor cores.

In the following screenshot, we can see the time of compilation with the default configuration.

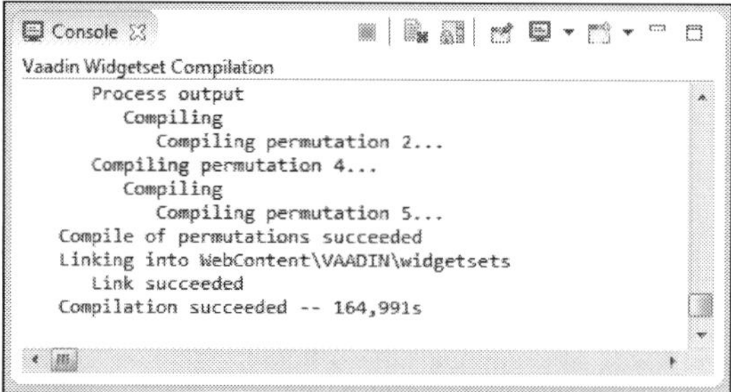

Getting ready

We create a widget, for example, a text field with counter, according to the *Creating a TextField with counter* recipe.

How to do it...

Carry out to following steps to speed up the widget set compilation:

1. The first way to speed up the widget set compilation is by reducing the number of permutation for web browser versions. We will compile it only for the Chrome web browser.
2. In the `*.gwt.xml` file, uncomment the `user.agent` property and set `safari` as a value.

```
<set-property name="user.agent" value="safari"/>
```

3. Run compilation by pressing *Ctrl* + *6* or by using the mouse. We can see the compilation process in the **Console** output.

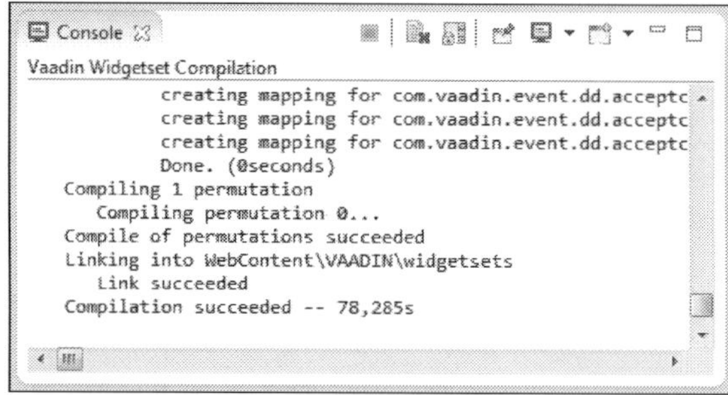

This compilation was faster than the first one.

4. The second way to speed up the compilation is by allowing the GWT compiler to use concurrent threads. It means that the different permutations are compiled in parallel. The default value of the Eclipse plug-in is that it uses as many cores as there are for compilation. But if we want to change it, we can do it in project properties:
    i. Right-click on the project. The context menu opens.
    ii. Select the last item **Properties**. The properties wizard opens.
    iii. In the menu, select the item **Vaadin.** The properties page for Vaadin project opens.
    iv. In the **Widgetsets** frame, select the number in the **Compiler threads:** fields. As shown in the following screenshot, the number **4** means that we'll use four threads. It depends on the CPU technology but the most common is that one thread uses one CPU core. The best performance is when we select as many threads as there are cores in the CPU.
    v. Press the **OK** or **Apply** button.

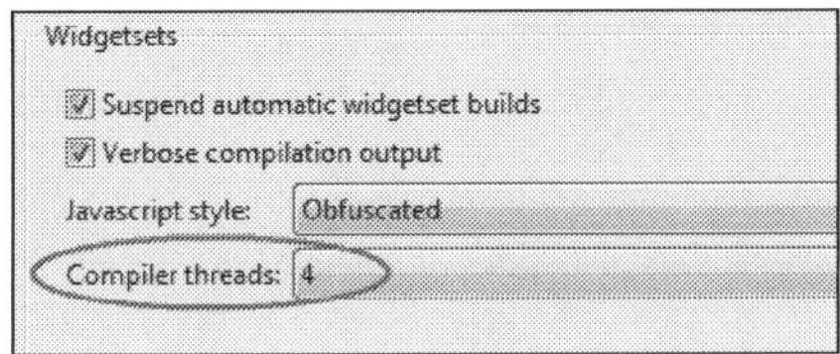

5. We can also set it by the command-line parameter as follows:

```
-localWorkers 4
```

How it works...

We have two ways to speed up widget set compilation. The first way is to reduce the number of permutations. We can compile an application for one type of web browser and for one i18n language. The second way is to use concurrent threads. The different permutations are compiled in parallel.

There's more...

For more browsers, we can use values separated by a comma:

```
<set-property name="user.agent" value="safari,gecko1_8"/>
```

The following is a table of supported web browsers:

Identifier	**Name**
`gecko1_8`	Mozilla Firefox 1.5 and later
`gecko`	Mozilla Firefox 1.0 (*obsolete*)
`ie6`	Internet Explorer 6
`ie8`	Internet Explorer 8
`safari`	Apple Safari and other Webkit-based browsers including Google Chrome
`opera`	Opera

When we use the i18n application, we can reduce the number of permutations to one language, for example, English:

```
<set-property name="locale" value="en" />
```

Internationalization of the GWT application is described at `https://developers.google.com/web-toolkit/doc/latest/DevGuideI18n`.

When we use development mode, compilation is not necessary. Debugging using the GWT development mode is described here at:

- `https://vaadin.com/wiki/-/wiki/Main/Using%20SuperDevMode`
- `https://vaadin.com/book/vaadin7/-/page/clientside.debugging.html`

5
Events

In this chapter, we will cover:

- Responding immediately to an event in TextArea
- Changing Label to TextField by double-clicking
- Lazy loading in a table
- Reordering columns and rows in a table
- Customizing shortcuts
- Adding click listener to the Link component
- Creating a custom context menu
- Updating a message in the menu bar using the ICEPush add-on
- Updating the noticeboard using the Refresher add-on

Introduction

In this chapter, we will learn how to work with events and listeners in Vaadin. We will use text change listener that will immediately react on users' inputs. Besides simple click listener, Vaadin provides a double-click listener. We will use it in the `Label` component. A very practical function is lazy loading in a table. It means that rows are loaded later after the user moves by slider on the side of table. We will also learn how to enable reordering columns and rows in a table. For users who want to control the application using the keyboard, we can add shortcuts for our actions. Actions can be grouped in the context menu. We will show how to use an add-on that adds a context menu to the text area. At the end, we will use two different ways to handle server-push events.

Responding immediately to an event in TextArea

It is very useful when surrounding components immediately respond to user input. For example, we can notify the user that the text in the editor has been changed. We will create a simple text area and button for saving. The button is enabled only if the value in the text area was changed as shown in the following screenshot:

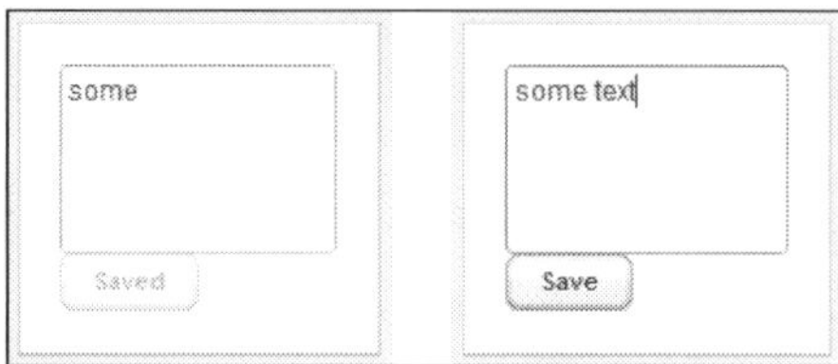

How to do it...

Carry out the following steps to create a TextArea that will immediately send an event respond:

1. We create a Vaadin project with a main UI class named Demo as follows:

   ```
   public class Demo extends UI {…}
   ```

2. We insert our text area and button to the VerticalLayout class. We start with creating a class named ImmediatelyTextArea which extends the VerticalLayout class.

   ```
   public class ImmediatelyTextArea extends
     VerticalLayout{…}
   ```

3. In the constructor, we create an instance of the TextArea class. We set this component to the immediate mode and the text change event to eager mode. It causes all text changes to be immediately fired to the listeners.

   ```
   public ImmediatelyTextArea() {
    TextArea textArea = new TextArea();
    textArea.setImmediate(true);
    textArea.setTextChangeEventMode
      (TextChangeEventMode.EAGER);
    …
   ```

4. Next we add a button with the caption **Saved**. In the initial state, it's disabled.

   ```
   final Button saveButton = new Button("Saved");
   saveButton.setEnabled(false);
   …
   ```

5. Now we add listeners, first for the text area. This listener will respond to changes in the text area. After each text change, the button is enabled and the caption is set to **Save**.

```
textArea.addTextChangeListener
  (new TextChangeListener() {
  @Override
  public void textChange(TextChangeEvent event) {
    saveButton.setCaption("Save");
    saveButton.setEnabled(true);
  }
});
...
```

6. The second listener is for the button. After each click, the button is disabled and the caption is set to **Saved**. Here we can add some other methods, for example, saving values to the database.

```
saveButton.addClickListener(new ClickListener() {
  @Override
  public void buttonClick(ClickEvent event) {
    saveButton.setCaption("Saved");
    saveButton.setEnabled(false);
  }
});
...
```

7. At the end of the constructor, we add our created components to the layout.

```
    layout.addComponent(textArea);
    layout.addComponent(saveButton);
  }
}
```

8. That's all. Now we can use our created `ImmediatelyTextArea` in the main UI `Demo` class.

```
public class Demo extends UI {

  @Override
  protected void init(VaadinRequest request) {
    setContent(new ImmediatelyTextArea());
  }
}
```

We run the server and open our application in the web browser.

How it works...

The text change event mode defines how quickly the changes are transmitted to the server and causes a server-side event. Lazier change events allow the sending of larger changes in one event if the user is typing fast, thereby reducing server requests. The allowed modes are defined in the `TextChangeEventMode` enum and are as follows:

- `LAZY` (default value): An event is triggered when there is a pause in editing the text
- `TIMEOUT`: A text change in the user interface causes the event to be communicated to the application after a timeout period
- `EAGER`: An event is triggered immediately for every change in the text content, typically caused by a key press

More information about event modes is available at the Vaadin web page (`https://vaadin.com/book/vaadin7/-/page/components.textfield.html`).

There's more...

We can also use `RichTextArea` instead of simple `TextArea`. In this case, the change value event is fired only if the `RichTextArea` loses focus. It can be confusing for users. Therefore, for this type of recipe, it is better to use a simple text area as described previously.

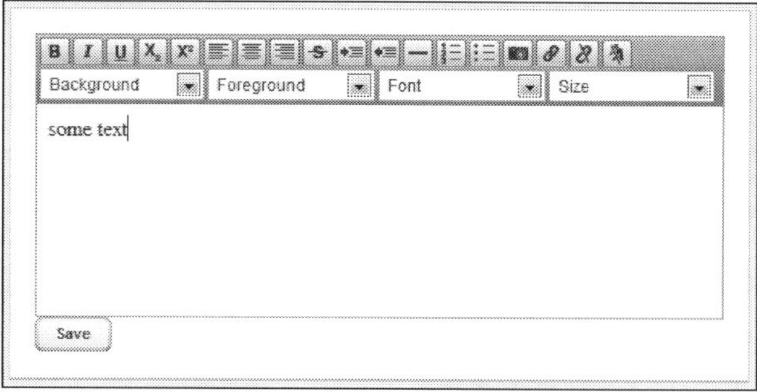

We can easily change the instance of `TextArea` to `RichTextArea` by rewriting the first line in the constructor.

```
public ImmediatelyTextArea() {
  RichTextArea textArea = new RichTextArea();
  textArea.setImmediate(true);
     ...
```

`RichTextArea` does not have a method for setting the change event mode. We can delete or comment it out.

```
//textArea.setTextChangeEventMode(TextChangeEventMode.EAGER);
```

And we need a different listener as follows:

```
textArea.addValueChangeListener(new ValueChangeListener() {
  @Override
  public void valueChange(ValueChangeEvent event) {
    saveButton.setCaption("Save");
    saveButton.setEnabled(true);
  }
});
```

That's all. Now we can run the server and, in the web browser, we can see the rich text area.

See also

- More information about text field and text area is described on the Vaadin's web pages at `https://vaadin.com/book/vaadin7/-/page/components.textfield.html` and `https://vaadin.com/book/vaadin7/-/page/components.textarea.html`
- Architecture of events and listeners is described at `https://vaadin.com/book/vaadin7/-/page/architecture.events.html`

Changing Label to TextField by double-clicking

We will create an editable `Label` class. It will be possible to edit this `Label`, because after double-clicking on it, the `Label` will become a `TextField`. After losing focus, it again becomes a `Label`. But how to add click listener to the `Label` or to a similar component that doesn't support such a listener? In those cases we can use `LayoutClickListener`. This listener is added to the layout in which the component is placed. It's called whenever the user clicks inside the layout.

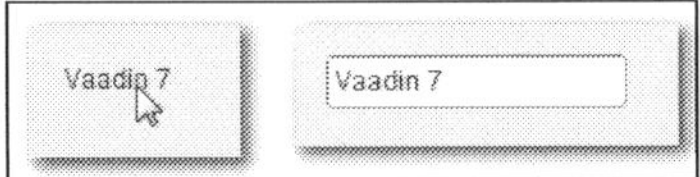

How to do it...

Carry out the following steps to create an editable `Label`:

1. We create a Vaadin project with a main UI class called `Demo` as follows:

   ```
   public class Demo extends UI {…}
   ```

2. Next, we create the `EditableLabel` class. It extends `VerticalLayout`.

   ```
   public class EditableLabel extends VerticalLayout {…}
   ```

3. Firstly, we need two variables: `label` and `textField`.

```
private Label label = new Label();
private TextField textField = new TextField();
```

4. Then, we create a simple constructor. Through the parameter we set the value of the `label` and we add it to the layout. We set `label` as a property data source of `textField`. It ensures that `textField` and `label` will always show the same string. At the end, we call a separate method for adding listeners.

```
public EditableLabel(String value) {
  label.setValue(value);
  label.setSizeUndefined();
  textField.setPropertyDataSource(label);
    addComponent(label);
    addListeners();
}
```

5. We continue with the creation of the `addListeners()` method. In this method, we create two listeners. The first is the click listener for the layout. In the `layoutClick()` event, we check whether the event is double-click and whether the clicked component is a `Label` because we want to use this click listener only for the `Label` component. Then we replace the label by a text field and we set a focus on it.

```
addLayoutClickListener(new LayoutClickListener() {
    @Override
    public void layoutClick(LayoutClickEvent event) {
      if (event.isDoubleClick()
      && event.getClickedComponent() instanceof Label){
        removeComponent(label);
        addComponent(textField);
        textField.focus();
      }
    }
  });
    ...
```

6. The second listener is for the text field. This listener is triggered when a text field loses the keyboard focus. In the `blur()` event, we replace the text field by the label.

```
    textField.addBlurListener(new BlurListener() {
      @Override
      public void blur(BlurEvent event) {
        removeComponent(textField);
        addComponent(label);
      }
    });

  }
```

7. That's all. We can use our created class in the main UI class `Demo`.

```
public class Demo extends UI {
  @Override
  protected void init(VaadinRequest request) {
    setContent(new EditableLabel("Vaadin 7"));
  }
}
```

Now we run the server and open our application in the web browser.

How it works...

The `Label` component does not allow using click listener. Therefore, we do a little trick. We will not add listener to a `Label`, but on the layout in which the label is located. The key method in this recipe is `addLayoutClickListener()`. This method is in the abstract class `AbstractOrderedLayout`, which is an ancestor of the `VerticalLayout` class. The click listener is called whenever the user clicks inside the layout. An event is also triggered when the click targets a component inside a nested layout, provided the targeted component does not prevent the click event from propagating. The child component that was clicked is included in the `LayoutClickEvent`.

See also

- The API of `LayoutClickListener` is available at `https://vaadin.com/api/7.0.0/com/vaadin/event/LayoutEvents.LayoutClickListener.html`
- The API of `AbstractOrderedLayout` is available at `https://vaadin.com/api/7.0.0/com/vaadin/ui/AbstractOrderedLayout.html`

Lazy loading in a table

When we work with tables, we often want to load rows quickly, no matter how big the tables are. In tables with a few rows, it isn't problem, but when we have thousands of rows, it can freeze the web browser. For such cases, there is support for lazy loading in Vaadin's tables. Lazy loading means that rows are loaded later. `Table` loads only the visible rows plus some rows are buffered for scrolling. The rest of the rows are loaded on demand.

In this recipe, we will create a table with ten thousand rows. It's big table, but as shown in the following screenshot, only the required part of the table is loaded. When we scroll to the rows that are not loaded, we will see an empty table with a row number range which will be loaded afterwards.

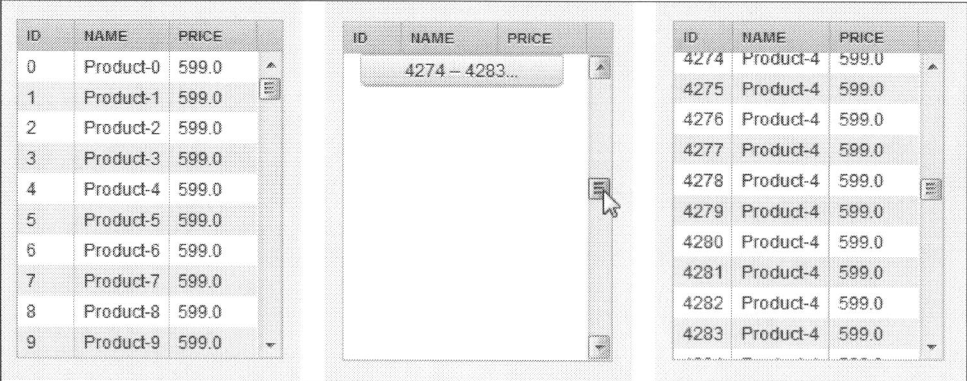

How to do it...

Carry out the following steps to learn how to use the lazy loading feature of `Table`:

1. We create a Vaadin project with a main UI class named `Demo` as follows:

```
public class Demo extends UI {…}
```

2. We need a bean item for the data table container. Therefore, we create a bean `Product` for our example. It consists of `id`, `name`, and `price`. We insert constructor, getter, and setter methods to this class.

```
public class Product {

  private int id;
  private String name;
  private double price;

  public Product(int id, String name, double price) {
    this.id = id;
    this.name = name;
    this.price = price;
  }

  <insert getters and setter for id, name and price>
}
```

3. Next, we create our `ProductTable` which extends `Table`.

```
public class ProductTable extends Table {…}
```

4. For the table container, we use the `BeanItemContainer` class. It constructs a container for beans of the `Product` type.

```
private BeanItemContainer<Product> tableContainer = new
  BeanItemContainer<Product>(Product.class);
```

5. The main functionality is in the constructor. Here we fill our table container with 10,000 rows by a separate method. Through the `setPageLength()` method, we set the number of visible rows in the table. Through the `setCacheRate()` method, we set the number of cached rows. The amount of cached rows will be `cacheRate` multiplied by `pageLength`. At the end of the constructor, we use our filled table.

```
public ProductTable() {
  fillTableContainer(tableContainer, 10000);
  setPageLength(10);
  setCacheRate(4);
  setContainerDataSource(tableContainer);
}
```

6. Next, we create a method for filling the table container. This method needs two parameters: a reference to the table container and a count of the generated rows.

```
  private void fillTableContainer(
    BeanItemContainer<Product> container, int count) {
    for (int i = 0; i < count; i++) {
      container.addItem(new Product
        (i, "Product-" + i,599));
    }
  }
```

7. Now we can use our lazy loading table in the main UI class `Demo`.

```
public class Demo extends UI {
  @Override
  protected void init(VaadinRequest request) {
    setContent(new ProductTable());
  }
}
```

Then, we run the server and open the application in a web browser.

How it works...

As described in Vaadin's documentation, the `setCacheRate(double cacheRate)` method adjusts a possible caching mechanism of table implementation.

The `Table` component may fetch and render some rows outside the visible area. In complex tables (for example, containing layouts and components), the client side may become unresponsive. Setting the value lower will make the UI more responsive. With higher values scrolling in, the client will hit the server less frequently.

The amount of cached rows will be `cacheRate` multiplied by `pageLength`, both below and above the visible area. The default value for `cacheRate` is `2`. The `setPageLength(int pageLength)` method sets the page length. Setting the page length to `0` disables paging. The page length represents the number of currently visible rows without scrolling in the rendered `Table`. The default length is 15 rows.

See also

- More information about Table is described in Vaadin's API `https://vaadin.com/api/7.0.0/com/vaadin/ui/Table.html`

Reordering columns and rows in a table

It is very user-friendly if users can adjust components by themselves. One such component is a `Table`. There are situations where some users want to see the name of items in the first column, other users want to see IDs, other users want to see prices, and so on. In other cases, the user can set, for example, the priority of items by reordering rows. If the row is above, it has a higher priority. In this recipe, we will see how to allow a user to reorder columns and rows in a table.

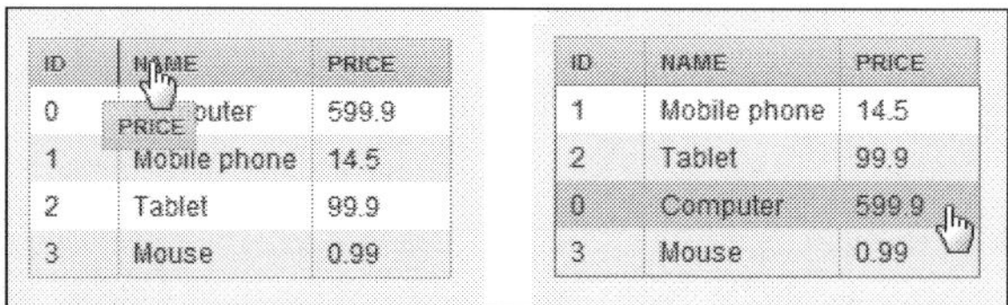

How to do it...

Carry out the following steps to allow reordering columns and rows in the `Table`:

1. We create a Vaadin project with a main UI class called `Demo` as follows:

   ```
   public class Demo extends UI {…}
   ```

2. We need a bean item for the data table container. We create the same bean as created in the *Lazy loading in a table* recipe.
3. Next, we create our `ReorderTable` class which extends the `Table` class.

   ```
   public class ReorderTable extends Table {…}
   ```

4. For the table container, we use the `BeanItemContainer` class. It constructs a container for beans of the `Product` type.

```
private BeanItemContainer<Product> container = new
  BeanItemContainer<Product>(Product.class);
```

5. In the constructor, we fill the table container by a separate method. We adjust the length of the table according to the current size of the table. Next, we set the datasource container. If we want to allow a user to reorder columns, we can do it by the `setColumnReorderingAllowed()` method with the argument `true`. To allow the reordering of rows, we have to set the drag mode of the table and set the drop handler.

```
public ReorderTable() {
  fillTableContainer(container);
  setPageLength(size());
  setContainerDataSource(container);
  setColumnReorderingAllowed(true);
  setDragMode(TableDragMode.ROW);
  setDropHandler(createDropHandler());
}
```

6. The drop handler will be created in the following method. Here we insert the implementation of the `DropHandler` interface. It consists of two methods. In the first `getAcceptiCriterion()` method, we return the value that says that we accept all drops anywhere on the component.

```
private DropHandler createDropHandler() {
  DropHandler dropHandler = new DropHandler() {

    @Override
    public AcceptCriterion getAcceptCriterion() {
      return AcceptAll.get();
    }
    ...
```

7. In the second method, we insert the implementation of the `drop()` method. In the beginning, we get a unique ID of the source-dragged object `Product`. Next, we get the ID of the target object `Product`. If the IDs are the same, we do nothing. If the source object is dropped at the bottom of the target, we insert it after the target object in the table container. If the source object is dropped exactly on the target or at the top of the target, we insert it before this target in the table container.

```
    @Override
    public void drop(DragAndDropEvent event) {
      DataBoundTransferable transferable =
      (DataBoundTransferable) event.getTransferable();
      Product sourceItemId =
      (Product) transferable.getItemId();
```

```
            AbstractSelectTargetDetails dropData =
            (AbstractSelectTargetDetails)
              event.getTargetDetails();
            Object targetItemId = dropData.getItemIdOver();

            if (sourceItemId == targetItemId) {
              return;
            }

            switch (dropData.getDropLocation()) {
              case BOTTOM:
              container.removeItem(sourceItemId);
              container.addItemAfter(
                targetItemId, sourceItemId);
              break;
              case MIDDLE:
              case TOP:
              container.removeItem(sourceItemId);
              Object prevItemId =
              container.prevItemId(targetItemId);
              container.addItemAfter(
                prevItemId, sourceItemId);
              break;
            }
          }
        };

        return dropHandler;
      }
```

8. At the end of this class, we create a method for filling the table container with some rows.

```
  private void fillTableContainer(
                BeanItemContainer<Product> container) {
    int id = 0;
    container.addItem(new Product
      (id++, "Computer",599.90));
    container.addItem(new Product(id++, "Mobile", 14.5));
    container.addItem(new Product
      (id++, "Tablet", 99.90));
    container.addItem(new Product(id++, "Mouse", 0.99));
  }
```

9. All is done. Now we can use our created `ReorderTable` in the main UI `Demo` class.

```
public class Demo extends UI {
  @Override
```

```
    protected void init(VaadinRequest request) {
      setContent(new ReorderTable());
    }
  }
```

We can run the server and open the application in a web browser.

How it works...

If `setColumnReorderingAllowed(true)` is set, the user can reorder table columns by dragging them with the mouse on the column header.

To reorder table rows, we have to implement the drop handler. As described in the Vaadin documentation, `DropHandler` contains the actual business logic for drag-and-drop operations. The `drop(DragAndDropEvent)` method is used to receive the transferred data and the `getAcceptCriterion()` method contains the (possibly client side-verifiable) criterion as to whether the dragged data will be handled at all.

See also

- More information about drag-and-drop is described in the *Dragging-and-dropping between different layouts* recipe in *Chapter 2, Layouts* and in the *Drag-and-drop from the desktop* recipe *Chapter 3, UI Components*
- More detailed information about Table is described at the Vaadin web page (`https://vaadin.com/book/vaadin7/-/page/components.table.html`)
- More information about API is available at `https://vaadin.com/api/7.0.0/com/vaadin/ui/Table.html`

Customizing shortcuts

Some users want to use the mouse as little as possible. They prefer to use the keyboard. For these users, we can improve our application by adding keyboard shortcuts. In this recipe, we will show how to add shortcuts on components in Vaadin's application. We will add two actions. The first action is for saving and the second action is for showing the window with **Help**.

How to do it...

Carry out the following steps to create custom shortcuts:

1. Create a Vaadin project with a main UI class named `Demo` as follows:

   ```
   public class Demo extends UI {…}
   ```

2. We create a class called `ShortcutPanel` which extends the `Panel` class and implements the `Handler` interface. We extend the `Panel` class because the keyboard actions can currently be attached only to `Panel` and `Window`.

   ```
   public class ShortcutPanel extends Panel implements
     Handler {…}
   ```

3. At the beginning of the class, we create two objects. The first one is a window for showing **Help**. This instance is created by a separate method. The second object is for an action that will show the help window. The help window will be bounded with the *F1* key. When the user uses this key outside our panel, the web browser opens its own help page.

   ```
   private Window helpWindow = createHelpWindow();
   private static final Action ACTION_HELP =
           new ShortcutAction("Help", KeyCode.F1, null);
   ```

4. In the constructor, we create all the necessary components. First we define layout. It will be `VerticalLayout` with a margin around the panel.

   ```
   public ShortcutPanel() {
     VerticalLayout layout = new VerticalLayout();
     layout.setMargin(true);
     setContent(layout);
      …
   ```

5. Then we create the text area and the Save button. On the button, we add a click listener that shows notification and we bind this listener with a keyboard shortcut through the `setClickShortcut()` method. At the end of the constructor, we set the size of the panel and add components and an action handler to this panel.

   ```
   TextArea textArea = new TextArea();
   Button saveButton = new Button("Save");
   saveButton.setClickShortcut
     (KeyCode.S,ModifierKey.CTRL);
   saveButton.addClickListener(new ClickListener() {
     @Override
     public void buttonClick(ClickEvent event) {
       Notification.show("Saved");
     }
   });
   ```

```
    setSizeUndefined();
    layout.addComponent(textArea);
    layout.addComponent(saveButton);
    addActionHandler(this);
}
```

6. Next, we create an implementation of methods from the `Handler` interface. The first is the `getActions()` method. In this method, we return the list of actions applicable to this handler.

```
@Override
public Action[] getActions(Object target, Object sender)
  {
  return new Action[] { ACTION_HELP };
}
```

7. Secondly, we implement the `handleAction()` method, which handles an action for the given target. When the action is an instance of our help action, the help window is shown in the web browser.

```
@Override
public void handleAction(
      Action action, Object sender, Object target) {
  if (action == ACTION_HELP) {
    UI.getCurrent().addWindow(helpWindow);
  }
}
```

8. In the next method, we create a subwindow with the help content.

```
private Window createHelpWindow() {
  Window window = new Window("Help");
  VerticalLayout layout = new VerticalLayout();
  layout.addComponent(new Label("Save: Ctrl+S"));
  layout.addComponent(new Label("Help: F1"));
  window.setContent(layout);
  window.center();
  return window;
}
```

9. Now we can use our created class in the main UI class `Demo`.

```
public class Demo extends UI {
  @Override
  protected void init(VaadinRequest request) {
    setContent(new ShortcutPanel());
  }
}
```

We run the server and open the application in the web browser.

See also

- More information about shortcuts is described at the Vaadin web page (`https://vaadin.com/book/vaadin7/-/page/advanced.shortcuts.html`)

Adding click listener to the Link component

Vaadin provides support for the `Link` component. We can make hyperlinks via this component. References to locations are represented as resource objects. The `Link` component is a regular HTML hyperlink, that is, an `<a href>` anchor element that is handled natively by the browser. Unlike when clicking a `Button`, clicking a `Link` does not cause an event on the server side. However, if we need to cause an event we have two ways to do it. We will take a look at them in this recipe.

Getting ready

We create a Vaadin project with a topmost class named `Demo`.

```
public class Demo extends UI {…}
```

How to do it...

The first way to do it, is to use an instance of the class `Button` and set the CSS style to `Reindeer.BUTTON_LINK`. So we get a component that looks like a link that has listeners for catching events.

```
public class Demo extends UI {

  @Override
  public void init(VaadinRequest request) {
    Button button = new Button("Vaadin");
    button.addClickListener(new ClickListener() {

      @Override
      public void buttonClick(ClickEvent event) {
        getPage().open("http://vaadin.com", "Vaadin");
      }
```

```
        });
        button.setStyleName(Reindeer.BUTTON_LINK);
        setContent(button);
    }
}
```

The second way is to use an add-on, `ActiveLink`. We can download the JAR file from Vaadin's directory at `http://vaadin.com/addon/activelink`.

`ActiveLink` is a `Link` with some additional features. When clicked, it will send an event to the server, rather as if it was a `Button` click. Details will be in the event.

This component has an advantage compared to the previous one: when we move the mouse over the link, we can see the path to the target source in the status bar.

```
public class Demo extends UI {

  @Override
  public void init(VaadinRequest request) {

    ActiveLink link = new ActiveLink("Vaadin",
new ExternalResource("http://vaadin.com"));
    link.setTargetName("_blank");
    link.addListener(new LinkActivatedListener() {
      public void linkActivated(LinkActivatedEvent event) {
        Notification.show("Link was opened in a new window");
      }
    });

    setContent(link);
  }
}
```

See also

- The author of the `ActiveLink` add-on is *Marc Englund*. We can download it from Vaadin's directory (`http://vaadin.com/addon/activelink`)
- For more information on how to use Vaadin add-ons, see `http://vaadin.com/directory/help/using-vaadin-add-ons`
- More information about Link is described here `https://vaadin.com/book/vaadin7/-/page/components.link.html`

Creating a custom context menu

Vaadin supports a simple context menu (mouse right-click) only for table, tree, and calendar. The menu items are handled as actions by an action handler. To enable a context menu, we have to implement a Vaadin `Action.Handler` and add it to the component with the `addActionHandler()` method. However, if we need a complex context menu on a different component, we can use the `ContextMenu` add-on created by *Peter Lehto*. In this recipe, we will create a context menu for the text area. We will add the context menu with three actions. One action cleans the text area and the two others insert a date and a name in the text area.

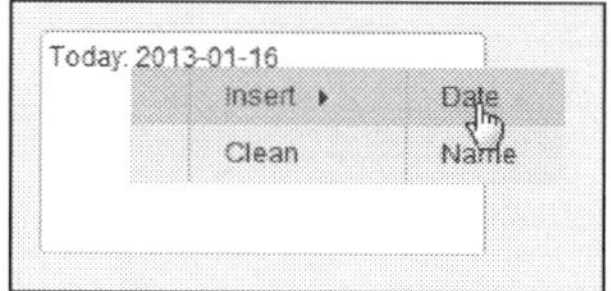

Getting ready

1. We create a Vaadin project with a main UI class called `Demo`.

   ```
   public class Demo extends UI {…}
   ```

2. We will use the `ContextMenu` add-on. We download it from the Vaadin directory (`http://vaadin.com/addon/contextmenu`) and put the JAR file to our web project under the `WebContent/WEB-INF/lib` directory.

   Alternatively, we can add Maven dependency according to the instructions on the mentioned web page.

3. Then we recompile this add-on. In Eclipse, we can do it by pressing *Ctrl* + *6* or by clicking on the button with the **Compile Vaadin widgets** tool tip in the top menu bar.

How to do it...

Carry out the following steps to create a custom context menu in the text area:

1. We create a class named `ContextMenuTextArea` that is based on `TextArea`.

   ```
   public class ContextMenuTextArea extends TextArea {…}
   ```

2. At the beginning of the class, we initialize the objects of the context menu and menu items. In the first level, we have two actions: `insert` and `clean`. The other actions `insert date` and `insert name` are submenus of `insert item`. The constant called `NAME` will be used for the action that will insert a name in the text area.

   ```
   private ContextMenu menu = new ContextMenu();
   private ContextMenuItem insertItem =
   ```

```
                              menu.addItem("Insert");
private ContextMenuItem cleanItem =
                              menu.addItem("Clean");
private ContextMenuItem dateItem =
                              insertItem.addItem("Date");
private ContextMenuItem nameItem =
                              insertItem.addItem("Name");
private static final String NAME = "Vaadin";
```

3. In the constructor, we add extensions into the text area and in a separate method we add all required listeners to the context menu items.

```
public ContextMenuTextArea() {
  addExtension(menu);
  addListeners();
}
```

4. Now we create a method that adds listeners to the context menu items. First we add a click listener to the `dateItem`, which is an instance of the `ContextMenuItem` class. On the click event in this listener, we insert formatted text in the text area.

```
private void addListeners(){

  dateItem.addItemClickListener(
           new ContextMenuItemClickListener() {
    @Override
    public void contextMenuItemClicked(
                 ContextMenuItemClickEvent event) {
      SimpleDateFormat format =
                 new SimpleDateFormat("yyyy-MM-dd");
      insertText(format.format(new Date()));
    }
  });
...
```

5. Next, we add a click listener to `nameItem`. On this click event we insert a name, for example, **Vaadin**.

```
  nameItem.addItemClickListener(
           new ContextMenuItemClickListener() {
    @Override
    public void contextMenuItemClicked(
                 ContextMenuItemClickEvent event) {
      insertText(NAME);
    }
  });
...
```

6. The last listener is about cleaning the whole text area. We add it to `cleanItem`.

```
    cleanItem.addItemClickListener(
              new ContextMenuItemClickListener() {
      @Override
      public void contextMenuItemClicked(
              ContextMenuItemClickEvent event) {
        setValue("");
        focus();
      }
    });
  }
```

7. The separate method ,`insertText()` helps us to insert some text into the text area to the last cursor position.

```
  private void insertText(String text) {
    int position = getCursorPosition();
    String value = getValue();
    setValue(value.substring(0, position)
              + text + value.substring(position));
    focus();
  }
```

8. That's all. Now we can use our new text area in the main UI class `Demo`.

```
public class Demo extends UI {

  @Override
  public void init(VaadinRequest request) {
    TextArea area = new ContextMenuTextArea();
    area.setWidth(200, Unit.PIXELS);
    area.setHeight(100, Unit.PIXELS);
    setContent(area);
  }
}
```

We run the server and open our application in the web browser.

How it works...

`ContextMenu` is a Vaadin 7 `Extension` that can be added to any Vaadin component. An `Extension` is an entity that is not a full-fledged UI component, but is instead used to enhance or extend the functionality of an existing component. In this book, `ContextMenu` version 4.1.1 is used that supports `Table`, in addition to `Layouts`, for which the context menu can be customized based on the selected `Item` and `Property`.

`ContextMenu` supports hierarchical menu structures and item-level click listeners as well as on-the-fly management of menu items.

See also

- The author of the add-on `ContextMenu` is *Peter Lehto*. We can download it from Vaadin's directory:
  `http://vaadin.com/addon/contextmenu`
- Here is information how to use Vaadin add-ons:
  `http://vaadin.com/directory/help/using-vaadin-add-ons`
- Here is a demo of ContextMenu on the Table and Tree components:
  `http://demo.vaadin.com/sampler/#TableActions`
  `http://demo.vaadin.com/sampler/#TreeActions`

Updating messages in the menu bar using the ICEPush add-on

Communication between the client and server in Vaadin is asynchronous. UI changes made on the server side are not reflected at the client side. This communication works well for most situations. However, it is a problem for applications that need push information from the server without the user's input. In this example, we will use the `ICEPush` add-on, which is a component that adds push support from the server to the client. We will insert a counter of new messages on the menu bar. This message counter will be updated only when a new message is received.

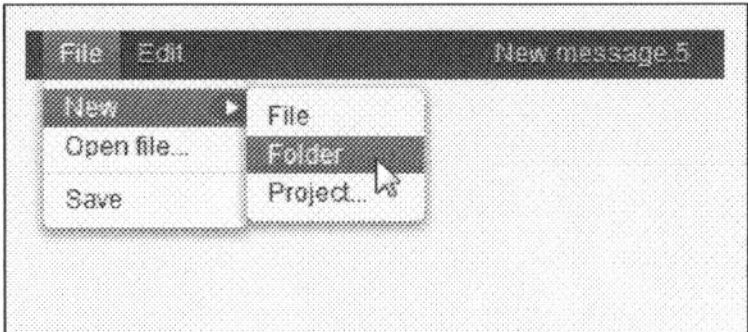

Getting ready

1. We create a Vaadin project with main UI class called `Demo`.

   ```
   public class Demo extends UI {…}
   ```

2. We will use the `ICEPush` add-on. We can download it from the Vaadin directory at `http://vaadin.com/addon/icepush` or add Maven dependency according to instructions on the mentioned web page.

3. After downloading the ZIP file, we unzip it and put all JAR files in to our web project under the `WebContent/WEB-INF/lib` directory.
4. We have to use `org.vaadin.artur.icepush.ICEPushServlet` instead of `com.vaadin.server.VaadinServlet` in the `WebContent/WEB-INF/web.xml` file.

Then we recompile this add-on. In Eclipse, we can do this by pressing *Ctrl + 6* or by clicking on the button with the **Compile Vaadin widgets** tool tip in the top menu bar.

How to do it...

Carry out the following steps to learn how to use the `ICEPush` add-on for updating messages in the menu bar:

1. We have to use a separate bar for the message, because each update of the message text repaints the whole menu. And we want to repaint only the message. Therefore, we use `HorizontalLayout` on which we place the menu bar and message bar side by side.

```
public class MessageMenuBar extends HorizontalLayout {…}
```

2. Next, we create instances of the `MenuBar` class, `ICEPush`, and prepare other variables, which will be used globally in the class.

```
private MenuBar menubar = new MenuBar();
private MenuBar messageBar = new MenuBar();
private ICEPush pusher = new ICEPush();
private MenuBar.MenuItem messageMenu;
```

3. The `menuCommand` object is used only for auxiliary purposes for the menu items.

```
private Command menuCommand = new Command() {
  public void menuSelected(MenuItem selectedItem) {
    Notification.show
      ("Action " + selectedItem.getText());
  }
};
```

4. In the constructor, we set the full width of our horizontal layout and the full size of the menu bar. The menu will be filled in a separate method `fillMenu()`. Then, we add all the created components. `Refresher` is added as an extension. Finally, we start the `MessageCounter` thread.

```
public MessageMenuBar() {
  setWidth("100%");
  menubar.setSizeFull();
  fillMenu();
```

```
    addComponent(menubar);
    addComponent(messageBar);
    addExtension(pusher);

    new MessageCounter().start();
  }
```

5. The separate method `fillMenu()` fills the main menu with some items and also creates one item for the message bar.

```
  private void fillMenu(){
    final MenuBar.MenuItem fileItem =
                            menubar.addItem("File", null);
    final MenuBar.MenuItem newItem =
                            fileItem.addItem("New", null);

    fileItem.addItem("Open file...", menuCommand);
    fileItem.addSeparator();

    newItem.addItem("File", menuCommand);
    newItem.addItem("Folder", menuCommand);
    newItem.addItem("Project...", menuCommand);

    fileItem.addItem("Save", menuCommand);

    final MenuBar.MenuItem edit =
                            menubar.addItem("Edit", null);
    edit.addItem("Cut", menuCommand);
    edit.addItem("Copy", menuCommand);
    edit.addItem("Paste", menuCommand);

    messageMenu = messageBar.addItem(
      "New message: 0", null);
  }
```

6. At the end, we have to create the inner `Thread` that will update text in the message counter. For this purpose, we create a helper method that will continually increase the variable `count` in a specified interval. In a production system, this method can be replaced by another one. For example, the `by` method will access the database or another system, which will return some message for the user. So, we need the `count` variable for new messages, the `nextTime` variable, which will time new message updates, and a constant for the time interval between message updates.

```
   public class MessageCounter extends Thread {

    private int count;
    private long nextTime;
    private static final int TIME_INTERVAL = 5000;
```

7. Next we override the `run()` method. This method will be called in a separate thread by the `start()` method. We will create an infinite loop in which we will check whether the count of messages has been changed. If it was changed, then we update the message in the menu and we push this change of UI to the client side using the `pusher` object. When the UI is updated from a background thread, we have to lock the application appropriately by using the session lock as follows.

```
@Override
public void run() {
  int oldCount = count;
  while (true) {
    updateMessageCount();
    if (oldCount != count) {
      getUI().getSession().getLockInstance().lock();
      try {
        oldCount = count;
        messageMenu.setText("New message:" + count);
        pusher.push();
      } finally {
      getUI().getSession()
       .getLockInstance().unlock();
     }
    }
  }
}
```

8. The `updateMessageCount()` method is used only for auxiliary purpose. It can be replaced by another method, for example, with database access. In our example, we update the count of new messages at the set interval.

```
    private void updateMessageCount() {
      long currentTime = System.currentTimeMillis();
      if (currentTime > nextTime ) {
        count++;
        nextTime = currentTime + TIME_INTERVAL;
      }
    }

  }

}
```

9. That is all. Now we can use our created class in the main UI `Demo` class.

```
public class Demo extends UI {
  @Override
  protected void init(VaadinRequest request) {
    setContent(new MessageMenuBar());
  }
}
```

We run the server and open the application in a web browser. We can see that the count on the message bar is updated automatically.

There's more...

There is a preliminary plan to implement server-push functionality directly into Vaadin. It's expected in Version 7.1. This book is written for Version 7.0.

More information about new features is on the roadmap web page at `https://vaadin.com/roadmap`.

See also

- The author of the ICEPush add-on is *Artur Signell*. You can download it from `http://vaadin.com/addon/icepush`

Updating the noticeboard using the Refresher add-on

This recipe is about the online sharing of information between more applications. We will create a public noticeboard, as in the following screenshot. Users can open this application in web browsers on different computers. Each of them sees the same, shared board. Users can move and edit any note and other users can see it live. In this recipe, we will see how to use the `Refresher` add-on. This component makes it possible to make UI changes, even if the user does not start a transaction.

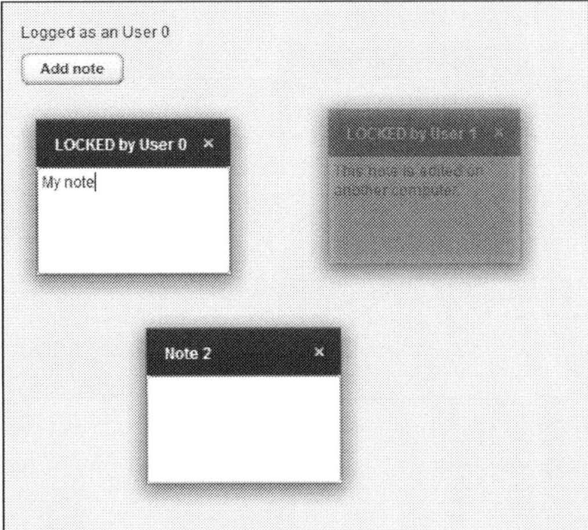

Getting ready

1. We create a Vaadin project with main UI class called `Demo`.

   ```
   public class Demo extends UI {…}
   ```

2. We will use the `Refresher` add-on. We download it from the Vaadin directory at `http://vaadin.com/addon/refresher` and put the JAR file in our web project under the `WebContent/WEB-INF/lib` directory.
3. Or we can add Maven dependency according to instructions on the mentioned web page.
4. Then we recompile this add-on. In Eclipse, we can do it by pressing *Ctrl* + *6* or by clicking on the button with the **Compile Vaadin widgets** tool tip in the top menu bar.

How to do it...

Carry out the following steps to create a noticeboard that can be shared between more web browsers using the `Refresher` add-on:

1. First, we have to create a `Note` class. It's a common JavaBean. These notes will be placed on the noticeboard. Each note has a unique ID. It also holds x and y positions on the noticeboard, the `caption` of the window, content as simple `text`, and information on whether note is locked by the user. If note isn't locked, then the value is set to `-1`; otherwise it is set to the user ID that locked it.

   ```
   public class Note implements Serializable {

     private int id;
     private int positionX;
     private int positionY;
     private String caption;
     private String text = "";
     private int lockedByUser = -1;

     public Note(int id) {
       this.id = id;
       caption = "Note " + id;
     }

     public Note(int id, int positionX, int positionY,
       String text) {
       this.id = id;
       this.positionX = positionX;
       this.positionY = positionY;
       this.text = text;
   ```

```
    }
    <Insert getters and setters for all fields.>
    ...
}
```

2. Next, we create a `Noticeboard` class.

   ```
   public class Noticeboard extends VerticalLayout {...}
   ```

3. At the beginning of the class, we insert some variables. Very important is list of notes simply called `notes`. This object is set as `static` because we want to share it with each browser session.

Using static variables isn't good for production systems. It's used here only as an example.

4. It works because Vaadin is inherently multi-threaded (each session gets its own thread). Next is a list of windows. Each session has its own list of windows. The `userCount` variable (the count of all users using this application) and `noteId` the (ID of the latest note) are also shared. In `userId`, the ID of the currently logged user is stored. At the end, we create the `refresher` object. This `refresher` object will refresh the web page after the interval in milliseconds specified in the constant `UPDATE_INTERVAL`.

   ```
   private static List<Note> notes = new ArrayList<>();
   private List<Window> windows = new ArrayList<>();
   private static int userCount;
   private int userId;
   private static int noteId = 1;
   private Refresher refresher = new Refresher();
   private static final int UPDATE_INTERVAL = 2000;
   ```

5. Next, we create the constructor. The constructor is called in each new session. Here we set the ID of the currently logged user. We insert a label with a message about the user ID, a button for adding new notes, and an extension `refresher`. For each note (created on the click event on the button), we create a window and add it to the list of windows and to the current UI. At the end of the constructor, we start the `NoticeboardUpdater` thread.

   ```
   public Noticeboard() {
     refresher.setRefreshInterval(UPDATE_INTERVAL);
     userId = userCount++;
     setSpacing(true);
     setMargin(true);
     addComponent(
   ```

```
            new Label("Logged as an User " + userId));
    Button addNoteButton = new Button("Add note");

    addNoteButton.addClickListener(new ClickListener() {
      @Override
      public void buttonClick(ClickEvent event) {
        Note note = new Note(noteId++);
        notes.add(note);
        Window window = createWindow(note);
        windows.add(window);
        UI.getCurrent().addWindow(window);
      }
    });

    addComponent(addNoteButton);
    addExtension(refresher);
    new NoticeboardUpdater().start();
  }
```

6. Next, we insert a method for creating new windows. Each new window is created according to the information in the `note` object. We set content, disable resizability, and set the position of the window on the noticeboard. Next, we add two listeners. `BlurListener` will be called after losing focus in the note window and `FocusListener` will be called when the note window gains focus.

```
private Window createWindow(final Note note) {
  final Window window = new Window(note.getCaption());
  Layout layout = new VerticalLayout();
  layout.addComponent(createContentNote(note, window));
  window.setContent(layout);
  window.setResizable(false);
  window.setPositionX(note.getPositionX());
  window.setPositionY(note.getPositionY());
  window.setData(note);
  window.addBlurListener(createBlurListener(window));
  window.addFocusListener(createFocusListener(window));
  return window;
}
```

7. In the next method, we create a content of the note. It's a simple text area. The value of content is set according to the text value of the note. We also add two listeners as in the previous method.

```
private TextArea createContentNote(
                final Note note, final Window window) {
  TextArea contentNote = new TextArea();
```

```
    contentNote.setSizeFull();
    contentNote.setValue(note.getText());
    contentNote.setImmediate(true);
    contentNote.setTextChangeEventMode(
                TextChangeEventMode.EAGER);
    contentNote.addBlurListener(
                createBlurListener(window));
    contentNote.addFocusListener(
                createFocusListener(window));
    contentNote.addTextChangeListener(
                new TextChangeListener() {
      @Override
      public void textChange(TextChangeEvent event) {
        note.setText(event.getText());
      }
    });
    return contentNote;
  }
```

8. Next, we insert two methods that create the required listeners. `BlurListener` is called when the component loses focus. After this event, we unlock the note.

```
  private BlurListener createBlurListener(
                      final Window window) {
    return new BlurListener() {
      @Override
      public void blur(BlurEvent event) {
        unlockNote(window);
      }
    };
  }
```

9. And `FocusListener` is called when the component gets the focus. In this case, we lock the note for the currently logged user.

```
  private FocusListener createFocusListener(
                       final Window window) {
    return new FocusListener() {
      @Override
      public void focus(FocusEvent event) {
        lockNote(window);
      }
    };
  }
```

10. Now we create a method that locks the note for the currently logged user. In the note, we store the user ID that locked the note. And we inform other users by the text in the caption that this note is locked.

    ```
    private void lockNote(Window window) {
      Note note = (Note) window.getData();
      note.setLockedByUser(userId);
      String caption = "LOCKED by User " + userId;
      note.setCaption(caption);
      window.setCaption(caption);
    }
    ```

11. In the method that unlocks the note, we set the user ID that locked the note to `-1`. We have to copy the current position of the window to the `note` object, because we need to store the last position of the window. And we also inform other users by the text in the caption that this note is unlocked.

    ```
    private void unlockNote(Window window) {
      Note note = (Note) window.getData();
      note.setLockedByUser(-1);
      note.setPositionX(window.getPositionX());
      note.setPositionY(window.getPositionY());
      note.setCaption("Note " + note.getId());
      window.setCaption("Note " + note.getId());
    }
    ```

12. Now we add the key method that will update the noticeboard. This method will be called from the `NoticeboardUpdater` thread. Here we iterate all shared `notes` and update private UI windows accordingly.

    ```
    private void updateNoticeboard() {
      for (Note note : notes) {
       ...
    ```

13. At first, we get a window object that is bound with the note and we update the content of the text area in this window.

    ```
        Window window = getWindow(note);
        updateTextArea(window, note);
          ...
    ```

14. If there isn't any window for the selected note, then we create one and bind it with the note.

    ```
        if (window == null) {
          window = createWindow(note);
          windows.add(window);
          UI.getCurrent().addWindow(window);
        }
         ...
    ```

15. If the note is locked by another user, then we disable this window. Other windows will be enabled.

```
if (note.getLockedByUser() > -1
        && note.getLockedByUser() != userId) {
  window.setEnabled(false);
} else {
  window.setEnabled(true);
}
...
```

16. If the selected note is locked by the same user as the logged user, then it means that we work with a focused note. We get the bound note from the current window. And we copy appropriate information from the window to the note. If it isn't a focused note, we copy appropriate information from the note to the window.

```
      if (note.getLockedByUser() == userId) {
        Note focusedNote = (Note) window.getData();
        focusedNote.setPositionX(window.getPositionX());
        focusedNote.setPositionY(window.getPositionY());
        focusedNote.setCaption(window.getCaption());
      }else {
        window.setPositionX(note.getPositionX());
        window.setPositionY(note.getPositionY());
        window.setCaption(note.getCaption());
      }
    }
  }
```

17. Next, we insert a method for updating the text area inside the window. It sets the value of this text area according to the text value in the note.

```
private void updateTextArea(Window window, Note note) {
  if (window == null)
    return;
  Layout layout = (Layout) window.getContent();
  TextArea area = (TextArea) layout.iterator().next();
  area.setValue(note.getText());
}
```

18. The `getWindow()` method iterates all current windows and finds window bound with the selected note.

```
private Window getWindow(Note note) {
  for (Window window : windows) {
    if (window.getData().equals(note)) {
      return window;
    }
```

```
    }
    return null;
  }
```

19. Now we create the inner class. It is an updater for the noticeboard. This is an infinite loop, in which, after the specified interval, all the notes on the board are updated. Changes made outside the UI thread must first acquire the thread lock. After the operation, the lock must be released.

```
public class NoticeboardUpdater extends Thread {
  @Override
  public void run() {
    while (true) {
      try {
        Thread.sleep(UPDATE_INTERVAL);
      } catch (InterruptedException e) {
        e.printStackTrace();
      }
          getUI().getSession().getLockInstance().lock();
      try {
        updateNoticeboard();
      } finally {
        getUI().getSession().getLockInstance().unlock();
      }
    }
  }
}
```

20. That is all. Now we can use our application in the main UI `Demo` class.

```
public class Demo extends UI {
  @Override
  public void init(VaadinRequest request) {
    setContent(new Noticeboard());
  }
}
```

21. We run the server and open the application in two different web browsers. We can update notes and we can see that notes are shared between browsers.

How it works...

We can share information between computers because we used a `static` list of `Note` objects. It works because Vaadin is inherently multi-threaded (each session gets its own thread). And each thread can share a static class field. In contrast, UI windows are unique for each session. They are updated according to the information in the shared notes. The `Refresher` add-on is an extension that adds server-push support to the Vaadin application. The `refresher` object updates the web page after a specified interval.

The main difference between the `Refresher` and `ICEPush` add-ons is that `Refresher` updates the UI page in the specified intervals, whereas `ICEPush` can update UI only when we call the `push()` method.

See also

- The author of the `Refresher` add-on is *Henrik Paul*. You can download it from `http://vaadin.com/addon/refresher`
- Another nice theory about communication in Vaadin is written by *Matti Tahvonen* on his blog at `https://vaadin.com/web/matti/blog/-/blogs/to-push-or-dontpush`

6
Messages

In this chapter, we will cover:

- Showing validation messages
- Styling system messages
- Showing a login form in pop-up view
- Customizing tray notifications
- Making a confirmation window
- Showing a rich tooltip with an image
- Informing about file transfers by a progress bar
- Waiting for an indeterminate process
- Showing information about browsers

Introduction

Our application users must be, in most cases, kept informed about the status of the application. For example, when a user inserts non-valid data into a field, then an error message should be shown. In that moment the user needs to get feedback on what is wrong.

In this chapter, we will go through how to show validation errors in fields, pop-up views, tray notifications, tooltips, and progress bars.

Showing validation messages

In this recipe, we will make an input text field for a PIN code with the following rules:

- It can contain only numbers. When a user enters letters, then a **Just numbers allowed** error is shown.
- When there are less than four numbers, a **Too few numbers** error is shown.
- When there are more than four numbers, a **Too many numbers** error is shown.
- The content of the field is valid only when it contains exactly four numbers.

These rules will be part of validation and the error message will appear together with the field. So when we move over the field, the error pops up, as shown in the following screenshot:

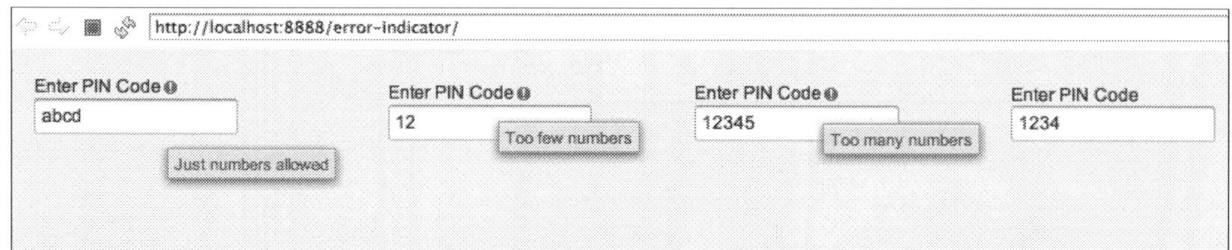

How to do it...

Carry out the following steps:

1. First, we create a `TextField` with an **Enter PIN Code** label. Then, we need to set `setImmediate` to `true`, so the requests from UI are sent immediately to the server.

```
public class MyVaadinUI extends UI {

  @Override
  protected void init(VaadinRequest request) {
    final VerticalLayout layout = new VerticalLayout();
    layout.setMargin(true);
    setContent(layout);

    TextField txt = new TextField("Enter PIN Code");
    txt.setImmediate(true);
    layout.addComponent(txt);
  }
}
```

2. Then, we create our custom validator named `PinValidator` which implements the rules mentioned previously.

```
public class PinValidator implements Validator {

  @Override
  public void validate(Object value) throws
    InvalidValueException {
    String text = (String) value;
    if (text == null || "".equals(text.trim())) {
      return;
    }
    if (!text.matches("\\d*")) {
      throw new InvalidValueException
        ("Just numbers allowed");
    }
    if (text.length() < 4) {
      throw new InvalidValueException("Too few numbers");
    } else if (text.length() > 4) {
      throw new InvalidValueException
        ("Too many numbers");
    }
  }
}
```

3. Add the newly created `PinValidator` to the text field.

```
txt.addValidator(new PinValidator());
```

4. We can run the application and test the implemented behavior.

How it works...

Every component that extends `com.vaadin.ui.AbstractField` can have multiple validators. The `Validator` interface defines just one method named `validate` into which the user input is passed. In addition, there are two inner classes. The first one is an exception called `InvalidValueException` and should be thrown when the user input is not according to the validation rules. The second is the `EmptyValueException` class which is just an extension of `InvalidValueException`. `EmptyValueException` should be thrown when the value is empty (it is up to us to define what input is considered as an empty value).

There's more...

The fields might be part of `FieldGroup`, which is basically a replacement for the `Form` class from Vaadin 6. We can call the `commit()` method on an instance of the `FieldGroup` class that invokes validation and validation errors are propagated to the user.

Luckily, we don't need to implement all the validators from scratch. Vaadin implements validators that cover many validation scenarios. There are validators such as `NullValidator`, `EmailValidator`, `StringLengthValidator`, and `RegexpValidator`. These together with the other validators can be found in the `com.vaadin.data.validator` package.

In some cases, it might be clever to consider implementing more validators instead of just one `PinValidator`. Each validator would be responsible for one validation rule. We will create a new validator that would just check the presence of input other than numeric.

```
public class NumericValidator implements Validator {
  @Override
  public void validate(Object value) throws
    InvalidValueException {
    String text = (String) value;
    if (!text.matches("\\d*")) {
      throw new InvalidValueException("Just numbers allowed");
    }
  }
```

Then we can use the `addValidator` method and add multiple validators to a field.

See also

- Validation is not done after each key press. The `SuperImmediateTextField` add-on can be used in case we need to validate the user's input after each key is entered. More information is available on the add-on page at `http://vaadin.com/directory#!addon/15`

Styling system messages

System messages are a special kind of message in Vaadin. These messages are typically shown when something really serious happens in the system. There can be problems in the communication between client and server, expired sessions, authentication errors, cookies are not enabled, or the server and the client are not synchronized. For example, the communication problem might occur when the application server went down and the client (the Vaadin application running in a browser) is trying to communicate with that server.

The following screenshot shows how the system message looks, when the client is not able to reach the server:

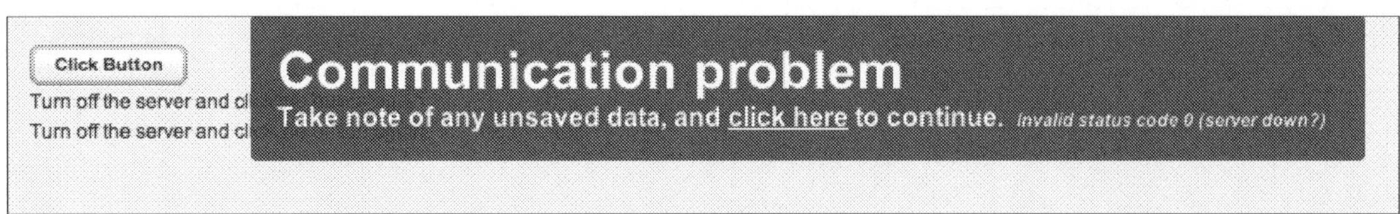

It might happen that we don't like the default design of system messages or we need to change the default text messages. It could be that the red color, which is used by default, is too red. And we would rather have it in a different color schema, as shown in the following screenshot:

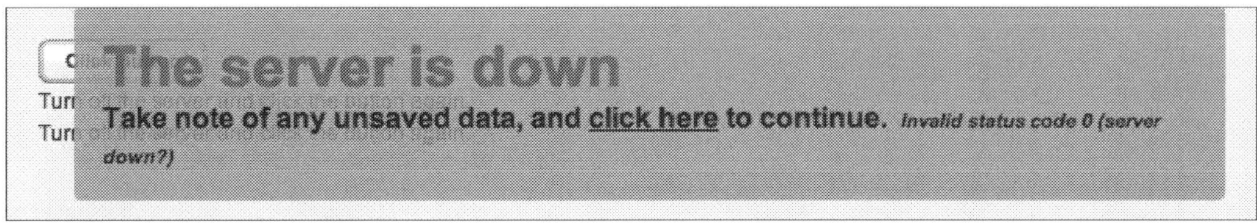

Getting ready

1. First, create a new CSS file, `VAADIN/themes/mytheme/styles.scss`.
2. Then, create a new Vaadin project with new class `MyVaadinUI` that is annotated with `@Theme("mytheme")`.

```
@Theme("mytheme")
public class MyVaadinUI extends UI {…}
```

How to do it...

Carry out the following steps:

1. Create a new class `MySystemMessagesProvider` that implements `SystemMessagesProvider`. Then implement the `getSystemMessages` method in which we make a new instance of `CustomizedSystemMessages`. All the customizable texts are accessible via the set and get methods; we change only the captions.

```
public class MySystemMessagesProvider implements
  SystemMessagesProvider {

  @Override
  public SystemMessages getSystemMessages
    (SystemMessagesInfo info) {
```

```
    CustomizedSystemMessages messages = new
      CustomizedSystemMessages();
    messages.setCommunicationErrorCaption
      ("The server is down");
    messages.setInternalErrorCaption("Internal error");
    messages.setSessionExpiredCaption
      ("Session has expired");
    messages.setOutOfSyncCaption
      ("Out of synchronization");
    messages.setCookiesDisabledCaption
      ("Cookies disabled");
    messages.setAuthenticationErrorCaption
      ("Authentication error");
    return messages;
  }
}
```

2. Then we add CSS that changes the design of default system messages. Insert the following code in the `styles.scss` file:

```
@import "../reindeer/reindeer.scss";

@include reindeer;

.v-app .v-Notification-system {
  background-color: #b43432;
  color: black;
}

.v-app .v-Notification-system h1 {
  color: #E3F708;
}
```

3. Now we need to create a new servlet, where we apply the system message provider we have created in the first step. Create a new class called `com.app.MyVaadinServlet`.

```
public class MyVaadinServlet extends VaadinServlet {

  class MySessionInitListener implements
    SessionInitListener {

    public void sessionInit(SessionInitEvent e)
           throws ServiceException {
      VaadinService service = e.getService();
      MySystemMessagesProvider provider = new
          MySystemMessagesProvider();
      service.setSystemMessagesProvider(provider);
```

```
        }
    }

    @Override
    protected void servletInitialized() throws
        ServletException {
      super.servletInitialized();

      VaadinServletService service = getService();
      MySessionInitListener listener = new
        MySessionInitListener();
      service.addSessionInitListener(listener);
    }
}
```

4. Add a reference to the `web.xml` file to `com.app.MyVaadinServlet`.

```
<servlet>
  <servlet-name>Vaadin Application Servlet</servlet-name>
  <servlet-class>com.app.MyVaadinServlet</servlet-class>
```

Now we can run the application and test whether the communication problem is shown correctly. Deploy the application on the application server. Open the application in a browser and click on the button. Turn off the application server. Now click on the button and system messages about the communication problem are shown.

How it works...

Vaadin 7 introduces a new way to customize system messages. It is done by the `SystemMessagesProvider` interface that defines the `getSystemMessages` method. Therefore we can make a new implementation of the `SystemMessagesProvider` interface and return our customized instance of `SystemMessages`. Most likely, we just create a new instance of `CustomizedSystemMessages` and set there all the texts we need to change.

Most probably, we will need to localize the system messages, so people who don't speak English don't have to read the default English messages. There is a method that receives an instance of the `getSystemMessages` method `SystemMessagesInfo`. From that instance, we can get `Local`. Then we just get the localized values from our localization properties files and pass them into the instance of the `CustomizedSystemMessages` class.

In order to change the color schema of the system message, we just customize the CSS file. In this recipe, we have just changed colors.

Showing a login form in pop-up view

We can easily add any component into the pop-up view. Let's create an application that has one pop-up view with the text **Click me!**. When the user clicks on the **Click me!** text, the login form is shown.

The pop-up view might be also used for showing a long description of a field within a form or any other component.

The following screenshot shows the **Click me!** text:

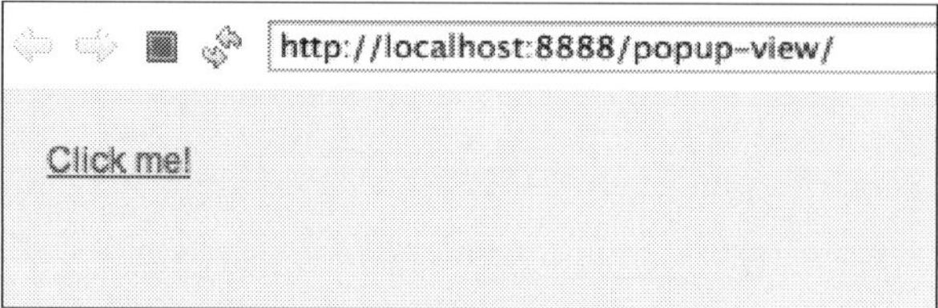

When we click on it, the following login window appears in the browser:

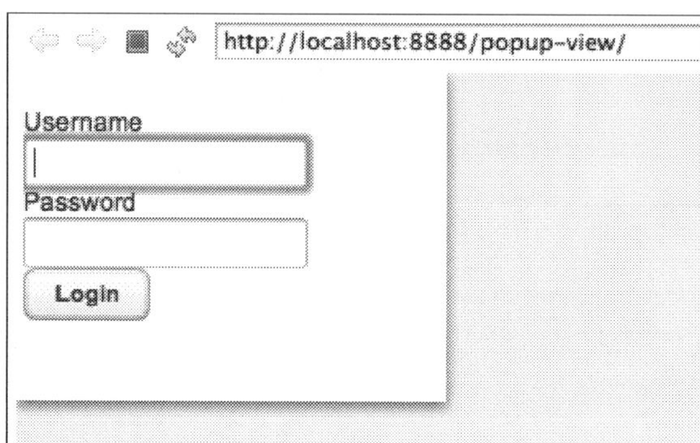

How to do it...

Carry out the following steps:

1. Create a new vertical layout in the `init` method and set it as the content of `UI`.

```
final VerticalLayout layout = new VerticalLayout();
layout.setMargin(true);
setContent(layout);
```

2. Then create the login form.

```
VerticalLayout login = new VerticalLayout();
TextField txtUsername = new TextField("Username:");
login.addComponent(txtUsername);
TextField txtPassword = new TextField("Password:");
login.addComponent(txtPassword);
Button btnLogin = new Button("Login");
login.addComponent(btnLogin);
```

3. Create a pop-up view component with the **Click me!** text and login form. The login form disappears after the user moves out from the login form (send a false value into the `setHideOnMouseOut` method if you want the login form to stay).

```
PopupView popup = new PopupView("Click me!", login);
addComponent(popup);
```

4. Run the application and click on the text displayed. The login form will appear.

How it works...

The main purpose of `PopupView` is to show the HTML string (**Click me!** in our case) and the login form. The HTML string can be understood as a minimized view of the pop up. Conversely, the login form can be called as a maximized view of the popup, which is shown when the user clicks on the **Click me!** text.

Customizing tray notifications

In this recipe, we will see how to make a tray notification with a custom design. When the user clicks on the **Click me!** button, the tray notification is shown in the top-right corner (instead of the default bottom-right corner).

Normally, the user has to click on the tray notification window in order to close it. We will change the default behavior, so the tray notification disappears immediately after the user moves with the cursor.

We also change the color of the tray notification from dark gray to light gray.

Getting ready

1. First, create a new CSS file `VAADIN/themes/mytheme/styles.scss`.
2. Then, create a new Vaadin project with the root class `TrayNotificationsUI` that is annotated with `@Theme("mytheme")`.

```
@Theme("mytheme")
public class TrayNotificationsUI extends UI {…}
```

How to do it...

Carry out the following steps:

1. We implement a simple click listener that handles button clicks. Then, we change the default behavior, so we set the delay to `0` ms, the position to top-right corner, and add a new CSS style name.

```
public class NotifyListener implements ClickListener {

  @Override
  public void buttonClick(ClickEvent event) {
    Notification notification = new Notification(
      "Well done!",
      "You have clicked on the button.",
    Notification.Type.TRAY_NOTIFICATION);

    notification.setDelayMsec(0);
    notification.setPosition(Position.TOP_RIGHT);
    notification.setStyleName("mynotification");

    notification.show(Page.getCurrent());
  }
}
```

2. Create a new button and add the click listener we have created in the previous step.

```
Button btn = new Button("Click me!");
btn.addClickListener(new NotifyListener());

addComponent(btn);
```

3. We will change the design of the tray notification by adding the following CSS. We change the background, color, and size of the font.

```
@import "../reindeer/reindeer.scss";

@include reindeer;

.v-app .v-Notification.mynotification {
  background-color: #C0C0C0;
  color: #818181;
  font-size: 75%;
}
```

4. Now we can run the application and test the behavior. The tray notification should be displayed when we click on the button.

How it works...

Vaadin notifications are temporary messages that are shown to the user. Every notification has a default setup and we do not have to touch it. We could create a notification just by writing a single line of code, as follows:

```
Notification.show("Good job!",
  Notification.Type.TRAY_NOTIFICATION);
```

But when we need to customize the notification we have to have an instance of the `Notification` class. That is why we have to get the current page and pass it to the `show` method.

```
notification.show(Page.getCurrent());
```

There's more...

We can do the following things with the notifications:

- Customize the notification design
- Set the delay after which the notification should disappear
- Set the position when the notification is shown
- Add an icon to the notification

Making a confirmation window

We are going to have a look at how to show a confirmation window after we click on an item in a table.

In this recipe, consider that fetching details of a database entity is an expensive operation and therefore we want to get the confirmation from the user before the application starts fetching the data.

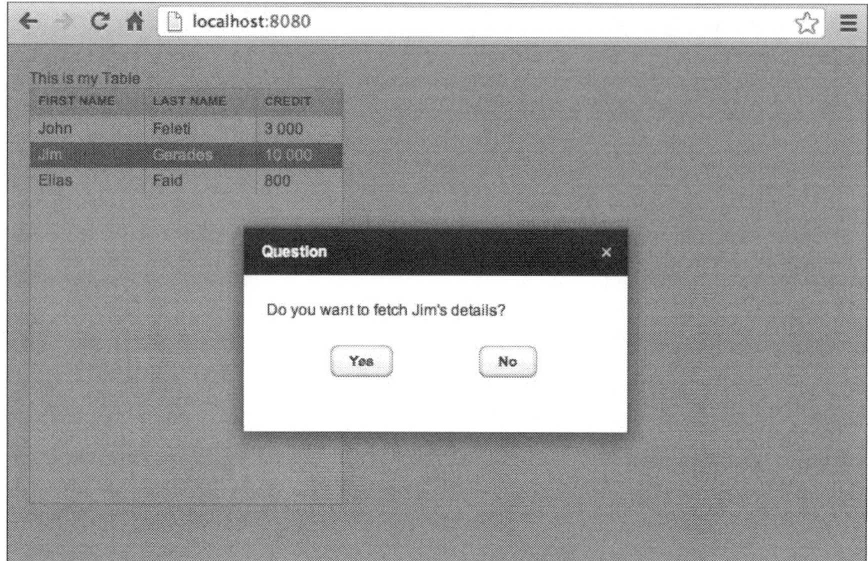

The confirmation window is going to be a useful component in many other scenarios, such as confirmation before removing, saving, and showing information messages.

How to do it...

Carry out the following steps:

1. Create a new class `Decision` that will implement two methods for possible decisions (we will simplify it to yes and no decisions).

```
public class Decision {

  public void yes(Button.ClickEvent event) {
  }
  public void no(Button.ClickEvent event) {
  }
}
```

2. Create a new class that represents the confirmation window. There will be two buttons to handle yes and no actions. Then we add click listeners to the buttons, so we can forward the click action to the instance of the decision.

```
public class ConfirmWindow extends Window {

  private Decision decision;
  private Button btnYes = new Button();
  private Button btnNo = new Button();
  private VerticalLayout layout = new VerticalLayout();
  private HorizontalLayout buttonsLayout = new
    HorizontalLayout();

  public ConfirmWindow(String caption, String question,
    String yes, String no) {
    setCaption(caption);
    btnYes.setCaption(yes);
    btnYes.focus();
    btnNo.setCaption(no);
    setModal(true);
    center();

    buttonsLayout.addComponent(btnYes);
    buttonsLayout.setComponentAlignment
      (btnYes, Alignment.MIDDLE_CENTER);
    buttonsLayout.addComponent(btnNo);
    buttonsLayout.setComponentAlignment
      (btnNo, Alignment.MIDDLE_CENTER);

    layout.addComponent(new Label(question));
    layout.addComponent(buttonsLayout);
    setContent(layout);

    layout.setMargin(true);
    buttonsLayout.setMargin(true);
    buttonsLayout.setWidth("100%");
    setWidth("300px");
    setHeight("160px");
    setResizable(false);

    btnYes.addClickListener(new Button.ClickListener() {
      @Override
      public void buttonClick(Button.ClickEvent event) {
        decision.yes(event);
        close();
      }
    });
```

```
    btnNo.addClickListener(new Button.ClickListener() {
      @Override
      public void buttonClick(Button.ClickEvent event) {
        decision.no(event);
        close();
      }
    });
    addShortcutListener(new ShortcutListener("Close",
      ShortcutAction.KeyCode.ESCAPE, null) {
      @Override
      public void handleAction(Object sender, Object
        target) {
        close();
      }
    });
    UI.getCurrent().addWindow(this);
  }

  void setDecision(Decision decision) {
    this.decision = decision;
  }
}
```

3. Create a table and add a few items. We need to add container properties so the table is aware of the column names, contained types, and default values. Then, we add the items together with IDs.

```
Table table = new Table("This is my Table");

table.addContainerProperty("First Name", String.class,
  null);
table.addContainerProperty("Last Name", String.class,
  null);
table.addContainerProperty("Credit", Integer.class,
  null);

table.addItem(new Object[] { "John", "Feleti", 3000 },
  1);
table.addItem(new Object[] { "Jim", "Gerades", 10000 },
  2);
table.addItem(new Object[] { "Elias", "Faid", 800 }, 3);
table.addValueChangeListener(new
  PeopleTableListener(table));
```

4. Create a new class for handling the `valueChange` events on the table. We will show people in the table, so let's call the `PeopleTableListener` class.

```
public class PeopleTableListener implements
  Property.ValueChangeListener {...}
```

5. Create a constructor for `PeopleTableListener` and add the `Table` type as the parameter. That way, we connect the listener with the table.

```
private final Table table;

public UserTableListener(Table table) {
  this.table = table;
}
```

6. We are implementing `Property.ValueChangeListener` and therefore we need to implement the `valueChange` method. That method is called always when the user selects an item in the table. First we get the selected value ID from the table and obtain the item.

```
@Override
public void valueChange(ValueChangeEvent event) {
  Object itemId = table.getValue();
  Item item = table.getItem(itemId);
```

7. Now we want to get confirmation from the user on whether to fetch data from the database. We get the value from the first column of the selected row. Then we make a new confirmation window and define what should happen when the user clicks on the **yes** or **no** buttons.

```
  Collection<String> columns = (Collection<String>)
    item.getItemPropertyIds();
  String column = (String) columns.toArray()[0];
  Property<?> itemProperty =
    item.getItemProperty(column);
  Object value = itemProperty.getValue();

  ConfirmWindow window = new ConfirmWindow("Question",
    "Do you want to fetch " + value + "'s details?",
    "Yes", "No");
  window.setDecision(new Decision() {
    @Override
    public void yes(ClickEvent event) {
      // fetch user
    }

    @Override
    public void no(ClickEvent event) {
```

```
            // do nothing?
        }
    });
}
```

8. Now we can run the application and click on the item in the table. The confirmation window is shown and we can make the decision whether to fetch the details of the selected user or not.

How it works...

We had to always set the main window in Vaadin 6 and adding subwindows was done via the `addWindow` method on the `Application` class. That has been completely changed in Vaadin 7. Now we just get the current instance of UI and add the window.

That way we have made our own confirmation window component as a feature of normal Vaadin components.

Showing a rich tooltip with an image

We are going to implement a rich tooltip that will appear when we point to the basic `Label` component with the cursor, in the browser. The tooltip will show information in a different font size and color. There will also be an image on it.

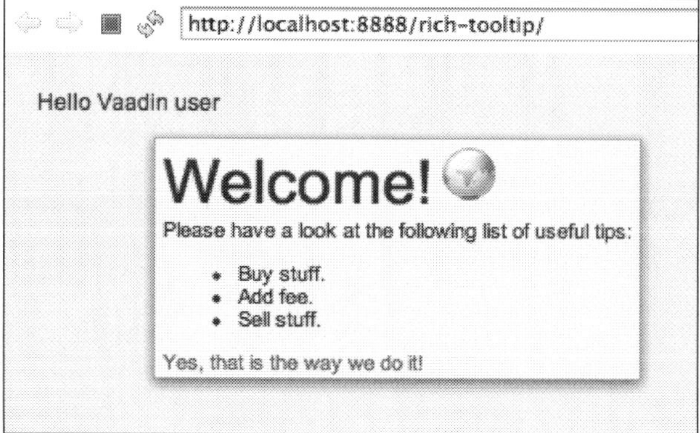

How to do it...

Carry out the following steps:

1. Create a new `Label` instance and place it on the UI.

   ```
   Label label = new Label("Hello Vaadin user");
   addComponent(label);
   ```

2. Then construct the tooltip HTML string and set it as a description on the label.

```
String tooltip = "<span style=\"font-
  size:30px;\">Welcome!</span>"
+ "<img src=\"VAADIN/themes/runo/icons/32/globe.png\"/>"
+ "<br/>"
+ "Please have a look at the following list of useful
  tips:"
+ "<ul>"
+ "<li>Buy stuff.</li>"
+ "<li>Add fee.</li>"
+ "<li>Sell stuff.</li>"
+ "</ul>"
+ "<span style=\"color:green;\">Yes, that is the way we
  do it!</span>";
SafeHtml html = SafeHtmlUtils.fromSafeConstant(tooltip);
abel.setDescription(html.asString());
```

3. Run the application and point the cursor on the label. The tooltip should be shown.

How it works...

Vaadin tooltips are implemented via HTML. So we just make the tooltip in HTML code and set it as tooltip via the `setDescription` method.

We should be careful when dealing with HTML strings in Java code. The code can become messy when we add a lot of HTML lines to it. It might be good practice to extract HTML to external files and fetch HTML code from them.

We have used the `SafeHtml` interface and the `fromSafeConstant` method from the `SafeHtmlUtils` class that returns a compile-time constant string wrapped as `SafeHtml`. More info about `SafeHtml` can be found at `https://developers.google.com/web-toolkit/doc/latest/DevGuideSecuritySafeHtml`.

There's more...

We might want to change the background or text shown on the tooltip. Adjust the content of the `style.scss` file in order to do that. The following code shows an example CSS code:

```
.v-app .v-tooltip {
  background-color: purple;
  border: 1px solid white;
  font-size: 11px;
  color: #white;

}
```

The following screenshot is the result of our lovely tooltip:

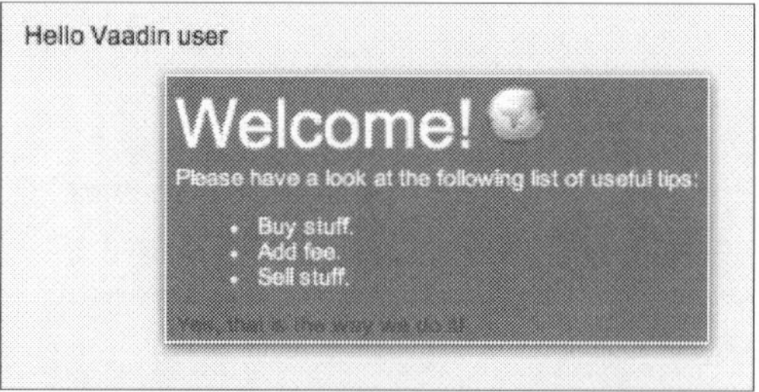

Informing about file transfers by a progress bar

We will implement file uploading in this recipe. The application will notify the user about the progress and will also display messages when the user starts uploading the file and when the upload has finished.

In this recipe, we first choose a file for upload. We click on the **Upload** button and then the file is going to be stored on the server.

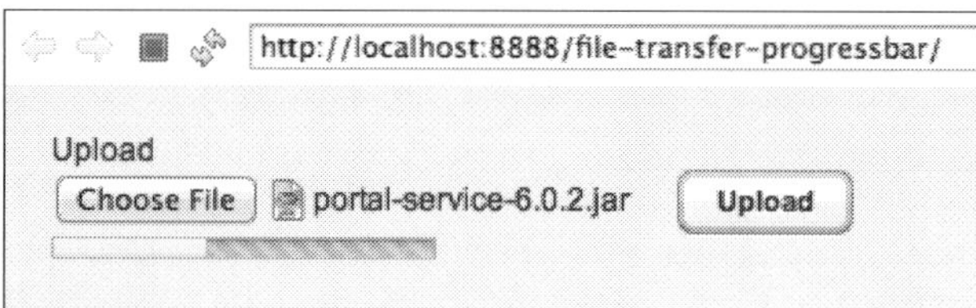

How to do it...

Carry out the following steps:

1. The key part of the upload mechanism is the receiver. The receiver will implement more than the `Receiver` interface. We want to be notified about the progress, so we also implement `ProgressListener`. Then we want to be notified when the upload starts and ends, so we implement another two interfaces, `StartedListener` and `FinishedListener`.

```
class UploadReceiver implements Receiver,
  ProgressListener, StartedListener, FinishedListener
```

2. We need access to the progress indicator from the upload receiver. So we make a reference from `UploadReceiver` to `ProgressIndicator` by creating a private field called `indicator` and adding it to the constructor. So `UploadReceiver` can't be created without the progress indicator.

```
private final ProgressIndicator indicator;

public UploadReceiver(ProgressIndicator indicator) {
  this.indicator = indicator;
}
```

3. The receiver interface defines the `receiveUpload` method. We need to implement it and state how and where the file is going to be stored on the server. The `filename` parameter is just the name of the received file. If we want to specify the directory in which to save the file, we need to add the full path to the directory followed by `filename`.

```
@Override
public OutputStream receiveUpload
  (String filename, String mimeType) {
  FileOutputStream fos = null;
  try {
    File file = new File(filename);
    fos = new FileOutputStream(file);
  } catch (FileNotFoundException e) {
    Notification.show(e.getMessage(),
    Notification.Type.ERROR_MESSAGE);
    return null;
  }
  return fos;
}
```

4. The `ProgressListener` interface defines the `updateProgress` method. That method is invoked when the user needs to be notified about the progress. So we update the progress indicator by the current state of the upload process. Note that the `try-catch` block is there just to slow down the upload, so we can test it on our local machines. The `try-catch` block should be removed before pushing code to the source code repository or before going into production.

```
@Override
public void updateProgress
  (long readBytes, long contentLength) {
  try {
    // let's slow down upload a bit
    Thread.sleep(100);
  } catch (InterruptedException e) {
    e.printStackTrace();
```

```
  }
  float newValue = readBytes / (float) contentLength;
  indicator.setValue(newValue);
}
```

5. There are two methods, `uploadStarted` and `uploadFinished`, from `StartListener` and `FinishedListener`. We will add the progress indicator when the upload starts (the `layout` variable is a layout on which we add the progress indicator components). Also we notify the user about the start or end of the upload. Then we remove the indicator and show information about finished upload when the upload is done.

```
@Override
public void uploadStarted(StartedEvent event) {
  layout.addComponent(indicator);
  Notification.show("Upload started.",
    Type.TRAY_NOTIFICATION);
}

@Override
public void uploadFinished(FinishedEvent event) {
  layout.removeComponent(indicator);
  Notification.show("Upload finished.",
    Type.TRAY_NOTIFICATION);
}
```

6. Create a new progress indicator with the default value set to `0` (so no progress is shown when the component is on the UI).

```
ProgressIndicator indicator = new
  ProgressIndicator(0.0f);
```

7. Then we make a new instance of the upload receiver that will be implemented in the next steps.

```
UploadReceiver uploadReceiver = new
  UploadReceiver(indicator);
Upload upload = new Upload("Upload", uploadReceiver);
upload.addProgressListener(uploadReceiver);
upload.addFinishedListener(uploadReceiver);
upload.addStartedListener(uploadReceiver);
layout.addComponent(upload);
```

8. We can finally run the application and try to upload few files.

How it works...

`ProgressIndicator` needs to implement `Receiver`. The rest of the implemented listeners are optional and they are just keeping the user more informed about what is happening with his/her upload.

There's more...

There are two more interfaces that can be implemented:

- `FailedListener`: This is implemented so that we can notify the user that the upload has failed
- `SucceededListner`: This notifies the user that the upload has been successful

Waiting for an indeterminate process

Sometimes we are not able to get the information about the progress of a task. Therefore, we are not able to use the normal progress indicator that starts at 0.0 and ends at 1.0, because we don't have the value to be set to the progress indicator.

For example, we perform sophisticated calculations on the server (see the following screenshot) and we want to let the user know that something is happening on the server and the user should wait for the result.

How to do it...

Carry out the following steps:

1. Let's implement the price calculation. The calculation will be done in a separate thread and therefore we implement the `Runnable` interface and place the calculation code into the `run()` method.

```
class PriceCalculation implements Runnable {

  private long calculated = 0;
  private final ProgressIndicator indicator;
  private final Label label;
```

```
    public PriceCalculation(ProgressIndicator indicator,
      Label label) {
      this.indicator = indicator;
      this.label = label;
    }

    public void addResult(int result) {
      calculated += result;
    }

    @Override
    public void run() {
      // TODO: fetch data from DB or do some real stuff
      int data = 200000;

      // perform calculation
      for (int i = 0; i < data; i++) {
        for (int j = 0; j < data; j++) {
          int result = i + j;
          addResult(result);
        }
      }

      getSession().getLockInstance().lock();
      try {
        // inform UI about result
        label.setValue("Result is: " + calculated);
        indicator.setVisible(false);
      } finally {
        getSession().getLockInstance().unlock();
      }
    }
  }
```

2. Now we implement `StartCalculationListener` that is invoked when the button is clicked. `StartCalculationListener` makes the progress indicator visible, creates a new thread, and starts up the calculation.

```
public class StartCalculationListener implements
  ClickListener {

  private final ProgressIndicator indicator;
  private final Label label;

  public StartCalculationListener
    (ProgressIndicator indicator, Label label) {
```

```
        this.indicator = indicator;
        this.label = label;
    }

    @Override
    public void buttonClick(ClickEvent event) {
        indicator.setVisible(true);
        Thread thread = new Thread
          (new PriceCalculation(indicator, label));
        thread.start();
    }
}
```

3. Now we put all the classes together. Make a new progress indicator and set `indeterminate` to `true`, and then hide it. We want to make the progress indicator visible after the user clicks on the button. Then we add a label for the calculation result and a button that starts up the calculation.

```
VerticalLayout layout = new VerticalLayout();

ProgressIndicator indicator = new ProgressIndicator();
Label label = new Label();

Button button = new Button("Start calculation");
layout.addComponent(button);

indicator.setIndeterminate(true);
indicator.setVisible(false);
layout.addComponent(indicator);

layout.addComponent(label);

button.addClickListener(new
  StartCalculationListener(indicator, label));}
```

4. Run the application and click on the button. A little circle should appear below the button that indicates that the calculation is in progress. The result should appear after the calculation is done.

How it works...

`StartCalculationListener` starts the calculation when we click on the button by starting up a new thread that will do all the work.

Note that we have obtained a lock from the session. Because we are accessing UI components from outside the normal request handling, we have to be careful about locking. We need to protect the data of the current session from concurrent access.

Showing information about browsers

It could happen that we need browser information in our application. Knowing more about the user can help us with making applications more user-friendly. For example, we could exclude some components in case the browser window is too small or we could display different content to Mac users.

Let's have a look at how to list all the available information about a client web browser.

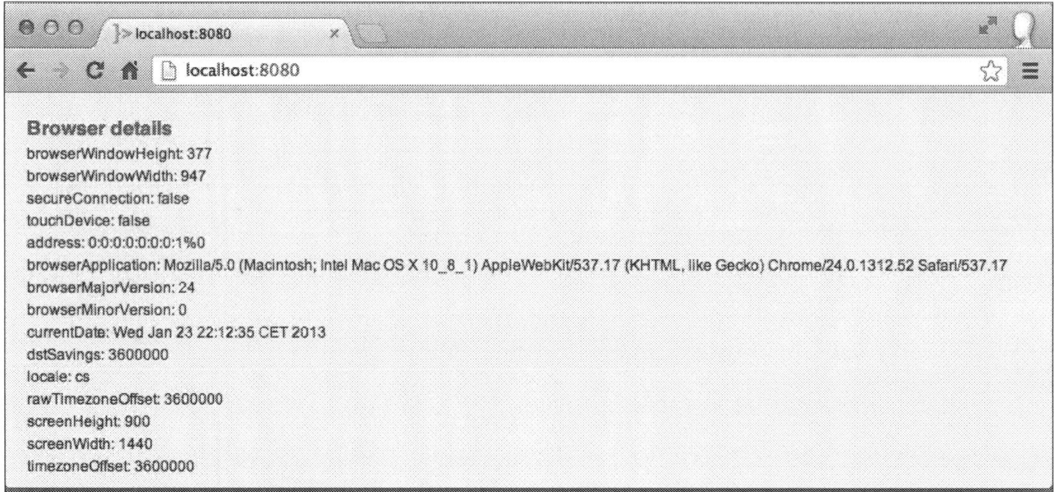

How to do it...

Carry out the following steps:

1. First, we get the current page and call the `getBrowserWindowHeight` and `getBrowserWindowWidth` methods. As the names of the methods suggest, these two methods return the browser width and height.

   ```
   Page page = Page.getCurrent();
   int browserWindowHeight = page.getBrowserWindowHeight();
   int browserWindowWidth = page.getBrowserWindowWidth();
   ```

2. Then, we get the instance of the web browser. The `WebBrowser` class represents the client's browser and there are many interesting getters there. Let's go through a few of them one by one.

   ```
   WebBrowser webBrowser = page.getWebBrowser();
   ```

3. The `getAddress()` method returns the IP address of the web browser. It is equivalent to the `getRemoteAddr` method from the `javax.servlet.http.HttpServletRequest` class.

   ```
   String address = webBrowser.getAddress();
   addComponent(new Label("address: " + address));
   ```

4. The `getBrowserApplication()` method is equivalent to the `getHeader("user-agent")` method from the `HttpServletRequest` class. It returns detailed information about the browser software.

   ```
   String browserApplication =
     webBrowser.getBrowserApplication();
   ```

   If we want, we can get more details about the browser.

   ```
   int browserMajorVersion =
     webBrowser.getBrowserMajorVersion();
   int browserMinorVersion =
     webBrowser.getBrowserMinorVersion();
   ```

5. The `getCurrentDate()` method returns the client's current date and time. It might be handy in case we don't want to work with server time but rather with client time.

   ```
   Date currentDate = webBrowser.getCurrentDate();
   ```

6. The `getLocale()` method returns the client's localization (the language that is set in browser preferences):

   ```
   Locale locale = webBrowser.getLocale();
   ```

7. We can also obtain the screen height and width. Note that it is not browser height and width. It is really the screen height and width.

   ```
   int screenHeight = webBrowser.getScreenHeight();
   int screenWidth = webBrowser.getScreenWidth();
   ```

8. Then, we might need to know the operating system and the browser used by the user. There are special methods for this purpose.

   ```
   boolean ie = webBrowser.isIE();
   boolean firefox = webBrowser.isFirefox();
   boolean safari = webBrowser.isSafari();
   boolean chrome = webBrowser.isChrome();
   boolean chromeFrame = webBrowser.isChromeFrame();
   boolean opera = webBrowser.isOpera();
   boolean macOSX = webBrowser.isMacOSX();
   boolean linux = webBrowser.isLinux();
   boolean windows = webBrowser.isWindows();
   ...
   ```

How it works...

The Page class gets a reference to WebBrowser via VaadinSession and WebBrowser delegates many methods to the VBrowserDetails class. VBrowserDetails is the class that parses data from a request. WebBrowser is initialized in VaadinServlet in its service method.

7
Working with Forms

In this chapter, we will cover:

- Creating a simple form
- Generating fields from a bean
- Binding fields to a bean
- Using field validation
- Using bean validation
- Creating a custom validation
- Creating a CRUD form
- Filtering items using ComboBox

Introduction

Forms are used for collecting requests from users of a website. We'll learn how to create various forms with different fields. We'll start with creating a simple login form. Then we'll show how to create a form very quickly and easily by generating fields from a bean. Validation of the user input is very important in each application. In Vaadin, we can check values on the fields, we can use JSR-303 (Java Specification Request) validation, or we can create our own custom validator. So we'll look more deeply at these validation techniques. Next we'll create a form that is based on the CRUD concept. **Create, read, update, and delete** (**CRUD**) are the four basic functions of storage. Finally, we'll learn how to use the `ComboBox` component to filter items.

Creating a simple form

When we need to pass data from the user to the server, we use input fields. When we have more fields, we arrange them into forms. Creating forms in Vaadin is very easy. In this recipe, we will create a simple login form panel as shown in the following screenshot:

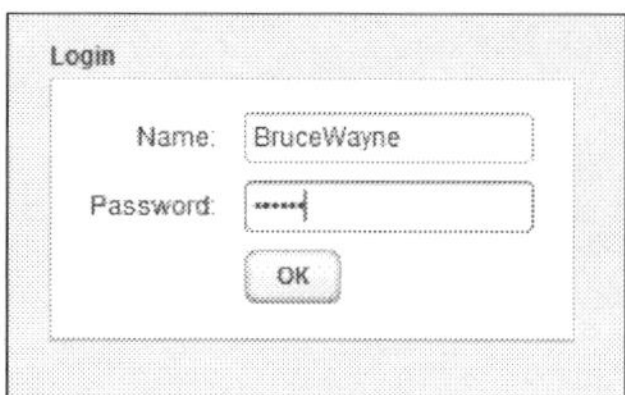

How to do it...

Carry out the following steps to create a simple login form:

1. We create a Vaadin project with a main UI class named `Demo`.

   ```
   public class Demo extends UI {…}
   ```

2. Our form will be wrapped in the `Panel` container. Therefore, we create a `LoginFormPanel` class that extends the `Panel` class.

   ```
   public class LoginFormPanel extends Panel {…}
   ```

3. All the parts of the form lie in the constructor. First, we set the name and size of the form.

   ```
     public LoginFormPanel() {
       super("Login");
       setSizeUndefined();
       …
   ```

4. We will use `FormLayout` for the fields. In this layout, captions are rendered to the left of their respective components. Margin `top` and margin `bottom` are by default set to `true`. Through the `setMargin(true)` method, we can set the margin on all four sides.

   ```
       FormLayout layout = new FormLayout();
       layout.setMargin(true);
       setContent(layout);
       …
   ```

5. The first field is for the name. We set this field as `final` because it will be used in the button's listener. We also set a focus on this field, because it is very useful for the user.

```
final TextField nameField = new TextField("Name:");
nameField.focus();
layout.addComponent(nameField);
...
```

6. The next field is for the password. Here, we use an instance of `PasswordField`. This field is used to enter secret text information. The entered letters are replaced by dots.

```
PasswordField passwordField =  new PasswordField("Password:");
    layout.addComponent(passwordField);
    ...
```

7. At the end, in the constructor, we insert a button for the form confirmation. We add a click listener and we bind it with a shortcut `Enter`, which is another useful feature for the user.

```
    Button okButton = new Button("OK");
    okButton.setClickShortcut(KeyCode.ENTER, null);
    okButton.addClickListener(new ClickListener() {
      @Override
      public void buttonClick(ClickEvent event) {
        Notification.show("Login user " + nameField.getValue());
      }
    });
    layout.addComponent(okButton);
  }
```

8. Now we will use our simple login form in the main UI class `Demo`. If we want to place this form at the center, we can do it through the vertical layout and align the component by the `setComponentAlignment()` method.

```
public class Demo extends UI {
@Override
protected void init(VaadinRequest request) {
VerticalLayout layout = new VerticalLayout();
setContent(layout);

LoginFormPanel loginPanel = new LoginFormPanel();
layout.addComponent(loginPanel);
layout.setSizeFull();
layout.setComponentAlignment(loginPanel, Alignment.MIDDLE_CENTER);
}
}
```

That is all. We can run the server and open the application in the web browser.

Generating fields from a bean

In some situations, we need to create a form very quickly. For example, when we are creating a proof of concept, a prototype of an application, or when we need only a simple form and we don't want to spend a lot of time on UI work. In those cases, we don't need to create each field, but we can generate them through the Java Bean. It's quick and easy. In this recipe, we will see how to generate a simple form for the Bean Product. Our generated form will look like the following screenshot:

How to do it...

Carry out the following steps to generate a form from the Java Bean:

1. Create a Vaadin project with a main UI class called `Demo`.

   ```
   public class Demo extends UI {…}
   ```

2. We start with a bean. This bean is for `Product` that has attributes `code`, `name`, `price`, and `date`. Names of the `getter` methods (without the prefix 'get' and 'is') will be used as captions for the generated fields.

   ```
   public class Product {

     private int code;
     private String name;
     private double price;
     private Date date = new Date();

     public Product(int code, String name, double price) {
       this.code = code;
       this.name = name;
       this.price = price;
     }
      <insert getters and setters>
     …
   }
   ```

3. Next, we create our main class named `GeneratedProductForm` as follows. We will extend `FormLayout`. In this layout, captions are rendered to the left of their respective components.

   ```
   public class GeneratedProductForm extends FormLayout {…}
   ```

4. The main parts of the form are in the constructor. Here, we set the size and the margin on all four sides of the form.

   ```
   public GeneratedProductForm() {
       setSizeUndefined();
       setMargin(true);
       …
   ```

5. Now we create an instance of the `FieldGroup` class. `FieldGroup` provides an easy way of binding fields to data and handling commits of these fields. As a field factory, we use our `CustomFieldGroupFieldFactory` class that is created in the inner class. The field factory is only used when `FieldGroup` creates a new field.

   ```
       FieldGroup fieldGroup = new BeanFieldGroup
       <Product>(Product.class);
       fieldGroup.setFieldFactory(new
   CustomFieldGroupFieldFactory());
       …
   ```

6. Next, we set the item through the `setItemDataSource()` method. This method updates the item that is used by this `FieldGroup` class and rebinds all fields to the properties in the new item.

   ```
       fieldGroup.setItemDataSource(new BeanItem<Product>(
       new Product(1, "Tablet", 299.99)));
       …
   ```

7. Adding components to the layout is simple. We build and bind them through the `fieldGroup` object.

   ```
       for (Object propertyId : fieldGroup.getUnboundPropertyIds()) {
         addComponent(fieldGroup.buildAndBind(propertyId));
       }
     }
   ```

8. If we use only simple types of attributes in our bean, we can skip this step and we can use simply an instance of the `DefaultFieldGroupFieldFactory` class. However, we use the `Date` type. We have to instruct the `fieldGroup` object how to generate a field for the `Date` type. For this type, we will return the instance of the `DateField` class.

   ```
   class CustomFieldGroupFieldFactory extends
   DefaultFieldGroupFieldFactory {
     @Override
     public <T extends Field> T createField(Class<?> dataType,
   ```

```
Class<T> fieldType) {
    if (Date.class.isAssignableFrom(dataType)){
      return (T) new DateField();
    }
    return super.createField(dataType, fieldType);
  }
}
```

9. That's all. Now we can use our form in the `Demo` class.

```
public class Demo extends UI {
  @Override
  protected void init(VaadinRequest request) {
    setContent(new GeneratedProductForm());
  }
}
```

Now we run the server and open the application in the web browser.

There's more...

If we have this generated form, it is very easy and quick to insert another field. For example, we can add a new field, `salable`, by adding a new attribute and method to the `Product` bean.

```
public class Product {
  ...
  private boolean salable;
  public boolean isSalable() {
    return salable;
  }

  public void setSalable(boolean salable) {
    this.salable = salable;
  }
   ...
}
```

In the following screenshot, we can see that a new field, `salable`, was added as a checkbox, because it is a type of `boolean`.

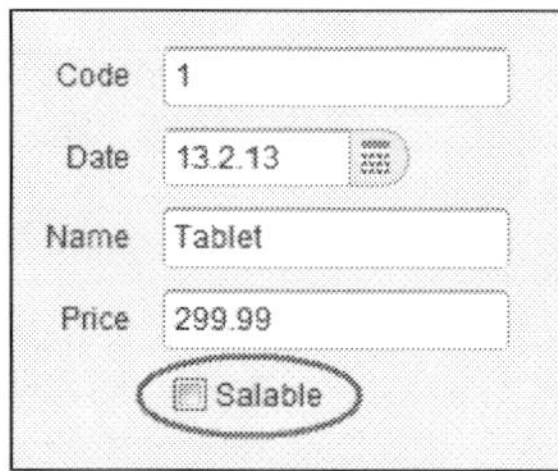

Binding fields to a bean

As mentioned in the previous recipe, generating fields in forms can be done very quickly. However, it is not very flexible. In some cases, we need to change, for example, the caption or the order of the fields. Therefore, when we want to create flexible forms, we can create each field separately and then bind them with a bean. In this recipe, we will create the same form as in the previous recipe, but we will change the caption of the fields.

How to do it...

Carry out the following steps to create form fields bound to a Java Bean:

1. Create a Vaadin project with a main UI class called `Demo`.

   ```
   public class Demo extends UI {…}
   ```

2. We start with a bean. This bean is for `Product` that has the attributes `code`, `name`, and `price`.

   ```
   public class Product {
     private int code;
     private String name;
     private double price;

     public Product(int code, String name, double price) {
       this.code = code;
       this.name = name;
       this.price = price;
     }
     <insert getters and setters>
      …
   }
   ```

3. Next, we create our main class of product form that is bound with a bean. This class is based on the `FormLayout` class. In this layout, captions are rendered to the left of their respective components.

   ```
   public class BoundProductForm extends FormLayout {…}
   ```

4. Now we create a field for each attribute from the bean. If the name of the field is the same as the name of an attribute, for example, the `code` field, then it will be automatically bound together.

> The name `code` is used only for demonstration. In a production application, it is preferable to use a more descriptive name such as `codeField` or `productCode`.

   However, if the name of field is different, we can bind it by the `@PropertyId` annotation. The value in the annotation must be the same as the name of the attribute in the bean.

```
private TextField code = new TextField("Product code:");
@PropertyId("name")
private TextField nameField = new TextField("Product name:");
@PropertyId("price")
private TextField priceField = new TextField("Price (USD):");
```

5. In the constructor, we set the size of the form to minimal height and width. Through the `setMargin(true)` method, we set the margin on all four sides.

```
public BoundProductForm() {
  setSizeUndefined();
  setMargin(true);
        ...
```

6. We continue with creating an instance of the `FieldGroup` class. `FieldGroup` provides an easy way of binding fields to data and handling commits of these fields. In this object, we also set `ItemDataSource`.

```
  FieldGroup fieldGroup =  new BeanFieldGroup
  <Product>(Product.class);
  fieldGroup.setItemDataSource(new BeanItem<Product>(
                  new Product(1, "Tablet", 299.99)));
  fieldGroup.bindMemberFields(this);
  ...
```

7. At the end, we add all the fields into the layout.

```
  addComponent(code);
  addComponent(nameField);
  addComponent(priceField);
}
```

8. That is all. We can use our created form in the main UI `Demo` class.

```
public class Demo extends UI {

  @Override
  protected void init(VaadinRequest request) {
    setContent(new BoundProductForm());
```

```
    }
  }
```

We can run the server and open our application in the web browser.

How it works...

FieldGroup provides an easy way of binding fields to data and handling commits of these fields. FieldGroup does not handle layouts in any way. The typical use case is to create a layout outside the FieldGroup class and then use FieldGroup to bind the fields to a data source. In our case, as a data source is used, an instance of BeanItem that adds all properties of a Java Bean to it. The properties are identified by their respective bean names. And finally using the FieldGroup.bindMemberFields() method, all (Java) member fields whose type extends Field are bound with the data source.

Using field validation

People make mistakes. Therefore, we have to check the user input. The important reason for validation is to make sure the data that should be stored in the database conforms to the rules of the data model. In Vaadin, it is possible to do it in several ways. The easiest way is to use predefined validators. We can validate, for example, the length of the string or the size of values; or we can compare the string against a regular expression. In this recipe, we will create a field that will check whether the given string is a syntactically valid email address.

How to do it...

Carry out the following steps to learn how to use validation in the form fields:

1. Create a Vaadin project with the main UI class called Demo.

   ```
   public class Demo extends UI {…}
   ```

2. We start with the main class named EmailField. This class is based on the TextField class. In the constructor, we set the caption of the field. We set this component to an immediate mode for a quick response. Through the addValidator() method, we easily add a new EmailValidator object. Through this parameter in the constructor, we pass an error message.

   ```
   public class EmailField extends TextField {

     public EmailField(String caption) {
       super(caption);
   ```

```
        setImmediate(true);
        addValidator(new EmailValidator("Invalid email"));
    }
}
```

3. Next, we can use our `EmailField` class in the `Demo` class. We use `FormLayout` that shows the caption on the left of the text field.

```
    @Override
    protected void init(VaadinRequest request) {
        FormLayout layout = new FormLayout();
        layout.setMargin(true);
        setContent(layout);
        EmailField field = new EmailField("Email:");
        layout.addComponent(field);
    }
}
```

That's all. We can run the server and open our application in the web browser.

How it works...

Validators are added using the `addValidator()` method inherited from the `AbstractField` class. All validators added to a field are checked each time its value changes. Another way of validation is to use converters. They are used to convert between the UI and the data model type.

There's more...

Here is a list of some useful predefined validators:

Validator	**Description**
`AbstractValidator`	Provides a basic Validator implementation. Since Vaadin 7, subclasses can either implement `validate(Object)` directly or implement `isValidValue(Object)` when migrating legacy applications. To check validity, `validate(Object)` should be used.
`AbstractStringValidator`	Base class for validating strings.
`StringLengthValidator`	Validates the length of strings.
`EmailValidator`	Checks that a string is a syntactically valid e-mail address.
`RegexpValidator`	Compares the string against a Java regular expression. Both complete matches and substring matches are supported.

For checking the type of numbers, we use converters on the field. This is an example of how to add a converter for double numbers:

```
TextField field = new TextField();
field.setConverter(Double.class);
```

See also

- Converters are a new feature in Vaadin 7. There is a separate recipe about it in *Chapter 9, Data Management*.
- Other practical recipe about field validation is the *Showing validation messages* recipe in *Chapter 6, Messages*.

Using bean validation

Java Bean Validation—JSR-303 is a framework that has been approved by the JCP (Java Community Process) and is accepted as a part of the Java EE 6 specification. Through this framework, we can easily add validation on the attributes in the bean. In this recipe, we will create a form for the `Product` bean and we will validate the attributes.

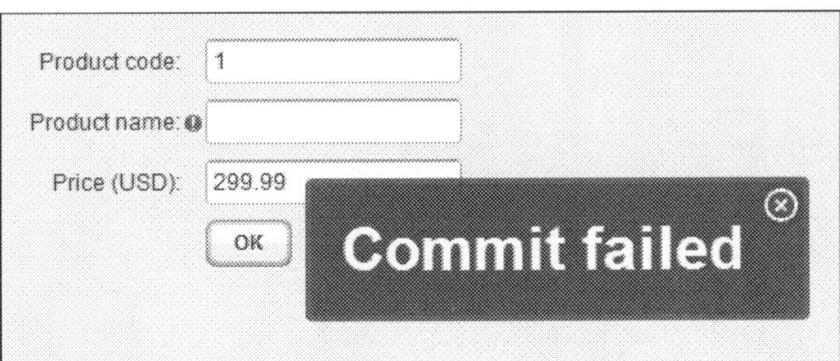

Getting ready

Before we start with bean validation, we need to download a Bean Validation implementation and add it to our project. For example, one of them is available at the following URL:

`http://code.google.com/p/agimatec-validation/downloads/list`

Alternatively, we can download the Hibernate Validator from the following URL:

`http://www.hibernate.org/subprojects/validator/download`

Or add the Maven dependency:

```
<dependency>
    <groupId>org.hibernate</groupId>
    <artifactId>hibernate-validator</artifactId>
    <version>4.3.1.Final</version>
</dependency>
```

Hibernate Validator requires `slf4j-api` and `slf4j-simple` JAR files available at the following URL:

`http://www.slf4j.org/download.html`

Or add the Maven dependency:

```
<dependency>
  <groupId>org.slf4j</groupId>
  <artifactId>slf4j-api</artifactId>
  <version>1.7.2</version>
</dependency>
```

After downloading, we add these JAR files into the lib folder in our project at `WebContent/WEB-INF/lib`.

How to do it...

Carry out the following steps to create a form with bean validation:

1. Create a Vaadin project with a main UI class named `Demo`.

   ```
   public class Demo extends UI {…}
   ```

2. We create a bean named `Product`. This bean has attributes `code`, `name`, and `price`. Using bean validation is very easy. For instance, if we want to add a not-null constraint to ensure a `null` value cannot be used on the `code` attribute, we place a `@NotNull` annotation on it. Using the `@Size` annotation with optional elements `min` and `max`, we can limit the length of the string `name`. To determine the minimum value of `price` we use an annotation, `@Min`.

   ```
   public class Product  {
     @NotNull
     private int code;
     @Size(min=2, max=10)
     private String name;
     @Min(0)
     private double price;
   ```

```
  public Product(int code, String name, double price) {
    super();
    this.code = code;
    this.name = name;
    this.price = price;
  }
  <insert getters and setter>
  ...
}
```

3. Next, we create our main class named `ProductForm`. This class is based on the `FormLayout` class. In this layout, captions are rendered to the left of their respective components.

```
public class ProductForm extends FormLayout {...}
```

4. We want to bind fields with bean attributes, so the names of the fields are the same as the attributes of the `Product` bean.

```
  private TextField code = new TextField("Product code:");
  private TextField name = new TextField("Product name:");
  private TextField price = new TextField("Price (USD):");
  private FieldGroup fieldGroup;
```

5. In the constructor, we set size of the form and, using the `setMargin(true)` method, we set a margin on all four sides.

```
  public ProductForm() {
    setSizeUndefined();
    setMargin(true);
    ...
```

6. Next, we create an instance of the `FieldGroup` class. `FieldGroup` provides an easy way of binding fields to data and handling commits of these fields. In this object, we also set the bean item.

```
    fieldGroup = new BeanFieldGroup<Product>(Product.class);
    fieldGroup.setItemDataSource(new BeanItem<Product>(product));
    fieldGroup.bindMemberFields(this);
    ...
```

7. At the end, we add all components to the layout.

```
    addComponent(code);
    addComponent(name);
    addComponent(price);
    addComponent(createOkButton());
  }
```

8. The `okButton` object is created in a separate method. We add a click listener on this button. In this listener, we commit all changes made to the bound fields. If some of the fields are not valid, the `FieldGroup.commit()` method throws `CommitException`.

```
private Button createOkButton() {
  Button okButton = new Button("OK");
  okButton.addClickListener(new ClickListener() {
    @Override
    public void buttonClick(ClickEvent event) {
      try {
        fieldGroup.commit();
        Notification.show("Product committed: " + product);
      } catch (CommitException e) {
        Notification.show(e.getMessage(), Type.ERROR_MESSAGE);
      }
    }
  });
  return okButton;
}
```

9. That is all. Now we can use our created form in the `Demo` class.

```
  @Override
  protected void init(VaadinRequest request) {
    setContent(new ProductForm());
  }
}
```

We run the server and open our application in the web browser.

How it works...

A table showing some bean validation constraints:

Constraint	Description	Example
`@AssertFalse`	The value of the field or property must be `false`.	`@AssertFalse` `boolean isUnsupported;`
`@Future`	The value of the field or property must be a date in the future.	`@Future` `Date eventDate;`
`@Min`	The value of the field or property must be an integer value greater than or equal to the number in the value element.	`@Min(5)` `int quantity;`

Constraint	Description	Example
@NotNull	The value of the field or property must not be null.	@NotNull String username;
@Size	The value can not exceed the value of one of the optional elements max or min.	@Size(min=2, max=240) String briefMessage;

The full list of the built-in Bean validation constraints is described on the Oracle's web page:

http://docs.oracle.com/javaee/6/tutorial/doc/gircz.html

See also

- The web page about Hibernate Validator is available at http://www.hibernate.org/subprojects/validator
- The web page about JSR-303: Bean Validation available at http://jcp.org/en/jsr/detail?id=303

Creating a custom validation

In some situations, we need our own special validation; for example, if we want to compare two fields, or if we want to validate some custom special component. In that case, we can add a custom validator and override the `validate(Object)` method. In this recipe, we will create a form for changing the password. We will add a custom validator that will match the new and confirmed password fields.

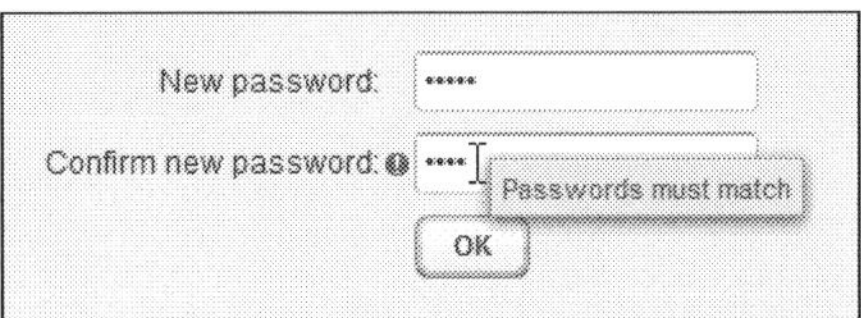

How to do it...

Carry out the following steps to create a form with a custom validation:

1. Create a Vaadin project with a main UI class called `Demo`.
   ```
   public class Demo extends UI {…}
   ```
2. We create a `ChangePasswordForm` class that is based on the `FormLayout` class.
   ```
   public class ChangePasswordForm extends FormLayout {…}
   ```

3. At first, we prepare some class fields. We create two instances of the `PasswordField` class for the new and confirmation password fields. In these fields, the characters are visually hidden. They are replaced by dots. Then we create the `okButton` object that will be used to call the `validate()` method. We also insert two string constants for confirmation and the error message for the validation process.

```
private PasswordField newPasswordField = new PasswordField
("New password:");
private PasswordField confirmPasswordField = new PasswordField
("Confirm new password:");
private Button okButton = new Button("OK");
private static final String CONFIRM_MESSAGE = "Passwords are the
same";
private static final String ERROR_MESSAGE = "Passwords must
match";
```

4. All the main functionality is in the constructor. For a better view of the form, we set height and width to a minimum size by the `setSizeUndefined()` method. And we also set an extra space around the whole form layout using the `setMargin()` method.

```
  public ChangePasswordForm() {
    setSizeUndefined();
    setMargin(true);
    ...
```

5. Next we create our custom validator and we add it to the confirmation password field. The confirmed password must be the same as the newly specified one. If they are different, the `validate()` method throws an `InvalidValueException` with an error message.

```
confirmPasswordField.addValidator(new Validator() {
      @Override
      public void validate(Object value) throws
InvalidValueException {
        String password = (String) value;
        if (!password.equals(newPasswordField.getValue())) {
          throw new InvalidValueException(ERROR_MESSAGE);
        }
      }
    });
    ...
```

6. Next we add a click listener to the `okButton` object. On the click event we'll validate the confirmation password field using the `validate()` method. This method calls the built-in validation and then our added validation. It checks the given field value against our validator. If the value is valid, it means that the confirmed password is the same as the newly specified one; the method does nothing. If the value is invalid, an `InvalidValueException` exception is thrown.

```
okButton.addClickListener(new ClickListener() {
  @Override
  public void buttonClick(ClickEvent event) {
    try {
      confirmPasswordField.validate();
      Notification.show(CONFIRM_MESSAGE);
    } catch (Exception e) {
      Notification.show(ERROR_MESSAGE,
      Type.ERROR_MESSAGE);
    }
  }
});
```

7. At the end of the constructor we insert all created components into the form layout.

```
    addComponent(newPasswordField);
    addComponent(confirmPasswordField);
    addComponent(okButton);
  }
```

8. That is all. Now we can use our created change password form in the topmost `Demo` class.

```
public class Demo extends UI {
  @Override
  protected void init(VaadinRequest request) {
    setContent(new ChangePasswordForm());
  }
}
```

We run the server and open the application in the web browser.

How it works...

Validators check the validity of input and, if the input is invalid, they can provide an error message through an exception. Validators are classes that implement the `Validator` interface. The interface has one method that we must implement:

- `validate()`: It reports a failure with an exception. The exception can be associated with an error message describing the details of the error.

Since Vaadin 7, the `isValid(Object)` method does not exist in the interface. Only `validate(Object)` should be used instead and the exception caught, where applicable. Concrete classes implementing `Validator` can still internally implement and use `isValid(Object)` for convenience or to ease migration from earlier Vaadin versions.

See also

- More information about the password field is described on the Vaadin web page at `https://vaadin.com/book/vaadin7/-/page/components.passwordfield.html`
- API of the `Validator` interface is available at `https://vaadin.com/api/7.0.0/com/vaadin/data/Validator.html`
- Another practical recipe about the custom field validation is also mentioned in the *Showing validation messages* recipe in *Chapter 6, Messages*.

Creating a CRUD form

CRUD is also known as `create`, `read`, `update`, and `delete`, which are four basic functions of storage. These methods are used by many user interfaces. We will create a form that is based on this concept. Data will be stored in a table. Adding and updating data will be implemented through a pop-up window with the form.

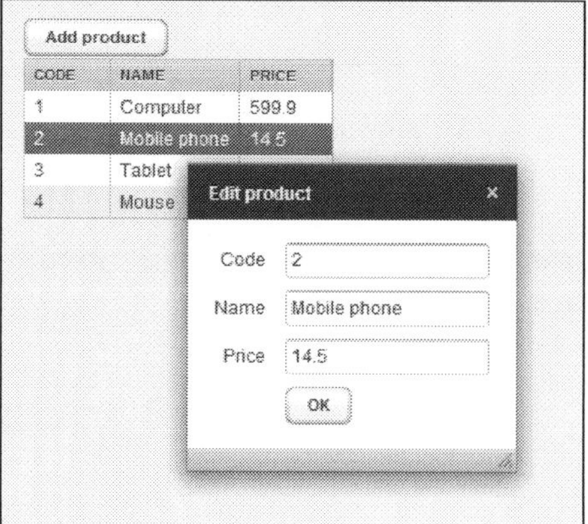

How to do it...

Carry out the following steps to create a CRUD form:

1. Create a Vaadin project with a main UI class called `Demo`.

```
public class Demo extends UI {…}
```

2. We start with the bean. This bean is for `Product` that has attributes `code`, `name`, and `price`. In each attribute, we add validation constrains.

```
public class Product  {
  @NotNull
  private int code;
  @Size(min=3, max=30)
  private String name = "";
  @Min(0)
  private double price;

  public Product(int code) {
    this.code = code;
  };

  public Product(int code, String name, double price) {
    this.code = code;
    this.name = name;
    this.price = price;
  }
  <insert getters and setters>
  ...
}
```

3. Next, we create our CRUD form. It extends `VerticalLayout`.

```
public class CrudForm extends VerticalLayout {...}
```

4. At first we prepare some components. The `Table` class will be used as a display of container items. Items will be stored in the `tableContainer` instance of `BeanItemContainer<Product>`. `FieldGroup` will be used for binding fields with attributes of `Product`. We also need one action for deleting items in the table. The value of `code` will start at `1` and the maximum number of rows in the table is set to `15`.

```
private Table table = new Table();
private BeanItemContainer<Product> tableContainer;
private FieldGroup fieldGroup;
private Action actionDelete = new Action("Delete");
private int code = 1;
private static final int MAX_PAGE_LENGTH = 15;
```

5. In the constructor, we initialize the values in the table. Then, we add a button for adding new items and a table into the layout. We also set the number of visible table rows according to the number of items in the table.

```
public CrudForm() {
  initTable();
  addComponent(createAddButton());
```

```
        addComponent(table);
        table.setPageLength(table.size());
    }
```

6. The table is initialized in a separate method. Here we set the table container and fill it with some data through the `fillTableContainer()` method.

```
    private void initTable() {
        tableContainer = new BeanItemContainer<Product>(Product.
class);
        fillTableContainer(tableContainer);
        table.setContainerDataSource(tableContainer);
        table.setSelectable(true);
        ...
```

7. Next, we add a click listener into this table. In this listener, we will react on the double-click of the mouse. We will open a pop-up window with the form on this event.

```
        table.addItemClickListener(new ItemClickListener() {
            @Override
            public void itemClick(ItemClickEvent event) {
                if (event.isDoubleClick()) {
                    openProductWindow(event.getItem(), "Edit product");
                }
            }
        });
```

8. Next, we add an action for deleting items from the `tableContainer` object. This action will appear in the context menu of the row in the table.

```
        table.addActionHandler(new Handler() {
            @Override
            public void handleAction(Action action, Object sender,
Object target) {
                if (actionDelete == action) {
                    tableContainer.removeItem(target);
                    updateTable();
                }
            }

            @Override
            public Action[] getActions(Object target, Object sender) {
                return new Action[] { actionDelete };
            }
        });
    }
```

9. A button for adding new items into the table is created in a separate method. We will open a pop-up window with the form after clicking on this button.

```
private Button createAddButton() {
  Button button = new Button("Add product");
  button.addClickListener(new ClickListener() {
    public void buttonClick(ClickEvent event) {
      openProductWindow(
          new BeanItem<Product>(new Product(code++)), "Add
product");
    }
  });
  return button;
}
```

10. Next, we insert a method for opening a pop-up window with the product form. This window is set as a modal because we don't want to allow the user to open another window. The body of this window consists of `FormLayout` that shows captions of fields on the left side. At the end, we add a button for confirming the values in the form.

```
private void openProductWindow(Item beanItem, String caption) {
  Window window = new Window(caption);
  window.setModal(true);

  FormLayout layout = new FormLayout();
  layout.setMargin(true);
  window.setContent(layout);

  fieldGroup = new BeanFieldGroup<Product>(Product.class);
  fieldGroup.setItemDataSource(beanItem);
  for (Object propertyId : fieldGroup.getUnboundPropertyIds()) {
    layout.addComponent(fieldGroup.buildAndBind(propertyId));
  }
  layout.addComponent(createOkButton(window));
  getUI().addWindow(window);
}
```

11. The confirmation button for the pop-up window is created in a separate method. In the click listener, we commit all changes made to the bound fields. If some of the fields are not valid, the `FieldGroup.commit()` method throws `CommitException`. If the commit is successful, the bean item is inserted into the table. The existing item is rewritten and the new item is added.

```
private Button createOkButton(final Window window) {
  Button okButton = new Button("OK");
  okButton.addClickListener(new ClickListener() {
    @Override
```

```
          public void buttonClick(ClickEvent event) {
          try {
            fieldGroup.commit();
            BeanItem<Product> beanItem =
                  (BeanItem<Product>) fieldGroup.getItemDataSource();
            tableContainer.addItem(beanItem.getBean());
            updateTable();
            window.close();
          } catch (CommitException e) {
            Notification.show(e.getMessage(), Type.ERROR_MESSAGE);
          }
        }
      });
      return okButton;
    }
```

12. The `updateTable()` method is used to flexibly change the length of the table. It changes the number of visible rows according to the number of items in the container. It is an optional method and this recipe can be used without calling this one. When we don't use it and an item will be removed from the container, then this item will be displayed as a blank row in the table.

    ```
    private void updateTable() {
      if (table.size() > MAX_PAGE_LENGTH) {
        table.setPageLength(MAX_PAGE_LENGTH);
      } else {
        table.setPageLength(table.size());
      }
      table.markAsDirtyRecursive();
    }
    ```

13. At the end, we insert a method for filling the table container with some data.

    ```
    private void fillTableContainer
    (BeanItemContainer<Product> tableContainer) {
      tableContainer.addItem(new Product(code++, "Computer",
599.90));
      tableContainer.addItem(new Product(code++, "Mobile phone",
14.5));
      tableContainer.addItem(new Product(code++, "Tablet", 99.90));
      tableContainer.addItem(new Product(code++, "Mouse", 0.99));
    }
    ```

14. That is all. Now we can use our CRUD form in the `Demo` class.

    ```
    public class Demo extends UI {
      @Override
      protected void init(VaadinRequest request) {
    ```

```
        setContent(new CrudForm());
    }
}
```

We run the server and open the application in the web browser.

How it works...

We created the CRUD application that implements four functions:

- `Create`: A new item (an instance of the `Product` class) is created by clicking on the **Add product** button. Then the form is generated using the `FieldGroup` class. The created item is added to the `BeanItemContainer<Product>` class by the `addItem(Object)` method.
- `Read`: All items in the `BeanItemContainer` class are displayed in the `Table` class.
- `Update`: Details of a specific item are displayed in the generated `TextField` class in the pop-up window. Here the user can change the values of the `Product` bean.
- `Delete`: Items can be removed from the `BeanItemContainer` class using the `Delete` action. This action is shown in a context menu on the `Table`.

There's more...

As well as in the *Generating fields from a bean* recipe when we have this generated form, it is very easy and quick to insert other fields. For example, we can add a new field `Salable` by adding new attributes and methods to the `Product` bean.

Filtering items using ComboBox

When we need to filter data in the fields, we can use `ComboBox`. In this component, items are filtered based on the user input and loaded dynamically (lazy loading) from the server. In this recipe, we will see how to use this component. In addition, we create two bound fields. The first one will be dynamically updated according to the second field.

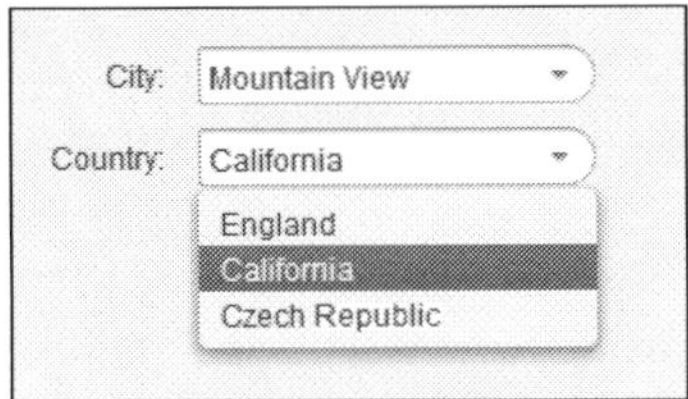

How to do it...

In this recipe, we will update the list of cities according to the country selected:

1. Create a Vaadin project with a main UI class called `Demo`.

   ```
   public class Demo extends UI {…}
   ```

2. We start with the `Country` class. In this class, we need two attributes, namely, `name` and `container` of cities. The property name will be used for a caption of countries in the **Country** combobox. The container will contain the name of cities related to this country.

   ```
   public class Country {
     private String name;
     private BeanItemContainer<String> citiesContainer =
                 new BeanItemContainer<>(String.class);
     public Country(String name, String... cities) {
       this.name = name;
       for (String city : cities) {
         citiesContainer.addItem(city);
       }
     }

     public BeanItemContainer<String> getCitiesContainer() {
       return citiesContainer;
     }

     public String getName() {
       return name;
     }
   }
   ```

3. Next, we create our form. It extends the `FormLayout` class.

   ```
   public class CountryForm extends FormLayout {…}
   ```

4. We need one container of Countries and two comboboxes.

   ```
     private BeanItemContainer<Country> countryContainer =
                 new BeanItemContainer<Country>(Country.class);
     private ComboBox countryBox = new ComboBox("Country:",
   countryContainer);
     private ComboBox cityBox = new ComboBox("City:");
   ```

5. In the constructor, we set the size and margin of the form. Next, we initialize comboboxes and add them to the layout.

```
public CountryForm() {
  setSizeUndefined();
  setMargin(true);

  initComboBoxes();
  addComponent(cityBox);
  addComponent(countryBox);
}
```

6. Comboboxes are initialized in a separate method. Here we fill the country container with `Country` objects and their cities. We can also use one of the filtering modes on the `ComboBox` class. This filter can filter words that start or contain the given input string. In our example we choose `FilteringMode.CONTAINS`. Then we disallow empty selection by the user. It is necessary because we will not need a null object in the `updateCityBox(Country)` method. Next, we update the combobox with cities according to the first country.

```
private void initComboBoxes() {
  fillCountryContainer(countryContainer);

  cityBox.setFilteringMode(FilteringMode.CONTAINS);
  cityBox.setNullSelectionAllowed(false);
  updateCityBox(countryContainer.getIdByIndex(0));
  ...
```

7. In the `countryBox` object, we select the first country. Then we set this `ComboBox` to the immediate mode. It means that value changes will be fired immediately. As in the previous `ComboBox`, we disallow empty selection by the user. Item captions will be read from the property specified with the `setItemCaptionPropertyId(Object propertyId)` method. In our case, we use the `name` property that returns the name of the country.

```
  countryBox.select(countryContainer.getIdByIndex(0));
  countryBox.setImmediate(true);
  countryBox.setNullSelectionAllowed(false);
  countryBox.setItemCaptionPropertyId("name");
```

8. At the end in the `initComboBoxes()` method, we add a value change listener on the `countryBox` because we want to update the combobox of cities after each change in the country combobox.

```
  countryBox.addValueChangeListener
  (new ValueChangeListener() {
    @Override
    public void valueChange(ValueChangeEvent event) {
```

```
            updateCityBox((Country) countryBox.getValue());
          }
        });
      }
```

9. The combobox of cities is updated by a separate method. Here we set the data source container of `cityBox` that is obtained from the `country` object. After setting the container, items of cities are immediately updated. Then we select the first city in the `ComboBox` object. Otherwise, the empty string will be shown in the `ComboBox` object.

```
private void updateCityBox(Country country) {
    cityBox.setContainerDataSource(country.getCitiesContainer());
    cityBox.select(country.getCitiesContainer().getIdByIndex(0));
  }
```

10. At the end, we insert the method that fills in the countries and cities.

```
  private void fillCountries() {
    container.addItem(new Country("England", "London", "Bristol",
    "Birmingham"));
    container.addItem(new Country("California", "San Francisco",
"San Jose",
    "Mountain View"));
    container.addItem(new Country("Czech republic", "Prague",
"Brno",
    "Ostrava"));
  }
```

11. That is all. We can use our `Country` form in the main `Demo` class.

```
@Override
  protected void init(VaadinRequest request) {
    setContent(new CountryForm());
  }
}
```

We run the server and open the application in the web browser.

How it works...

ComboBox is a drop-down list for a single selection with an input prompt. We can set three modes of filters that are used for filtering values in the list. Modes are contained in the `FilteringMode` enumerator:

- `STARTSWITH`: Only values that start with the given string are displayed. It's the default filter mode.

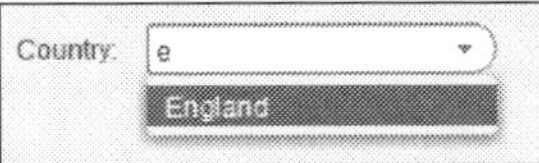

- `CONTAINS`: Only values that contain the given string are displayed.

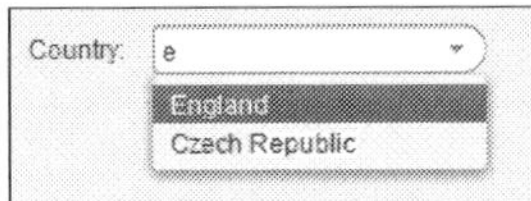

- `OFF`: Filter is turned off. No values are filtered. All values are displayed.

There's more...

If we want to allow the user to add additional items to the `ComboBox` class, we can do it easily by the `ComboBox.setNewItemsAllowed(boolean)` method. For example, this `cityBox.setNewItemsAllowed(true)` method allows the user to add new cities. The user can simply write a new name to the prompt line and press the *Enter* key. The changes are made after losing focus from `ComboBox`.

See also

- API of the `ComboBox` class is described at `https://vaadin.com/api/7.0.0/com/vaadin/ui/ComboBox.html`

8
Spring and Grails Integration

In this chapter, we will cover:

- Setting up a Vaadin project with Spring in Maven
- Handling login with Spring
- Accessing a database with Spring
- Internationalizing Vaadin applications with Spring
- Vaadin and Spring injector
- Internationalizing Vaadin in Grails
- Using Grails ORM in Vaadin application
- Using Grails Services in Vaadin
- Adding a Vaadin Add-on into Grails project

Introduction

In this chapter, we will cover the integration of Vaadin with Spring and Grails frameworks.

First, we show how to add Spring into the Maven project. Then we will show how to perform some basic operations with Spring, such as security, login, accessing database, localization, and dependency injection.

In the second part, we will explore the basics of Vaadin application development inside of a Grails project. We will show how to make localization, how to access database, how to work with services, and how to add an add-on.

Setting up a Vaadin project with Spring in Maven

We will set up a new Maven project for Vaadin application that will use the Spring framework. We will use a Java annotation-driven approach for Spring configuration instead of XML configuration files. This means that we will eliminate the usage of XML to the necessary minimum (for XML fans, don't worry there will be still enough XML to edit).

In this recipe, we will set up a Spring project where we define a bean that will be obtainable from the Spring application context in the Vaadin code. As the final result, we will greet a lady named Adela, so we display **Hi Adela!** text on the screen. The brilliant thing about this is that we get the greeting text from the bean that we define via Spring.

Getting ready

First, we create a new Maven project.

```
mvn archetype:generate \
  -DarchetypeGroupId=com.vaadin \
  -DarchetypeArtifactId=vaadin-archetype-application \
  -DarchetypeVersion=LATEST \
  -Dpackaging=war \
  -DgroupId=com.packtpub.vaadin \
  -DartifactId=vaadin-with-spring \
  -Dversion=1.0
```

More information about Maven and Vaadin can be found at `https://vaadin.com/book/-/page/getting-started.maven.html`.

How to do it...

Carry out the following steps, in order to set up a Vaadin project with Spring in Maven:

1. First, we need to add the necessary dependencies. Just add the following Maven dependencies into the `pom.xml` file:

```
<dependency>
  <groupId>org.springframework</groupId>
  <artifactId>spring-core</artifactId>
  <version>${spring.version}</version>
</dependency>

<dependency>
  <groupId>org.springframework</groupId>
  <artifactId>spring-context</artifactId>
  <version>${spring.version}</version>
</dependency>

<dependency>
  <groupId>org.springframework</groupId>
  <artifactId>spring-web</artifactId>
  <version>${spring.version}</version>
</dependency>

<dependency>
  <groupId>cglib</groupId>
  <artifactId>cglib</artifactId>
  <version>2.2.2</version>
</dependency>
```

2. In the preceding code, we are referring to the `spring.version` property. Make sure we have added the Spring version inside the `properties` tag in the `pom.xml` file.

```
<properties>
...
  <spring.version>3.1.2.RELEASE</spring.version>
</properties>
```

When we were writing this book, the latest version of Spring was 3.1.2. Check the latest version of the Spring framework at `http://www.springsource.org/spring-framework`.

3. The last step in the Maven configuration file is to add the new repository into `pom.xml`. Maven needs to know where to download the Spring dependencies.

```
<repositories>
...
  <repository>
  <id>springsource-repo</id>
  <name>SpringSource Repository</name>
  <url>http://repo.springsource.org/release</url>
  </repository>
</repositories>
```

4. Now we need to add a few lines of XML into the `src/main/webapp/WEB-INF/web.xml` deployment descriptor file. At this point, we make the first step in connecting Spring with Vaadin. The location of the `AppConfig` class needs to match the full class name of the configuration class.

```
<context-param>
  <param-name>contextClass</param-name>
  <param-value>
    org.springframework.web.context.support.Annotation
      ConfigWebApplicationContext
  </param-value>
</context-param>

<context-param>
  <param-name>contextConfigLocation</param-name>
  <param-value>com.packtpub.vaadin.AppConfig
    </param-value>
</context-param>

<listener>
  <listener-class>
    org.springframework.web.context.ContextLoaderListener
  </listener-class>
</listener>
```

5. Create a new class `AppConfig` inside the `com.packtpub.vaadin` package and annotate it with the `@Configuration` annotation. Then create a new `@Bean` definition as shown:

```
package com.packtpub.vaadin;
import org.springframework.context.annotation.Bean;
import org.springframework.context.annotation.Configuration;

@Configuration
public class AppConfig {
```

```
    @Bean(name="userService")
    public UserService helloWorld() {
      return new UserServiceImpl();
    }
  }
```

6. In order to have the recipe complete, we need to make a class that will represent a domain class. Create a new class called `User`.

```
public class User {
  private String name;
  // generate getters and setters for name field
}
```

7. `UserService` is a simple interface defining a single method called `getUser()`. When the `getUser()` method is called in this recipe, we always create and return a new instance of the user (in the future, we could add parameters, for example login, and fetch user from the database). `UserServiceImpl` is the implementation of this interface. As mentioned, we could replace that implementation by something smarter than just returning a new instance of the same user every time the `getUser()` method is called.

```
public interface UserService {

  public User getUser();
}
public class UserServiceImpl implements UserService {

  @Override
  public User getUser() {
    User user = new User();
    user.setName("Adela");
    return user;
  }
}
```

8. Almost everything is ready now. We just make a new UI and get the application context from which we get the bean. Then, we call the service and obtain a user that we show in the browser. After we are done with the UI, we can run the application.

```
public class AppUI extends UI {

  private ApplicationContext context;

  @Override
  protected void init(VaadinRequest request) {
    UserService service = getUserService(request);
    User user = service.getUser();
```

```
        String name = user.getName();
        Label lblUserName = new Label("Hi " + name + " !");
        VerticalLayout layout = new VerticalLayout();
        layout.setMargin(true);
        setContent(layout);
        layout.addComponent(lblUserName);
    }

    private UserService getUserService
      (VaadinRequest request) {
        WrappedSession session = request.getWrappedSession();
        HttpSession httpSession = ((WrappedHttpSession)
          session).getHttpSession();
        ServletContext servletContext =
          httpSession.getServletContext();
        context = WebApplicationContextUtils.getRequired
          WebApplicationContext(servletContext);

        return (UserService) context.getBean("userService");
    }
}
```

9. Run the following Maven commands in order to compile the widget set and run the application:

```
mvn package
mvn jetty:run
```

How it works...

In the first step, we have added dependencies to Spring. There was one additional dependency to `cglib`, Code Generation Library. This library is required by the `@Configuration` annotation and it is used by Spring for making the proxy objects. More information about `cglib` can be found at `http://cglib.sourceforge.net`.

Then, we have added `contextClass`, `contextConfigLocation` and `ContextLoaderListener` into `web.xml` file. All these are needed in order to initialize the application context properly. Due to this, we are able to get the application context by calling the following code:

```
WebApplicationContextUtils.getRequiredWebApplicationContext
  (servletContext);
```

Then, we have made `UserService` that is actually not a real service in this case (we did so because it was not in the scope of this recipe). We will have a look at how to declare Spring services in the following recipes.

In the last step, we got the application context by using the `WebApplicationContextUtils` class from Spring.

```
WrappedSession session = request.getWrappedSession();
HttpSession httpSession = ((WrappedHttpSession)
  session).getHttpSession();
ServletContext servletContext = httpSession.getServletContext();
context = WebApplicationContextUtils.getRequired
  WebApplicationContext(servletContext);
```

Then, we obtained an instance of `UserService` from the Spring application context.

```
UserService service = (UserService) context.getBean("userService");
User user = service.getUser();
```

We can obtain a bean without knowing the bean name because it can be obtained by the bean type, like this `context.getBean(UserService.class)`.

There's more...

Using the `@Autowire` annotation in classes that are not managed by Spring (classes that are not defined in `AppConfig` in our case) will not work, so no instances will be set via the `@Autowire` annotation.

See also

- There is one great add-on, which helps with Spring usage inside a Vaadin application. More information about it is on the Spring Stuff add-on page at `https://vaadin.com/directory#addon/spring-stuff`.

Handling login with Spring

We will create a login functionality in this recipe. The user will be able to log in as admin or client. We will not use a database in this recipe. We will use a dummy service where we just hardcode two users. The first user will be "admin" and the second user will be "client". There will be also two authorities (or roles), `ADMIN` and `CLIENT`.

We will use Java annotation-driven Spring configuration.

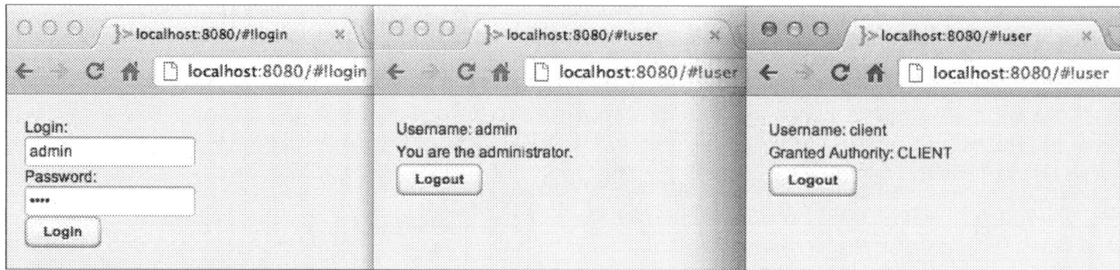

Getting ready

Create a new Maven project from the Vaadin archetype.

```
mvn archetype:generate \
  -DarchetypeGroupId=com.vaadin \
  -DarchetypeArtifactId=vaadin-archetype-application \
  -DarchetypeVersion=LATEST \
  -Dpackaging=war \
  -DgroupId=com.app \
  -DartifactId=vaadin-spring-login \
  -Dversion=1.0
```

Maven archetype generates the basic structure of the project. We will add the packages and classes, so the project will have the following directory and file structure:

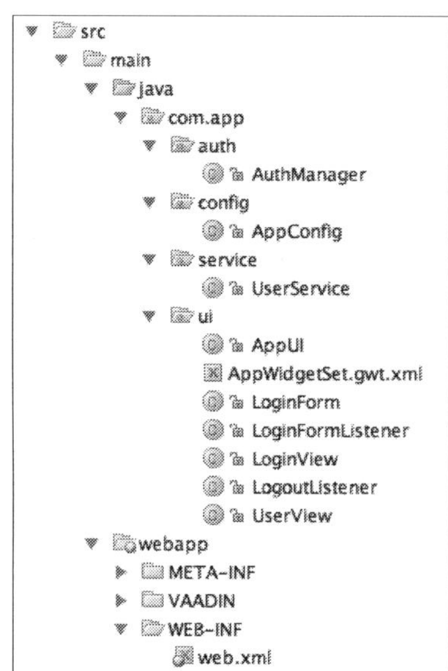

How to do it...

Carry out the following steps, in order to create login with Spring framework:

1. We need to add Maven dependencies in `pom.xml` to `spring-core`, `spring-context`, `spring-web`, `spring-security-core`, `spring-security-config`, and `cglib` (`cglib` is required by the `@Configuration` annotation from Spring).

```
<dependency>
  <groupId>org.springframework</groupId>
  <artifactId>spring-core</artifactId>
  <version>${spring.version}</version>
</dependency>
<dependency>
  <groupId>org.springframework</groupId>
  <artifactId>spring-context</artifactId>
  <version>${spring.version}</version>
</dependency>
<dependency>
  <groupId>org.springframework</groupId>
  <artifactId>spring-web</artifactId>
  <version>${spring.version}</version>
</dependency>
<dependency>
  <groupId>org.springframework.security</groupId>
  <artifactId>spring-security-core</artifactId>
  <version>${spring.version}</version>
</dependency>
<dependency>
  <groupId>org.springframework.security</groupId>
  <artifactId>spring-security-config</artifactId>
  <version>${spring.version}</version>
</dependency>
<dependency>
  <groupId>cglib</groupId>
  <artifactId>cglib</artifactId>
  <version>2.2.2</version>
</dependency>
```

2. Now we edit the `web.xml` file, so Spring knows we want to use the annotation-driven configuration approach. The path to the `AppConfig` class must match full class name (together with the package name).

```
<context-param>
  <param-name>contextClass</param-name>
  <param-value>
```

```
    org.springframework.web.context.support.Annotation
      ConfigWebApplicationContext
    </param-value>
  </context-param>

  <context-param>
    <param-name>contextConfigLocation</param-name>
    <param-value>com.app.config.AppConfig</param-value>
  </context-param>

  <listener>
    <listener-class>
      org.springframework.web.context.ContextLoaderListener
    </listener-class>
  </listener>
```

3. We are referring to the `AppConfig` class in the previous step. Let's implement that class now. `AppConfig` needs to be annotated by the `@Configuration` annotation, so Spring can accept it as the context configuration class. We also add the `@ComponentScan` annotation, which makes sure that Spring will scan the specified packages for Spring components. The package names inside the `@ComponentScan` annotation need to match our packages that we want to include for scanning. When a component (a class that is annotated with the `@Component` annotation) is found and there is a `@Autowire` annotation inside, the auto wiring will happen automatically.

```
package com.app.config;

import com.app.auth.AuthManager;
import com.app.service.UserService;
import com.app.ui.LoginFormListener;
import com.app.ui.LoginView;
import com.app.ui.UserView;
import org.springframework.context.annotation.Bean;
import org.springframework.context.
  annotation.ComponentScan;
import org.springframework.context.
  annotation.Configuration;
import org.springframework.context.
  annotation.Scope;

@Configuration
@ComponentScan(basePackages = {"com.app.ui" ,
  "com.app.auth", "com.app.service"})
public class AppConfig {
```

```
  @Bean
  public AuthManager authManager() {
    AuthManager res = new AuthManager();
    return res;
  }

  @Bean
  public UserService userService() {
    UserService res = new UserService();
    return res;
  }

  @Bean
  public LoginFormListener loginFormListener() {
    return new LoginFormListener();
  }
}
```

4. We are defining three beans in `AppConfig`. We will implement them in this step.

   `AuthManager` will take care of the login process.

```
package com.app.auth;

import com.app.service.UserService;
import org.springframework.beans.factory.
  annotation.Autowired;
import org.springframework.security.authentication.
  AuthenticationManager;
import org.springframework.security.authentication.
  BadCredentialsException;
import org.springframework.security.authentication.
  UsernamePasswordAuthenticationToken;
import org.springframework.security.core.Authentication;
import org.springframework.security.core.
  AuthenticationException;
import org.springframework.security.core.
  GrantedAuthority;
import org.springframework.security.core.
  userdetails.UserDetails;
import org.springframework.stereotype.Component;

import java.util.Collection;

@Component
public class AuthManager implements
  AuthenticationManager {
```

```
    @Autowired
    private UserService userService;

    public Authentication authenticate
    (Authentication auth) throws AuthenticationException {
      String username = (String) auth.getPrincipal();
      String password = (String) auth.getCredentials();

      UserDetails user =
      userService.loadUserByUsername(username);

      if (user != null && user.getPassword().
      equals(password)) {
        Collection<? extends GrantedAuthority>
        authorities = user.getAuthorities();
        return new UsernamePasswordAuthenticationToken
        (username, password, authorities);
      }
      throw new BadCredentialsException("Bad Credentials");
    }
  }
```

`UserService` will fetch a user based on the passed login. `UserService` will be used by `AuthManager`.

```
package com.app.service;

import org.springframework.security.core.
  GrantedAuthority;
import org.springframework.security.core.
  authority.GrantedAuthorityImpl;
import org.springframework.security.core.
  authority.SimpleGrantedAuthority;
import org.springframework.security.core.
  userdetails.UserDetails;
import org.springframework.security.core.
  userdetails.UserDetailsService;
import org.springframework.security.core.
  userdetails.UsernameNotFoundException;
import org.springframework.security.core.
  userdetails.User;
import org.springframework.stereotype.Service;

import java.util.ArrayList;
import java.util.List;

public class UserService implements UserDetailsService {
```

```
  @Override
  public UserDetails loadUserByUsername
  (String username) throws UsernameNotFoundException {
    List<GrantedAuthority> authorities = new
    ArrayList<GrantedAuthority>();
    // fetch user from e.g. DB
    if ("client".equals(username)) {
      authorities.add
      (new SimpleGrantedAuthority("CLIENT"));
      User user = new User(username, "pass", true, true,
      false, false, authorities);
      return user;
    }
    if ("admin".equals(username)) {
      authorities.add
      (new SimpleGrantedAuthority("ADMIN"));
      User user = new User(username, "pass", true, true,
      false, false, authorities);
      return user;
    } else {
      return null;
    }
  }
}
```

`LoginFormListener` is just a listener that will initiate the login process, so it will cooperate with `AuthManager`.

```
package com.app.ui;

import com.app.auth.AuthManager;
import com.vaadin.navigator.Navigator;
import com.vaadin.ui.*;
import org.springframework.beans.factory.annotation.Autowired;
import org.springframework.security.authentication.
  UsernamePasswordAuthenticationToken;
import org.springframework.security.core.Authentication;
import org.springframework.security.core.
  AuthenticationException;
import org.springframework.security.core.context.
  SecurityContextHolder;
import org.springframework.stereotype.Component;

@Component
public class LoginFormListener implements
  Button.ClickListener {
```

```
    @Autowired
    private AuthManager authManager;

    @Override
    public void buttonClick(Button.ClickEvent event) {
      try {
        Button source = event.getButton();
        LoginForm parent = (LoginForm) source.getParent();
        String username = parent.getTxtLogin().getValue();
        String password =
        parent.getTxtPassword().getValue();

        UsernamePasswordAuthenticationToken request = new
        UsernamePasswordAuthenticationToken
        (username, password);

        Authentication result =
        authManager.authenticate(request);

        SecurityContextHolder.getContext().
        setAuthentication(result);

        AppUI current = (AppUI) UI.getCurrent();
        Navigator navigator = current.getNavigator();
        navigator.navigateTo("user");

      } catch (AuthenticationException e) {
        Notification.show("Authentication failed: " +
        e.getMessage());
      }

    }
  }
```

5. The login form will be made as a separate Vaadin component. We will use the application context and that way we get bean from the application context by ourselves. So, we are not using auto wiring in `LoginForm`.

```
package com.app.ui;

import com.vaadin.ui.*;
import org.springframework.context.ApplicationContext;

public class LoginForm extends VerticalLayout {

  private TextField txtLogin = new TextField("Login: ");
  private PasswordField txtPassword = new
  PasswordField("Password: ");
  private Button btnLogin = new Button("Login");
```

```
    public LoginForm() {
      addComponent(txtLogin);
      addComponent(txtPassword);
      addComponent(btnLogin);

      LoginFormListener loginFormListener =
      getLoginFormListener();
      btnLogin.addClickListener(loginFormListener);
    }
    public LoginFormListener getLoginFormListener() {
      AppUI ui = (AppUI) UI.getCurrent();
      ApplicationContext context =
      ui.getApplicationContext();
      return context.getBean(LoginFormListener.class);
    }

    public TextField getTxtLogin() {
      return txtLogin;
    }

    public PasswordField getTxtPassword() {
      return txtPassword;
    }
  }
```

6. We will use `Navigator` for navigating between different views in our Vaadin application. We make two views. The first is for login and the second is for showing the user detail when the user is logged into the application. Both classes will be in the `com.app.ui` package.

   `LoginView` will contain just the components that enable a user to log in (text fields and button).

```
public class LoginView extends VerticalLayout
  implements View {
  public LoginView() {
    LoginForm loginForm = new LoginForm();
    addComponent(loginForm);
  }

  @Override
  public void enter(ViewChangeListener.ViewChangeEvent
  event) {
  }
};
```

`UserView` needs to identify whether the user is logged in or not. For this, we will use `SecurityContextHolder` that obtains the `SecurityContext` that holds the authentication data. If the user is logged in, then we display some data about him/her. If not, then we navigate him/her to the login form.

```
public class UserView extends VerticalLayout
  implements View {

  public void enter(ViewChangeListener.ViewChangeEvent
  event) {
    removeAllComponents();

    SecurityContext context =
    SecurityContextHolder.getContext();
    Authentication authentication =
    context.getAuthentication();

    if (authentication != null &&
    authentication.isAuthenticated()) {
      String name = authentication.getName();

      Label labelLogin = new Label("Username: " + name);
      addComponent(labelLogin);

      Collection<? extends GrantedAuthority> authorities
        = authentication.getAuthorities();

      for (GrantedAuthority ga : authorities) {
        String authority = ga.getAuthority();
        if ("ADMIN".equals(authority)) {
          Label lblAuthority = new Label("You are
                               the administrator. ");
          addComponent(lblAuthority);
        } else {
          Label lblAuthority = new Label("Granted
                Authority: " + authority);
          addComponent(lblAuthority);
        }
      }

      Button logout = new Button("Logout");
      LogoutListener logoutListener = new
      LogoutListener();
      logout.addClickListener(logoutListener);
            addComponent(logout);
    } else {
      Navigator navigator =
      UI.getCurrent().getNavigator();
```

```
        navigator.navigateTo("login");
      }
    }
  }
```

7. We have mentioned `LogoutListener` in the previous step. Here is how that class could look:

```
public class LogoutListener implements
  Button.ClickListener {

  @Override
  public void buttonClick(Button.ClickEvent clickEvent) {
    SecurityContextHolder.clearContext();
    UI.getCurrent().close();
    Navigator navigator = UI.getCurrent().getNavigator();
    navigator.navigateTo("login");
  }
}
```

8. Everything is ready for the final `AppUI` class. In this class, we put in to practice all that we have created in the previous steps.

   We need to get the application context. That is done in the first lines of code in the `init` method. In order to obtain the application context, we need to get the session from the request, and from the session get the servlet context. Then, we use the Spring utility class, `WebApplicationContextUtils`, and we find the application context by using the previously obtained servlet context.

   After that, we set up the navigator.

```
@PreserveOnRefresh
public class AppUI extends UI {

  private ApplicationContext applicationContext;

  @Override
  protected void init(VaadinRequest request) {
    WrappedSession session = request.getWrappedSession();
    HttpSession httpSession = ((WrappedHttpSession)
      session).getHttpSession();
    ServletContext servletContext =
      httpSession.getServletContext();
    applicationContext = WebApplicationContextUtils.
    getRequiredWebApplicationContext(servletContext);

    Navigator navigator = new Navigator(this, this);
    navigator.addView("login", LoginView.class);
    navigator.addView("user", UserView.class);
```

```
    navigator.navigateTo("login");
    setNavigator(navigator);
  }

  public ApplicationContext getApplicationContext() {
    return applicationContext;
  }
}
```

9. Now we can run the application. The password for usernames `client` and `admin` is `pass`.

```
mvn package
mvn jetty:run
```

How it works...

There are two tricky parts from the development point of view while making the application:

- First is how to get the Spring application context in Vaadin. For this, we need to make sure that `contextClass`, `contextConfigLocation`, and `ContextLoaderListener` are defined in the `web.xml` file. Then we need to know how to get Spring application context from the `VaadinRequest`. We certainly need a reference to the application context in UI, so we define the `applicationContext` class field together with the public getter (because we need access to the application context from other classes, to get Spring beans).
- The second part, which is a bit tricky, is the `AppConfig` class. That class represents annotated Spring application configuration (which is referenced from the `web.xml` file). We needed to define what packages Spring should scan for components. For this, we have used the `@ComponentScan` annotation. The important thing to keep in mind is that the `@Autowired` annotation will work only for Spring managed beans that we have defined in `AppConfig`. When we try to add the `@Autowired` annotation to a simple Vaadin component, the `autowired` reference will remain empty because no auto wiring happens. It is up to us to decide what instances should be managed by Spring and where we use the Spring application context to retrieve the beans.

We have used navigator for navigation between the views. More information about navigator can be found in the *Using Navigator for creating bookmarkable applications with back-forward button support* recipe in *Chapter 2, Layouts*.

Accessing a database with Spring

We will make a simple application that adds new orders to the database. A user just fills in a name of the order and clicks on the **Add New Order** button.

The orders will be stored in the in-memory database and it will be easy to switch the database, for example to MySQL. For accessing the database, we use `JdbcTempate` from Spring framework.

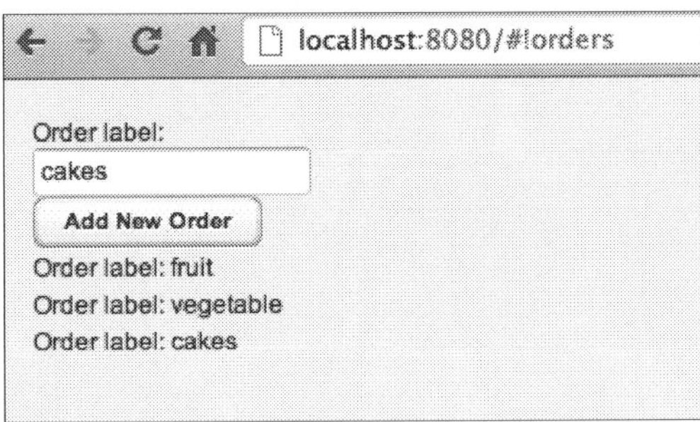

Getting ready

Create a new Maven project from the Vaadin archetype.

```
mvn archetype:generate \
 -DarchetypeGroupId=com.vaadin \
 -DarchetypeArtifactId=vaadin-archetype-application \
 -DarchetypeVersion=LATEST \
 -Dpackaging=war \
 -DgroupId=com.app \
 -DartifactId=vaadin-spring-database \
 -Dversion=1.0
```

The project structure will be as follows:

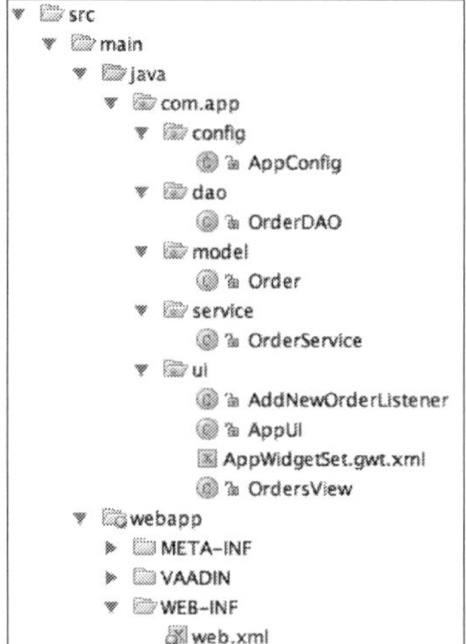

How to do it...

Carry out the following steps, in order to create a Vaadin application with access to the database with Spring framework:

1. Add the necessary dependencies to the Maven `pom.xml` file.

```
<dependency>
  <groupId>org.springframework</groupId>
  <artifactId>spring-core</artifactId>
  <version>${spring.version}</version>
</dependency>
<dependency>
  <groupId>org.springframework</groupId>
  <artifactId>spring-context</artifactId>
  <version>${spring.version}</version>
</dependency>
<dependency>
  <groupId>org.springframework</groupId>
  <artifactId>spring-web</artifactId>
  <version>${spring.version}</version>
</dependency>
<dependency>
  <groupId>cglib</groupId>
  <artifactId>cglib</artifactId>
  <version>2.2.2</version>
</dependency>
```

```
<dependency>
  <groupId>org.springframework</groupId>
  <artifactId>spring-jdbc</artifactId>
  <version>${spring.version}</version>
</dependency>
  <dependency>
  <groupId>com.h2database</groupId>
  <artifactId>h2</artifactId>
  <version>1.3.168</version>
</dependency>
```

2. Add the Spring context configuration to `web.xml`.

```
<context-param>
  <param-name>contextClass</param-name>
  <param-value>
    org.springframework.web.context.support.
    AnnotationConfigWebApplicationContext
  </param-value>
</context-param>
<context-param>
  <param-name>contextConfigLocation</param-name>
  <param-value>com.app.config.AppConfig</param-value>
</context-param>
<listener>
  <listener-class>
    org.springframework.web.context.ContextLoaderListener
  </listener-class>
</listener>
```

3. Specify the Spring context configuration in the `AppConfig` class.

```
package com.app.config;

import com.app.dao.OrderDAO;
import com.app.service.OrderService;
import org.springframework.beans.factory.
  annotation.Autowired;
import org.springframework.context.annotation.Bean;
import org.springframework.context.annotation.ComponentScan;
import org.springframework.context.
  annotation.Configuration;
import org.springframework.jdbc.core.JdbcTemplate;
import org.springframework.jdbc.datasource.
  DriverManagerDataSource;
```

```
import javax.sql.DataSource;
@Configuration
@ComponentScan(basePackages = {"com.app.ui",
  "com.app.service"})
public abstract class AppConfig {

  @Autowired
  private DriverManagerDataSource dataSource;

  @Bean
  public OrderService orderService() {
    OrderService res = new OrderService();
    return res;
  }

  @Bean
  public DriverManagerDataSource
  driverManagerDataSource() {
    String driverClassName = "org.h2.Driver";
    String url = "jdbc:h2:mem:test;DB_CLOSE_DELAY=-1";
    String username = "sa";
    String password = "";

    DriverManagerDataSource res = new
      DriverManagerDataSource();
    res.setDriverClassName(driverClassName);
    res.setUrl(url);
    res.setUsername(username);
    res.setPassword(password);
    return res;
  }

  @Bean
  public JdbcTemplate jdbcTemplate() {
    return new JdbcTemplate(dataSource);
  }

  @Bean
  public OrderDAO orderDAO() {
    return new OrderDAO ();
  }
}
```

4. The `Order` class will represent the domain model, which holds the values.

```
package com.app.model;

public class Order {
```

```
  private Integer id;
  private String label;

  // generate getters and setters for id an label
}
```

5. `OrderService` will provide a `findAll()` method that returns all the orders from the `OrderDAO` repository.

```
package com.app.service;

import com.app.dao.OrderDAO;
import com.app.model.Order;
import org.springframework.beans.factory.annotation.Autowired;
import org.springframework.stereotype.Service;

import java.util.List;

@Service
public class OrderService {

  @Autowired
  private OrderDAO orderDAO;

  public List<Order> findAll() {
    List<Order> res = orderDAO.findAll();
    return res;
  }
}
```

6. `OrderDAO` represents the repository for orders. We place there all the work with SQL and mapping data from `ResultSet` to the model classes.

```
package com.app.dao;

import com.app.model.Order;
import org.springframework.beans.factory.
  annotation.Autowired;
import org.springframework.jdbc.core.JdbcTemplate;
import org.springframework.jdbc.core.RowMapper;
import org.springframework.stereotype.Repository;

import java.sql.ResultSet;
import java.sql.SQLException;
import java.util.List;

@Repository
public class OrderDAO {
```

```
    @Autowired
    JdbcTemplate jdbcTemplate;

    public void createDbTable() {
      jdbcTemplate.execute("create table if not exists
      orders (id integer, label varchar(100))");
    }

    public List<Order> findAll() {
      String query = "select * from orders";
      RowMapper mapper = new RowMapper() {

        public Object mapRow(ResultSet rs, int rowNum)
        throws SQLException {
          Order order = new Order();
          order.setId(rs.getInt("id"));
          order.setLabel(rs.getString("label"));
          return order;
        }
      };
      return jdbcTemplate.query(query, mapper);
    }

    public void save(Order order) {
      String query = "insert into orders (label) values
      (?)";
      jdbcTemplate.update
      (query, new Object[]{order.getLabel()});
    }
  }
```

7. Now we implement the user interface for showing and adding the orders. `OrdersView` will contain a text field where we type the name of the order and button that invokes `AddNewOrderListener`.

   Once the user clicks on the button, we navigate back to `OrdersView` and that way we re-render the orders. Orders will be fetched from the database every time when rendering the `OrdersView`.

```
package com.app.ui;

import com.app.model.Order;
import com.app.service.OrderService;
import com.vaadin.navigator.View;
import com.vaadin.navigator.ViewChangeListener;
import com.vaadin.ui.*;
import org.springframework.context.ApplicationContext;
```

```
import java.util.List;

public class OrdersView extends VerticalLayout
  implements View {

  private TextField txtOrderLabel = new TextField
  ("Order label: ");

  public void enter(ViewChangeListener.ViewChangeEvent
  event) {
    removeAllComponents();

    addComponent(txtOrderLabel);

    Button btnAddNewOrder = new Button("Add New Order");
    btnAddNewOrder.addClickListener
    (new AddNewOrderListener());
    addComponent(btnAddNewOrder);

    AppUI current = (AppUI) UI.getCurrent();
    ApplicationContext context =
    current.getApplicationContext();
    OrderService service = context.getBean
    (OrderService.class);

    List<Order> all = service.findAll();
    for (Order o : all) {
      String label = o.getLabel();
      Label lbl = new Label("Order label: " + label);
      addComponent(lbl);
    }
  }

  public TextField getTxtOrderLabel() {
    return txtOrderLabel;
  }
}
```

8. As we have mentioned in the previous step, we need to handle the click action that should add a new order into the database. Therefore, we implement the `Button.ClickListener` interface. Create the `AddNewOrderListener` class.

```
package com.app.ui;

import com.app.dao.OrderDAO;
import com.app.model.Order;
import com.vaadin.ui.Button;
import com.vaadin.ui.TextField;
import com.vaadin.ui.UI;
```

```
import org.springframework.context.ApplicationContext;

public class AddNewOrderListener implements
  Button.ClickListener {

  @Override
  public void buttonClick(Button.ClickEvent event) {
    OrdersView view = (OrdersView)
    event.getButton().getParent();

    AppUI current = (AppUI) (UI.getCurrent());
    ApplicationContext context =
    current.getApplicationContext();

    OrderDAO orderDAO = context.getBean(OrderDAO.class);

    TextField txtOrderLabel = view.getTxtOrderLabel();
    String value = txtOrderLabel.getValue();

    Order order = new Order();
    order.setLabel(value);
    orderDAO.save(order);

    current.getNavigator().navigateTo("orders");
  }
}
```

9. It is time to create the `AppUI` class that extends the `UI` class from Vaadin. First, we get the Spring application context and then we get the `OrderDAO` bean from the context, so we can make the database table.

   At the end of the `init` method, we initialize the navigator and set it to the current UI.

```
package com.app.ui;

import com.app.dao.OrderDAO;
import com.vaadin.annotations.PreserveOnRefresh;
import com.vaadin.navigator.Navigator;
import com.vaadin.server.VaadinRequest;
import com.vaadin.server.WrappedHttpSession;
import com.vaadin.server.WrappedSession;
import com.vaadin.ui.UI;
import org.springframework.context.ApplicationContext;
import org.springframework.web.context.support.
   WebApplicationContextUtils;

import javax.servlet.ServletContext;
import javax.servlet.http.HttpSession;
```

```
@PreserveOnRefresh
public class AppUI extends UI {

  private ApplicationContext applicationContext;

  @Override
  protected void init(VaadinRequest request) {
    WrappedSession session = request.getWrappedSession();
    HttpSession httpSession = ((WrappedHttpSession)
    session).getHttpSession();
    ServletContext servletContext =
    httpSession.getServletContext();
    applicationContext = WebApplicationContextUtils.
    getRequiredWebApplicationContext(servletContext);

    OrderDAO orderDAO = applicationContext.getBean
    (OrderDAO.class);
    orderDAO.createDbTable();

    Navigator navigator = new Navigator(this, this);

    OrdersView userView = new OrdersView();
    navigator.addView("orders", userView);

    navigator.navigateTo("orders");
    setNavigator(navigator);
  }

  public ApplicationContext getApplicationContext() {
    return applicationContext;
  }
}
```

10. Now we can run the application.

```
mvn package
mvn jetty:run
```

How it works...

We have used two Spring annotations: `@Service` and `@Repository`. Both are just specifications of the `@Component` annotation. Both annotations are accepted by Spring while scanning the packages for the Spring components. In addition, when we mark our classes by one of these two annotations, the classes are more properly suited for processing by tools or associating with aspects.

More information about Spring annotations can be found in the Spring documentation at `http://static.springsource.org/spring/docs/3.1.x/spring-framework-reference/htmlsingle/spring-framework-reference.html#beans-stereotype-annotations`.

We have created the `createDbTable()` method in `OrderDAO`. This way of creating a database maybe fine when starting up a project but it should be moved definitely elsewhere, for example while installing SQL scripts.

There's more...

Here is an example of how to switch a database from H2 to MySQL. We need to add a Maven dependency in `pom.xml`.

```
<dependency>
  <groupId>mysql</groupId>
  <artifactId>mysql-connector-java</artifactId>
  <version>5.1.21</version>
</dependency>
```

And then change the `driverManagerDataSource()` bean definition in `AppConfig`.

```
@Bean
  public DriverManagerDataSource driverManagerDataSource() {
    String driverClassName = "com.mysql.jdbc.Driver";
    String url = "jdbc:mysql://localhost:3306/dbname";
    String username = "sa";
    String password = "";
```

We wanted to keep this recipe short so we have made `OrderDAO` and `OrderService` as classes without any abstraction. In real world, we would make `OrderDAO` and `OrderService` as interfaces and then we would create specific DAOs and services (for example, `OrderDAOH2` and `OrderDAOMySql`).

Inside the `OrdersView` class, we have fetched all the orders from the database and then we have added them on the screen as labels. In a real project, we would rather use a table or list to display the orders. More information about this approach can be found in the *Avoiding sluggish UI – lazy loaded tables* and *Avoiding sluggish UI – paged tables* recipes in *Chapter 10, Architecture and Performance*.

Internationalizing Vaadin applications with Spring

We will take a look at a simple example where we demonstrate how to perform internationalization (or also called localization) in the Vaadin application using Spring.

The application will be localized in two languages, English and Finnish. We will display *Name* in two languages. The second one is going to be the Finnish language, where the name can be translated as *Nimi*.

A user (developer or tester) has to change the language setting in the browser in order to see the localization properly.

In the following screenshot, we have changed the browser language to English in the browser setup window. When we refresh the page, the localized name appears on the screen.

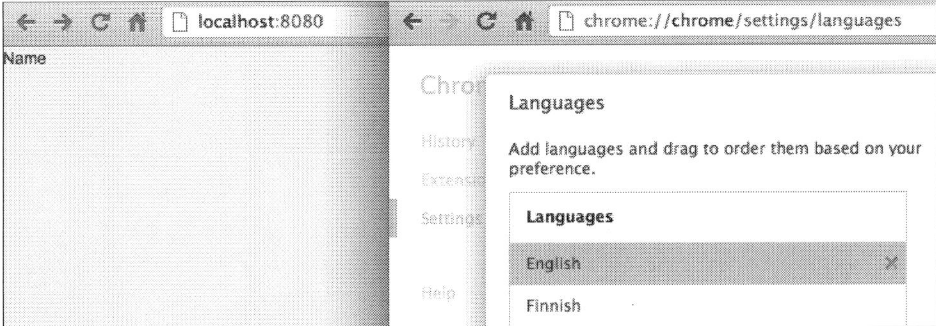

Then we have changed the language to Finnish and the appropriate localized string appears on the screen.

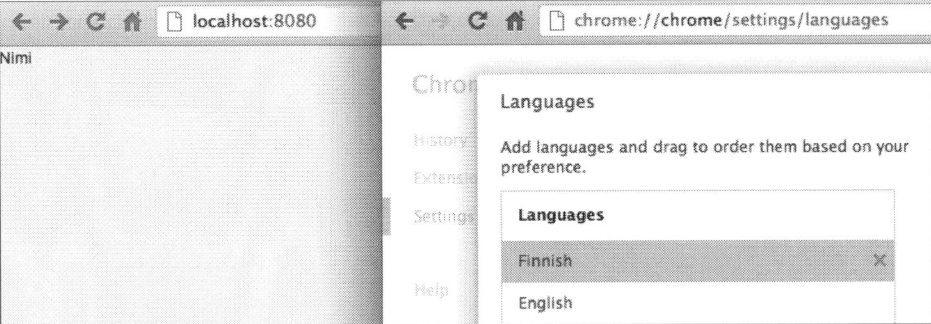

Getting ready

Create a new Maven project from the Vaadin archetype.

```
mvn archetype:generate \
 -DarchetypeGroupId=com.vaadin \
 -DarchetypeArtifactId=vaadin-archetype-application \
 -DarchetypeVersion=LATEST \
 -Dpackaging=war \
 -DgroupId=com.app \
 -DartifactId= vaadin-spring-internationalization \
 -Dversion=1.0
```

The project structure will be as follows:

How to do it...

Carry out the following steps, in order to create a localized Vaadin application with the Spring framework:

1. First, we add the necessary dependencies to `pom.xml`, so the Spring can be used in our project.

```
<dependency>
  <groupId>org.springframework</groupId>
  <artifactId>spring-core</artifactId>
  <version>${spring.version}</version>
</dependency>
<dependency>
```

```
    <groupId>org.springframework</groupId>
    <artifactId>spring-context</artifactId>
    <version>${spring.version}</version>
  </dependency>
  <dependency>
    <groupId>org.springframework</groupId>
    <artifactId>spring-web</artifactId>
    <version>${spring.version}</version>
  </dependency>
  <dependency>
    <groupId>cglib</groupId>
    <artifactId>cglib</artifactId>
    <version>2.2.2</version>
  </dependency>
```

2. Activate Spring by adding the context setup into the `web.xml` file.

```
<context-param>
  <param-name>contextClass</param-name>
  <param-value>
    org.springframework.web.context.support.
    AnnotationConfigWebApplicationContext
  </param-value>
</context-param>

<context-param>
  <param-name>contextConfigLocation</param-name>
  <param-value>
    com.app.AppConfig
  </param-value>
</context-param>

<listener>
  <listener-class>
    org.springframework.web.context.ContextLoaderListener
  </listener-class>
</listener>
```

3. Create the localization files `messages_en.properties` and `messages_fi.properties` for English and Finnish languages in the `src/main/resources/com/app` directory. There will be just one key-value pair as shown next:

```
messages_en.properties
label.name = Name
messages_fi.properties
label.name = Nimi
```

4. Create a Spring application context configuration class and define a new bean for `ReloadableResourceBundleMessageSource` from the `org.springframework.context.support` package.

```
@Configuration
public class AppConfig {

  @Bean
  public ReloadableResourceBundleMessageSource
  reloadableResourceBundleMessageSource() {
    ReloadableResourceBundleMessageSource messageSource =
    new ReloadableResourceBundleMessageSource();
    messageSource.setBasename
    ("classpath:com/app/messages");
    return messageSource;
  }
}
```

5. Now we create a very simple user interface that shows the localized string under the `label.name` key from the property files.

```
public class UserView extends HorizontalLayout {

  public UserView() {
    AppUI current = (AppUI) UI.getCurrent();
    ApplicationContext applicationContext =
    current.getApplicationContext();
    MessageSource messageSource =
    applicationContext.getBean
    (ReloadableResourceBundleMessageSource.class);

    Locale locale = LocaleContextHolder.getLocale();
    String localizedName = messageSource.getMessage
    ("label.name", null, locale);

    Label lblName = new Label(localizedName);
    addComponent(lblName);
  }

}
```

6. The final step is to create our UI class where we get the application context and set `UserView` as the content of the application.

```
public class AppUI extends UI {

  private ApplicationContext applicationContext;

  @Override
  protected void init(VaadinRequest request) {
```

```
        WrappedSession session = request.getWrappedSession();
        HttpSession httpSession = ((WrappedHttpSession)
        session).getHttpSession();
        ServletContext servletContext =
        httpSession.getServletContext();
        applicationContext = WebApplicationContextUtils.
        getRequiredWebApplicationContext(servletContext);

        setContent(new UserView());
      }

      public ApplicationContext getApplicationContext() {
        return applicationContext;
      }
    }
```

How it works...

All the work is actually done by `ReloadableResourceBundleMessageSource` from Spring. We just needed to set the path to our localization properties files. Note that we have set it to `com/app/messages` where `com` and `app` are the directories and `messages` is base-name for the localization files.

If we need to hardcode the locale, we can create a new locale as follows:

```
Locale locale = new Locale("fi", "FI");
```

Vaadin and Spring injector

We will make a simple application that shows the username on the screen. Our goal in the recipe is to auto inject or maybe (in better terms) autowire Spring beans in the Vaadin application.

Getting ready

Create new Maven project from the Vaadin archetype.

```
mvn archetype:generate \
 -DarchetypeGroupId=com.vaadin \
 -DarchetypeArtifactId=vaadin-archetype-application \
 -DarchetypeVersion=LATEST \
 -Dpackaging=war \
 -DgroupId=com.packtpub.vaadin \
 -DartifactId=vaadin-spring-injector \
-Dversion=1.0
```

How to do it...

Carry out the following steps, in order to make a Vaadin application with autowiring via injector:

1. First, we create a class representing a user.

```
public class User {
  private String name;
  // generate getters and setters for name field
}
```

2. Create a service that returns a new user always when the `getUser()` method is called.

```
public class UserService {

  public User getUser() {
    // TODO: here we could fetch data from e.g. database
    User user = new User();
    user.setName("Adela");
    return user;
  }
}
```

3. Make a new Spring configuration class that defines the new bean for `UserService`.

```
@Configuration
public class AppConfig {

  @Bean
  public UserService userService() {
    return new UserService();
  }
}
```

4. Create the `Injector` class, which handles the autowiring.

```
public class Injector {

  public static void inject(Object component) {
    ApplicationContext context = getApplicationContext();
    AutowireCapableBeanFactory beanFactory =
    context.getAutowireCapableBeanFactory();
    beanFactory.autowireBeanProperties(component,
    AutowireCapableBeanFactory.AUTOWIRE_BY_TYPE, false);
  }
```

```
  private static ApplicationContext
  getApplicationContext() {
    ServletRequestAttributes attributes =
    (ServletRequestAttributes) RequestContextHolder.
    currentRequestAttributes();
    HttpServletRequest request = attributes.getRequest();
    HttpSession session = request.getSession(false);
    ServletContext servletContext =
    session.getServletContext();
    WebApplicationContext context =
    WebApplicationContextUtils.
    getRequiredWebApplicationContext(servletContext);
    return context;
  }
}
```

5. Create a UI provider, which delegates the autowiring to the `Injector` class.

```
public class AppUIProvider extends UIProvider {

  @Override
  public Class<? extends UI>
  getUIClass(UIClassSelectionEvent event) {
    return AppUI.class;
  }

  @Override
  public UI createInstance(UICreateEvent event) {
    UI instance = super.createInstance(event);
    Injector.inject(instance);
    return instance;
  }
}
```

6. Now we add a reference to `UIProvider` in the `web.xml` file.

```
<servlet>
  <servlet-name>Vaadin Application Servlet</servlet-name>
  <servlet-class>com.vaadin.server.VaadinServlet
  </servlet-class>
  <init-param>
    <description>Vaadin UI to display</description>
    <param-name>UI</param-name>
    <param-value>com.app.AppUI</param-value>
  </init-param>
  <init-param>
    <description>Vaadin UI</description>
    <param-name>UIProvider</param-name>
```

```
    <param-value>com.app.AppUIProvider</param-value>
  </init-param>
</servlet>
```

7. Configure the Spring context inside the `web.xml` deployment descriptor file as follows:

```
<context-param>
  <param-name>contextClass</param-name>
  <param-value>
    org.springframework.web.context.support.
    AnnotationConfigWebApplicationContext
  </param-value>
</context-param>

<context-param>
  <param-name>contextConfigLocation</param-name>
  <param-value>
    com.app.AppConfig
  </param-value>
</context-param>

<listener>
  <listener-class>
    org.springframework.web.context.ContextLoaderListener
  </listener-class>
</listener>
<listener>
  <listener-class>
    org.springframework.web.context.request.
    RequestContextListener
  </listener-class>
</listener>
```

8. Create the `AppUI` class where we autowire the `UserService`. Then, we use the service to obtain a user, so we can display the username on the screen.

```
public class AppUI extends UI {

  @Autowired
  UserService userService;

  @Override
  protected void init(VaadinRequest request) {
    String name = userService.getUser().getName();
    Label lblUserName = new Label("Hi " + name + " !");
    setContent(lblUserName);
  }
}
```

9. Run the application with the following commands:

```
mvn package
mvn jetty:run
```

How it works...

We have created the `userService` field annotated with the `@Autowire` annotation in the `AppUI` class. The autowiring should happen automatically when the application is being started. The autowiring is initialized in `UIProvider`, which delegates the autowiring to the `Injector` class while the Vaadin application is starting up. The `Injector` class is using `RequestContextListener` that we have declared in the `web.xml` file to obtain the Spring application context. After we have access to the Spring application context, we use `AutowireCapableBeanFactory` to autowire the beans we have defined in the `AppConfig` configuration class.

Keep in mind that we need to call the `Injector` class in each component where we want to have the beans injected. We shall call the injector in the constructor of the class, which contains fields with the `@Autowire` annotation.

Internationalizing Vaadin in Grails

We have set up a new Grails project with Vaadin in *Chapter 1, Creating a Project in Vaadin*. Now let's have a look at how to perform localization.

We will see how to use the `i18n` method, which is provided by the Vaadin plugin. In order to do that, we will create a simple application, showing a few texts that will be localized. The first screen on the left-hand side in the following screenshot is localized in the Swedish language. The second one, on the right-hand side, is localized in the English language.

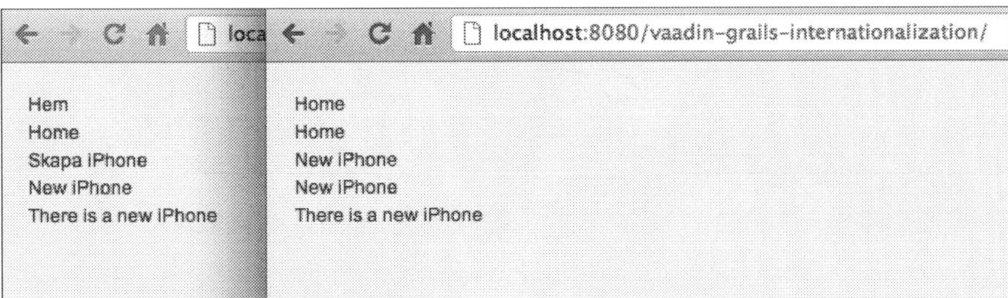

Getting ready

Make sure you have a project using the latest stable version of Grails and Vaadin.

Use `grails list-plugin-updates` to get the list of updates for the plugins installed in the project. Alternatively, just run `grails install-plugin vaadin` and a new version of the plugin will be installed.

We will place the code in the following section directly into the `init` method inside the `MyUI` class. The `MyUI` class is the generated class by Vaadin plugin, inside the Grails project.

There are many properties files available by default. We will use them so we don't have to create our own.

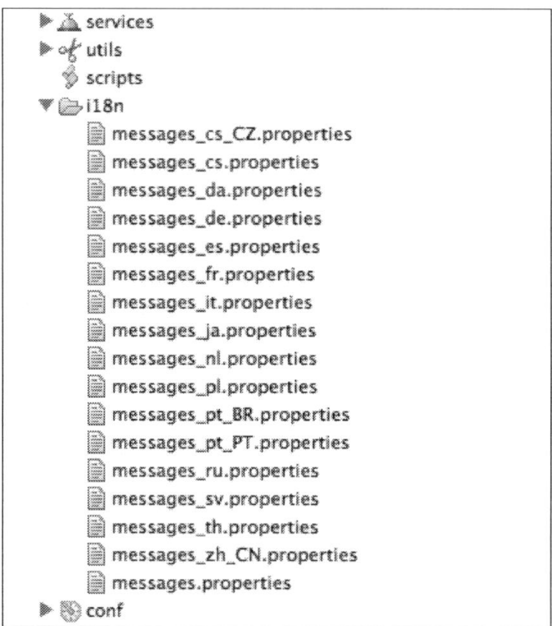

How to do it...

Carry out the following steps, in order to try out the possibilities of localization for Vaadin applications in Grails:

1. In most cases, we need to localize just a single string. Make sure there is a `default.home.label=Hem` key-value pair in the localization properties file that will be used for a specific user language setup in the browser.

```
String home = Grails.i18n("default.home.label")
Label lblHome = new Label(home)
addComponent(lblHome)
```

2. It might happen that we need to force Grails to use a specific localization. We dictate Grails to use the English locale in the following code:

```
String homeEng = Grails.i18n
  ("default.home.label", Locale.ENGLISH)
Label lblHomeEng = new Label(homeEng)
addComponent(lblHomeEng)
```

3. In order to use arguments in the localization strings, we just need to declare a key-value pair such as `default.new.label=Skapa {0}`. And `{0}` will be replaced by a string from the `newItemArgs` field, which we pass into the `i18n` method.

```
Object[] newItemArgs = ["iPhone"]
String newItem = Grails.i18n
  ("default.new.label", newItemArgs)
Label lblNewItem = new Label(newItem)
addComponent(lblNewItem)
```

4. We can also force a specific locale for localizations with arguments.

```
Object[] newItemArgsEng = ["iPhone"]
String newItemEng = Grails.i18n
  ("default.new.label", newItemArgs, Locale.ENGLISH)
Label lblNewItemEng = new Label(newItemEng)
addComponent(lblNewItemEng)
```

5. The last scenario is useful for cases when we know there will be more localization files and we don't want to provide localization for all the localization keys. For example, there is a key named `doesnt.exist` and it doesn't have localization in English. In that case, `"There is a new {0}"` will be used.

```
Object[] newItemArgsDef = ["iPhone"]
String newItemEngDef = Grails.i18n("doesnt.exist",
  newItemArgs, "There is a new {0}", Locale.ENGLISH)
Label lblNewItemEngDef = new Label(newItemEngDef)
addComponent(lblNewItemEngDef)
```

How it works...

The `Grails` class is provided by the Vaadin plugin and it uses Spring `MessageSource` to obtain the localized messages.

All we need to do is to import the `Grails` class and call the `i18n` method in order to get the localized texts.

There's more...

In case we request the localization key-value pair that doesn't exist (for example, "`label.home`"), we obtain the key in brackets (for example, "`[label.home]`") instead of a value from the `Grails.i18n()` method. So we do not have to localize key-value pairs while coding, the localization can be done after we are done with coding.

Using Grails ORM for Vaadin application

We will create a simple application that will have access to the database. In the database, there will be one entity, User. A visitor of our application will see the list of the users fetched from the database (it is going to be two women's names, Sara and Ester).

How to do it...

Carry out the following steps in order to connect a Vaadin application with the database in a Grails environment:

1. First, we need to make a new domain class named `User`. This class will be placed inside the domain folder.

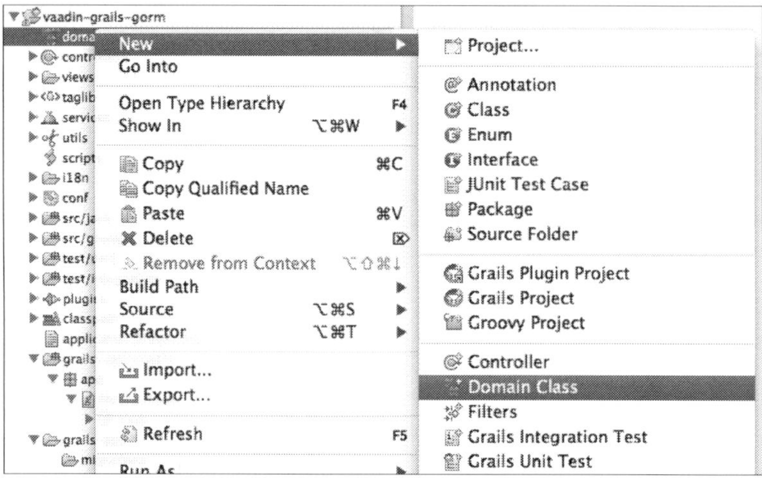

2. A new dialog window appears and we just type in `user`. The package name is automatically taken from the name of the project. If we want to specify a different package name, we just type the full name of the class, such as `mycomp.User`.

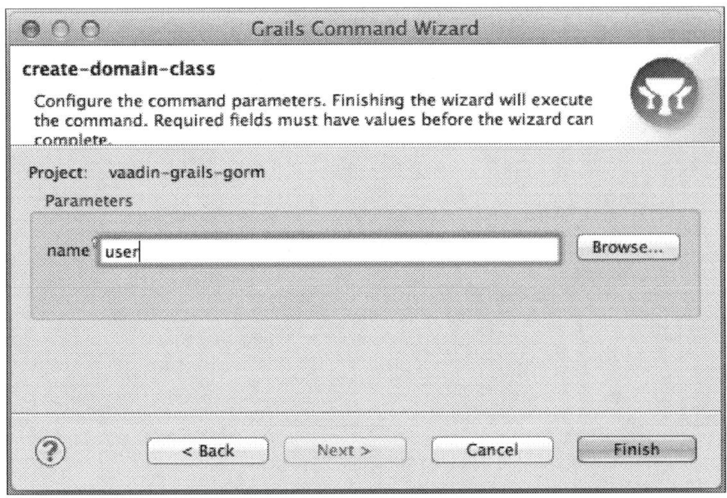

Alternatively, we can create the domain class from the Grails command line:

`grails create-domain-class user`

3. The `User` class has been generated into the domain folder inside the `vaadin.grails.gorm` package. We will add a new field that will represent the name of the user.

```
package vaadin.grails.gorm

class User {

  String name

  static constraints = {
  }
}
```

4. For the testing purpose, we create few users when the application starts up. We will create the test users only when we are in the development environment, not in the production. In order to do that, edit the `BootStrap` init method. The `BootStrap` script is located in the `conf` folder.

```
def init = { servletContext ->
  environments {
    development {
      User user1 = new User()
      user1.name = "Sara"
```

```
            user1.save(failOnError: true)

            User user2 = new User()
            user2.name = "Ester"
            user2.save(failOnError: true)
        }
    }
}
```

5. We are done and we can edit the `app.MyUI` class that is located in the `grails-app/vaadin` folder. We will use the `list()` method that returns all the records from the database for an entity and it is auto-generated by Grails.

```
@Override
protected void init(VaadinRequest vaadinRequest) {
  VerticalLayout layout = new VerticalLayout();
  layout.setMargin(true)

  List<User> users = User.list()
  for (User user : users) {
    String name = user.name
    layout.addComponent(new Label("User name: " + name))
  }
}
```

How it works...

Grails is a framework that follows the "convention over configuration" concept. What does it mean for this recipe? When we put a class into the `grails-app/domain` folder, Grails maps that class through ORM with the database. ORM stands for Object-relation mapping and Grails uses Hibernate for it. The nice thing is that we don't have to do Hibernate mapping manually. It all happens automatically because we have put our class that should be persistent into the domain folder.

More information about Grails ORM can be found at `http://grails.org/doc/latest/guide/GORM.html`.

There's more...

We can change the database setting in the `DataSource.groovy` script that is located in the `conf` folder. The following is an example of how the data source configuration could look in a real-world project:

`dataSource` defines common database setup. We could use `dataSource` without environments if we want to have just one database for all environments.

```
dataSource {
  pooled = true
  driverClassName = "org.h2.Driver"
  username = "sa"
  password = ""
}
hibernate {
  cache.use_second_level_cache = true
  cache.use_query_cache = true
  cache.region.factory_class =
  'net.sf.ehcache.hibernate.EhCacheRegionFactory'
}

environments {
  development {
    dataSource {
      dbCreate = "update"
      url = "jdbc:h2:mem:devDb;MVCC=TRUE;MODE=MYSQL"
    }
  }
  test {
    dataSource {
      dbCreate = "create-drop"
      url = "jdbc:h2:mem:testDb;MVCC=TRUE"
    }
  }
  production {
    dataSource {
      driverClassName = "com.mysql.jdbc.Driver"
      dbCreate = "update"
      username = "root"
      password = "secured_password"
      url = "jdbc:mysql://db_name"
      pooled = true
      properties {
        maxActive = -1
        minEvictableIdleTimeMillis = 1800000
        timeBetweenEvictionRunsMillis = 1800000
        numTestsPerEvictionRun = 3
        testOnBorrow = true
        testWhileIdle = true
        testOnReturn = true
```

```
            validationQuery = "SELECT 1"
          }
        }
      }
    }
```

Using Grails services in Vaadin

We will make a bit of an interactive application in this recipe. A client will be able to add new users into the database and the user interface will reflect the actual state of the `User` database table.

The following screenshot shows what we are going to develop in this recipe:

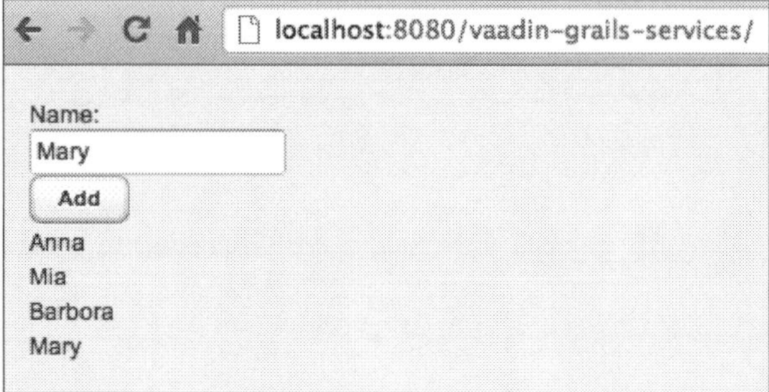

How to do it...

Carry out the following steps, in order to use Grails services inside Vaadin application:

1. Create a new domain class called `User` inside the `grails-app/domain` folder.

```
class User {

  String name

  static constraints = {
  }
}
```

2. Create a new service for the `User` class. We will implement the `getAll` method that returns all the users from the database and the `add` method that stores a new user in the database. The following screenshot shows how to make the service in Eclipse:

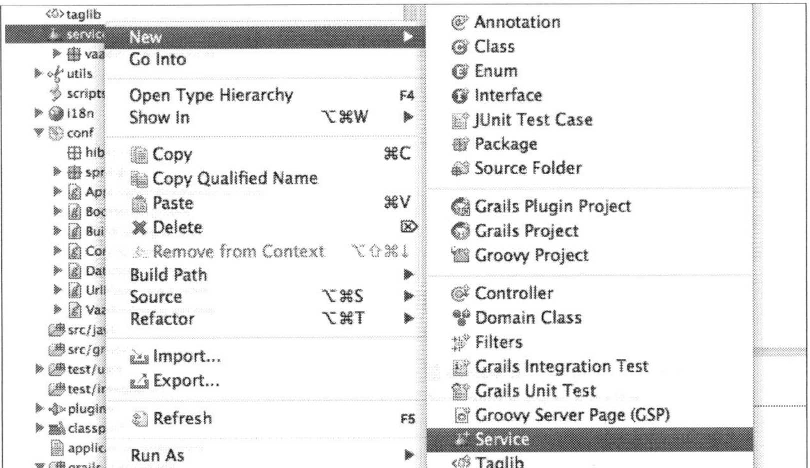

Now type the name of the domain class we want to make the service for.

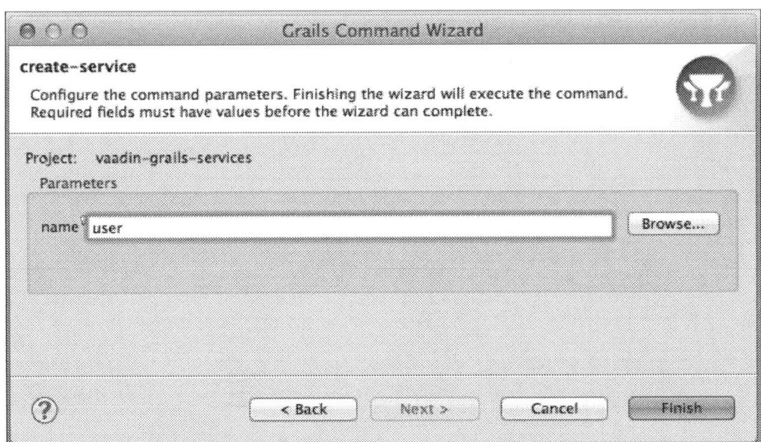

The following code shows what has been generated by the Grails framework. Add the `getAll` and `add` methods into the `UserService` class.

```
class UserService {

  List<User> getAll() {
    List<User> list = User.list()
    return list
```

```
    }

    User add(String name) {
      User user = new User(name: name)
      user.save(failOnError:true)
      return user
    }
}
```

3. Create a new click listener that will take care of creating new users by using the `add` method from `UserService`.

```
public class AddUserListener implements ClickListener {

  @Override
  public void buttonClick(ClickEvent event) {
    MyUI ui = (MyUI) UI.getCurrent()
    String value = ui.txtName.getValue()
    User user = Grails.get(UserService).add(value)
    ui.layout.addComponent(new Label(user.name))
  }
}
```

4. Now add the needed components in order to be able to add and display the users in the browser.

```
class MyUI extends UI {

  TextField txtName = new TextField("Name: ");
   VerticalLayout layout = new VerticalLayout()

  @Override
  protected void init(VaadinRequest vaadinRequest) {
    layout.margin = true
    setContent(layout)

    layout.addComponent(txtName);

    Button btnAdd = new Button("Add");
    layout.addComponent(btnAdd);
    btnAdd.addClickListener(new AddUserListener());

    List<User> users = Grails.get(UserService).getAll()
    for (User user : users) {
      layout.addComponent(new Label(user.name))
    }
  }
}
```

How it works...

Creating the persistent classes and related services is pretty easy and quick in Grails. Grails services are transactional by default. We can switch them off by adding the `transactional` static field into the `UserService` class.

```
static transactional = true
```

Alternatively, we can configure it via the `@Transactional` annotation from Spring.

More information about Grails services can be found at `http://grails.org/doc/latest/guide/services.html`.

Dependency injection in Vaadin is done via the `get()` method from the `Grails` class. The `Grails` class is provided by the Vaadin plugin for the Grails framework. The `Grails` class uses the Spring application context for obtaining the service instances.

Note that we should not make strong references to Grails services in Vaadin classes. Instead, use the `Grails.get()` method. Obtaining classes from the Spring application context is fast and we don't have to worry about performance. The reason to do so is that strong references (instance variables) might be serialized together with Vaadin components and after the services are deserialized, they would not work properly, because they would be out of Spring's control.

Adding a Vaadin add-on into Grails project

There are many Vaadin add-ons available at `http://vaadin.com/directory`. We will use the Vaadin Calendar add-on in this recipe.

First, we add dependencies and we connect it to the Grails project. Then, we will run the application without the widget set compilation, so we will see it is necessary to do the widget set compilation.

After we recompile the widget set and run the application, the Vaadin Calendar will appear in the browser.

Getting ready

Register on `http://vaadin.com`. It is necessary to have a profile there so you have access to the add-ons. Then, open `http://vaadin.com/directory#addon/vaadin-calendar` and expand the Maven POM link, so the maven dependency is visible.

How to do it...

Carry out the following steps in order to add the Calendar add-on into the Vaadin application inside the Grails project:

1. We need to add a dependency to our Grails project. Dependencies are managed in the `BuildConfig.groovy` script, which is in the `grails-app/conf` folder. Add a new maven repository and a new dependency there.

   ```
   mavenRepo "http://maven.vaadin.com/vaadin-addons"
   ```

2. We need to make sure that we use the proper version of the add-on. If needed, get the latest version from the Maven POM information box on the add-on page. Then add the dependency to `BuildConfig.groovy`.

   ```
   compile 'com.vaadin.addon:vaadin-calendar:2.0.0'
   ```

3. As we want to use a component that has its own widget set, we need to create a new widget set definition file. We will create it in the `grails-app/vaadin/app` directory and name it `AppWidgetSet.gwt.xml`.

```
<?xml version="1.0" encoding="UTF-8"?>
<!DOCTYPE module PUBLIC
    "-//Google Inc.//DTD Google Web Toolkit 1.7.0//EN"
    "http://google-web-toolkit.googlecode.com/svn/
    tags/1.7.0/distro-source/core/src/gwt-module.dtd">
<module>
  <inherits name="com.vaadin.DefaultWidgetSet" />
  <inherits name="com.vaadin.addon.calendar.gwt.
  CalendarWidgetset" />
</module>
```

4. We will not use the default widget set anymore, so we have to communicate this to Vaadin. Open `VaadinConfig.groovy` from the `conf` folder and add there a note about the new widget set file.

```
widgetset = "app.AppWidgetSet"
```

5. We are ready with the configuration for the first part. Now we can add the Vaadin Calendar on UI. We do this in the `MyUI` class from the `grails-app/vaadin/app` folder.

```
@Override
protected void init(VaadinRequest vaadinRequest) {
  VerticalLayout layout = new VerticalLayout()
  layout.setMargin(true)
  setContent(layout)
  Calendar calendar = new Calendar()
  layout.addComponent calendar
}
```

6. Try to run the application and open it in the browser. After a while, the following dialog window will be shown. It says that Vaadin has failed to load the widget set. That is because there is no widget set like the one we have defined in `VaadinConfig.groovy`:

7. Make a new folder called `libs-widgetset` (inside the project root) for libraries that are needed for the widget set compilation. Download all-in-one archive of Vaadin 7 from `https://vaadin.com/download` and move all the `.jar` files from the archive into the `libs-widgetset` folder. Do not forget to also move the `.jar` files from the `lib` folder from the archive.

8. We will use ANT for the widget set compilation. So make sure you have ANT installed on your computer. Create a new `build.xml` file with the following content:

```
<?xml version="1.0"?>
<project name="Widgetset compiler" basedir="."
  default="compile-widgetset">
  <target name="compile-widgetset">
    <path id="classpath">
      <pathelement path="grails-app/vaadin"/>
      <pathelement path="src/java"/>
      <pathelement path="target/classes"/>
      <fileset dir="libs-widgetset">
        <include name="*.jar"/>
      </fileset>
    </path>
    <echo>Compiling ${widgetset}...</echo>
    <property name="module" value="app.AppWidgetSet" />
    <property name="module.output.dir"
    location="web-app/VAADIN/widgetsets" />
    <property name="localWorkers" value="2" />
    <mkdir dir="${module.output.dir}" />
    <java classname="com.google.gwt.dev.Compiler"
    classpathref="classpath" failonerror="yes"
    fork="yes" maxmemory="512m">
      <arg value="-war" />
      <arg value="${module.output.dir}" />
      <arg value="-localWorkers" />
      <arg value="${localWorkers}" />
      <arg value="-strict" />
      <arg value="${module}" />
      <sysproperty key="vFailIfNotSerializable"
      value="true" />
      <jvmarg value="-Xss8M" />
      <jvmarg value="-XX:MaxPermSize=256M" />
      <jvmarg value="-Djava.awt.headless=true" />
    </java>
  </target>
</project>
```

9. Open the console inside the project root and run the `ant` command. The widget set compilation will start.

   Before you run the `ant` command, remove all the content of the `vaadin-grails-addon/web-app/VAADIN` folder.

   ```
   ant
   ```

10. We can start the application again and see if everything is running as expected.

   ```
   grails run-app
   ```

How it works...

The Ant build script takes all the `.jar` files and project files and sets up the class path. Then the build script calls the `Compiler` class from GWT in order to proceed with the widget set compilation.

There's more...

In case we place `AppWidgetSet.gwt.xml` to a different location, we need to change the Ant property module as follows:

```
<property name="module" value="app.other.AppWidgetSet" />
```

9

Data Management

In this chapter, we will cover:

- Binding property to a component
- Binding items to a component
- Binding a container to a component
- Creating a complex table – CRUD II
- Filtering data in the table
- Using converters
- Storing the last selected tab name in cookies

Introduction

Vaadin provides a useful concept of data model. It consists of three levels: `property`, `item`, and `container`. Container is composed of items. Item is composed of properties. And each property is defined by type and value. The data model is realized as a set of interfaces: `Property`, `Item`, and `Container`.

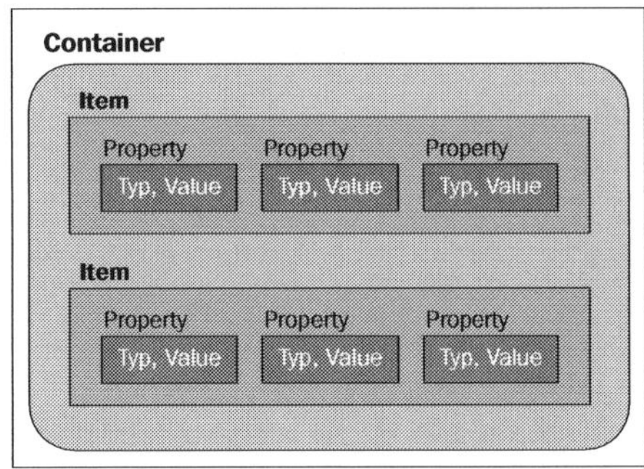

We will learn how to bind each level of the data model to UI components. One of the most complex UI components is a table. We'll show how to bind this component to the container, how to add actions to the context menu, and how to use custom filter values in the table. We'll also describe `Converters`. It's a new feature in Vaadin 7. It is used to convert between the UI and the data model type. At the end we'll learn how to read and write cookies in the web browser.

Binding property to a component

Through the `Property` interface, we can easily bind a single data object with a component. This property can be shared between multiple components. Changes in the property in one component are immediately visible in the other components. The `Property` interface is the base of the Vaadin Data Model. It provides a standardized API for a single data object that can be read (get) and written (set). In this recipe, we will work with one `ObjectProperty` that will store a string of an HTML page. We will create a simple editor of this page. It will consist of three tabs: a preview of a page, an HTML editor, and a Rich text editor as depicted in the following screenshot:

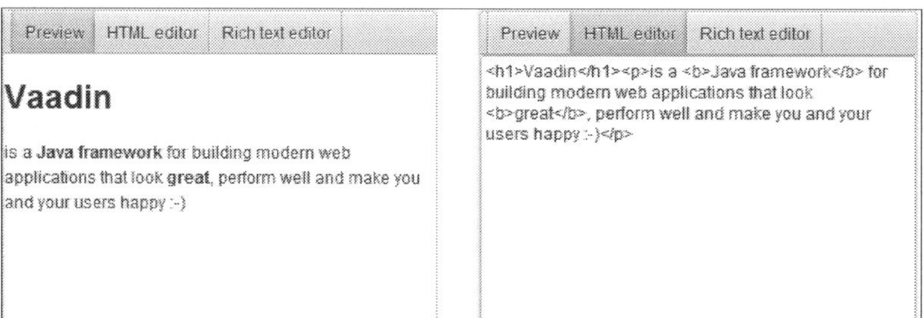

How to do it...

Carry out the following steps to create a simple HTML editor by binding property to a component:

1. Create a Vaadin project with a main UI class called `Demo` as follows:

   ```
   public class Demo extends UI {…}
   ```

2. We create a class named `Editor` that extends `TabSheet` as follows. Each section (preview and two editors) will have its own tab.

   ```
   public class Editor extends TabSheet {…}
   ```

3. Our HTML page will be stored in an instance of the `ObjectProperty` class. We call it `htmlPage` and we set the type of the value to `String`. Next, we add constant of tab page height.

   ```
   private ObjectProperty<String> htmlPage =
         new ObjectProperty<String>(
   ```

```
        "<h1>Vaadin</h1><p>is a <b>Java framework</b> for
                building modern web applications.</p>");
    private static final int HEIGHT = 300;
```

4. In the constructor, we create tabs. Each tab will be created in separated methods. In the first, we insert a preview of the HTML page. In the second will be plain text area with HTML editor and in the last tab we insert Vaadin's component Rich text editor.

```
public Editor() {
  addTab(createPreview());
  addTab(createHtmlEditor());
  addTab(createRichEditor());
}
```

5. The **Preview** tab is created through the `createPreview()` method. In all tabs, vertical layout is used. To clarify the code, we move the creation of this layout to the `createLayout()` method. The **Preview** tab consists of only one component. It is a `Label` that has set the shared property named `htmlPage`.

```
private Layout createPreview() {
  Layout layout = createLayout("Preview");
  Label label = new Label("", ContentMode.HTML);
  label.setPropertyDataSource(htmlPage);
  layout.addComponent(label);
  return layout;
}
```

6. The next tab is the **HTML editor**. It also has a vertical layout and consists of a simple text area with a set property `htmlPage`.

```
private Layout createHtmlEditor() {
  Layout layout = createLayout("HTML editor");
  TextArea editor = new TextArea();
  editor.setSizeFull();
  editor.setPropertyDataSource(htmlPage);
  layout.addComponent(editor);
  return layout;
}
```

7. The last tab is the **Rich text editor**. Here we use a nice Vaadin component `RichTextArea`. It has also a set property `htmlPage`.

```
private Layout createRichEditor() {
  Layout layout = createLayout("Rich text editor");
  RichTextArea editor = new RichTextArea();
  editor.setSizeFull();
  editor.setPropertyDataSource(htmlPage);
  layout.addComponent(editor);
  return layout;
}
```

8. In the common method for creating layout, we set the caption and height of the vertical layout which is used in all tabs. This caption is automatically used for the tab's name.

```
private Layout createLayout(String caption) {
  Layout layout = new VerticalLayout();
  layout.setCaption(caption);
  layout.setHeight(HEIGHT, Unit.PIXELS);
  return layout;
}
```

9. Now we can use our created `Editor` class in the main UI class `Demo`.

```
public class Demo extends UI {
  @Override
  protected void init(VaadinRequest request) {
    setContent(new Editor());
  }
}
```

We run the server and open the created application in the web browser.

How it works...

We created a simple HTML editor. The HTML source code is stored in an instance of the `ObjectProperty<String>` class. The `ObjectProperty` class is a simple data object containing one typed value. In our case, it is a `String` type. This property is bound with all three sections of our editor by the `setPropertyDataSource(Property)` method. If the user makes any changes in one of the editors, these changes are propagated into the other sections through `ValueChangeEvent`.

There's more...

In Vaadin, we can use other implementations of the `Property` interface. Some of them are described in the following table:

Name of class	Description
`AbstractProperty`	An abstract base class for `Property` implementations. Handles listener management for `ValueChangeListeners` and `ReadOnlyStatusChangeListeners`.
`MethodProperty`	Proxy class for creating properties from pairs of getter and setter methods of a `Bean` property. Accessing the object through the `Property` interface directly manipulates the underlying field.

Name of class	Description
`ObjectProperty`	A simple data object containing one typed value.
`TextFileProperty`	Property implementation for wrapping a text file. Supports reading and writing of a file from/to `String`.
`TransactionalPropertyWrapper` *(new in Vaadin 7)*	Wrapper class that helps implement two-phase commit for a non-transactional property. When accessing the property through the wrapper, getting and setting the property value take place immediately.

See also

- More information about `Properties` is described in Vaadin's book, available at `https://vaadin.com/book/vaadin7/-/page/datamodel.properties.html`
- API of the `Property` interface is available at `https://vaadin.com/api/7.0.0/com/vaadin/data/Property.html`
- API of `ObjectProperty` class is available at `https://vaadin.com/api/7.0.0/com/vaadin/data/util/ObjectProperty.html`

Binding items to a component

In the previous recipe, we described how to bind one property to the component. Now we will describe how to bind multiple properties. For this case, we will use the `Item` interface. The `Item` interface provides access to a set of named properties. We will create an Admin page for managing components through properties. These properties will be stored in the `PropertysetItem` class. We will be able to change the dimensions of the text area by changing the values in the text fields in a form. The item will be bound to the two components: `FieldGroup` that will be used to create a form in the Admin page and `CustomTextArea`, which is our managed component.

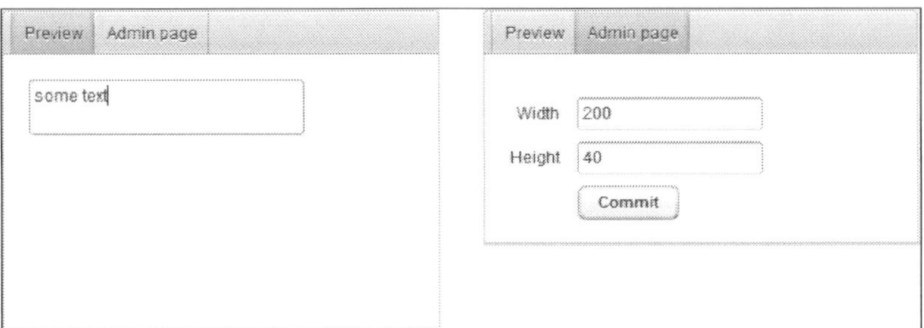

How to do it...

Carry out the following steps to learn how to bind items to a component:

1. Create a Vaadin project with a main UI class named `Demo`.

   ```
   public class Demo extends UI {…}
   ```

2. We start with creating the `CustomTextArea` class that extends `TextArea`.

   ```
   public class CustomTextArea extends TextArea {…}
   ```

3. We need two constants. One is for the width and the second is for the height. Both will be used for the name of the item's property. These properties will store the dimension of the custom text area.

   ```
   public static final String WIDTH = "width";
   public static final String HEIGHT = "height";
   ```

4. In the constructor, we only set reference to the item that is used as a data source.

   ```
   public CustomTextArea(Item itemDataSource) {
     setItemDataSource(itemDataSource);
   }
   ```

5. Data source is set by a separate method called `setItemDataSource()`. In this method, we get two properties from this item. The first is for the width and the second is for the height. We add a value change listener for each property. In these listeners, we set the dimension of the text area.

   ```
   public void setItemDataSource(Item itemDataSource) {
     ObjectProperty<?> widthProperty =
     (ObjectProperty<?>) itemDataSource.getItemProperty
       (WIDTH);
     widthProperty.addValueChangeListener
       (new ValueChangeListener() {
       @Override
       public void valueChange
         (com.vaadin.data.Property.ValueChangeEvent event) {
         Integer width = (Integer)
           event.getProperty().getValue();
         setWidth(width, Unit.PIXELS);
       }
     });

     ObjectProperty<?> heightProperty =
     (ObjectProperty<?>) itemDataSource.getItemProperty
       (HEIGHT);
     heightProperty.addValueChangeListener
       (new ValueChangeListener() {
   ```

```
      @Override
      public void valueChange
        (com.vaadin.data.Property.ValueChangeEvent event) {
        Integer height =  (Integer)
          event.getProperty().getValue();
        setHeight(height, Unit.PIXELS);
      }
    });
  }
```

6. Next, we create the `AdminPage` class that extends the `TabSheet` class. The first tab will be used for our managed component and in the second tab, we will have a form with values of the managed component.

   ```
   public class AdminPage extends TabSheet {…}
   ```

7. At first, we create global `item` that is an instance of the `PropertysetItem` class. This class is used for handling a set of identified properties. It also supports listeners who are interested in changes to the `Property` set managed by the class.

   ```
   private PropertysetItem item = new PropertysetItem();
   ```

8. In the constructor, we add two properties with default values into the item and then we insert content of a tab that is created by the separate method.

   ```
   public AdminPage() {
     item.addItemProperty(CustomTextArea.WIDTH,
                          new ObjectProperty<Integer>(50));
     item.addItemProperty(CustomTextArea.HEIGHT,
                          new ObjectProperty<Integer>(40));

     addTab(createPreview());
     addTab(createAdminEditor());
   }
   ```

9. The **Preview** tab is based on the vertical layout. The name of this layout is automatically used for naming the tab. We enable the spacing and margin for good looks. Next, we add our `CustomTextArea` that we bind with the item data source.

   ```
   private Layout createPreview() {
     VerticalLayout layout = new VerticalLayout();
     layout.setCaption("Preview");
     layout.setSpacing(true);
     layout.setMargin(true);
     CustomTextArea textArea = new CustomTextArea(item);
     layout.addComponent(textArea);
     return layout;
   }
   ```

10. The next tab, Admin editor is based on the `FormLayout` that is used to build a form easily. This form consists of text fields that are built and bound with the item's properties by the `FieldGroup` object.

```
private Layout createAdminEditor() {
  FormLayout layout = new FormLayout();
  layout.setCaption("Admin page");
  layout.setSpacing(true);
  layout.setMargin(true);

  FieldGroup group = new FieldGroup();
  group.setItemDataSource(item);
  for (Object propertyId :
    group.getUnboundPropertyIds()) {
    layout.addComponent
      (group.buildAndBind(propertyId));
  }
  layout.addComponent(createCommitButton(group));
  return layout;
}
```

11. The values of the text fields are transferred to the properties after calling the `FieldGroup.commit()` method. We will call this method on the click event in the `Button's` listener.

```
private Button createCommitButton
  (final FieldGroup group) {
  Button button = new Button("Commit");
  button.addClickListener(new ClickListener() {
    @Override
    public void buttonClick(ClickEvent event) {
      try {
        group.commit();
      } catch (CommitException e) {
        Notification.show(e.getMessage(),
          Type.ERROR_MESSAGE);
      }
    }
  });
  return button;
}
```

12. That is all. We can use our created `AdminPage` in the main UI `Demo` class.

```
public class Demo extends UI {
  @Override
  protected void init(VaadinRequest request) {
    setContent(new AdminPage());
  }
}
```

We run the server and open the application in the web browser.

How it works...

In our example, we used the `PropertysetItem` class for handling a set of identified properties. We added two properties, first for width and second for the height of custom text area. Both properties are a type of `Integer`. This instance of `PropertysetItem` called `item` is used to bind dimension of our custom text area with values in the form on the Admin page. If the user changes some values in this form and clicks on the **Commit** button, the dimension of the custom text area will be changed accordingly by the `ValueChangeEvent`.

There's more...

In Vaadin, we can use other implementations of the `Item` interface. Some of them are described in the following table:

Name of the class	Description
`BeanItem<BT>`	A wrapper class for creating an instance of `Item` from any Java Bean in such a way, that the bean fields become properties.
`FilesystemContainer.FileItem`	Wrapper for files in a filesystem.
`PropertysetItem`	Class for handling a set of identified properties.
`RowItem`	Represents one row of a result set obtained from a `QueryDelegate`.

The `FieldGroup` class is new in Vaadin 7 that constructs a field binder that uses the given `Item` data source.

See also

- Additional information about creating forms is described in *Chapter 7, Working with Forms*
- More information about the `Item` is described in the Vaadin book available at `https://vaadin.com/book/vaadin7/-/page/datamodel.items.html`
- API of `Item` interface is available at `https://vaadin.com/api/7.0.0/com/vaadin/data/Item.html`
- API of the `PropertysetItem` class is available at `https://vaadin.com/api/7.0.0/com/vaadin/data/util/PropertysetItem.html`

Binding a container to a component

It is easy and quick to create a table in Vaadin. Because `Table` is managed using the data model through the `Container`, we don't need to care about table rendering. We can manage only the `Container` and Vaadin provides other stuff such as nice default CSS style, sorting values by clicking on the head of the column, resizing width of columns by the mouse, and other great functions. In relation to the previous recipe, `Container` is a set of `Items`. In this recipe, we will show how to quickly and easily create a table by Vaadin `Container`.

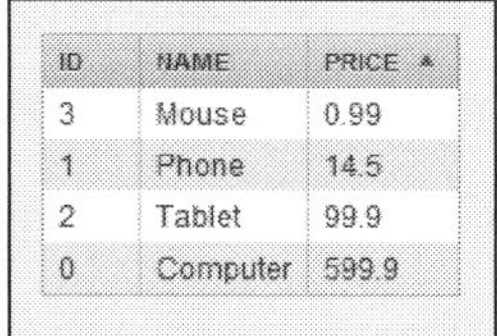

ID	NAME	PRICE ▲
3	Mouse	0.99
1	Phone	14.5
2	Tablet	99.9
0	Computer	599.9

How to do it...

Carry out the following steps to bind a container to a component:

1. Create a Vaadin project with main UI class named `Demo`.

```
public class Demo extends UI {…}
```

2. First, we need some Java Bean. For example, we can create a `Product` bean that is usually defined by `id`, `name`, and `price`. For each variable, we create the getter and setter methods.

```
public class Product {
  private int id;
  private String name;
  private double price;
```

```
  public Product(int id, String name, double price) {
    this.id = id;
    this.name = name;
    this.price = price;
  }

  <insert getters and setter>
  ...
}
```

3. Next, we create a class called `ProductTable` that extends the `Table` class.

   ```
   public class ProductTable extends Table {...}
   ```

4. As a data source we use an instance of the `BeanItemContainer` class. It is a container for JavaBeans. The properties of the container are determined automatically by introspecting the used Java Bean class. Only beans of the same type can be added to the container. In our example, it is the `Product` type.

   ```
   private BeanItemContainer<Product> products =
   new BeanItemContainer<Product>(Product.class);
   ```

5. In the constructor, we fill the container with some instances of the `Product` class. For a better look, we set the number of table rows according to the number of visible items in the table using the `setPageLength()` method.

   ```
     public ProductTable() {
       fillContainer(products);
       setContainerDataSource(products);
       setPageLength(size());
     }
   ```

6. Next, we create a method for filling the container.

   ```
     private void fillContainer(Container container) {
       int id = 0;
       container.addItem
         (new Product(id++, "Computer",599.90));
       container.addItem(new Product(id++, "Phone", 14.5));
       container.addItem(new Product
         (id++, "Tablet", 99.90));
       container.addItem(new Product(id++, "Mouse", 0.99));
     }
   ```

7. That is all. Now we can use our created table in the main UI `Demo` class.

```
public class Demo extends UI {
  @Override
  protected void init(VaadinRequest request) {
```

```
        setContent(new ProductTable());
    }
}
```

We run the server and open the created application in the web browser.

How it works...

We created `Table` that consists of `Product` items. In our example `Product` is a typical Java Bean with three fields: `id`, `name`, and `price`. This bean is used to create an instance of `BeanItemContainer` as a data source. We don't need to care about rendering the table. It's all done by passing data source to the table's container.

There's more...

The `Container` interface is the highest containment level of the Vaadin Data Model, for containing items (rows) which in turn contain properties (columns). In Vaadin, we can use other implementations of the `Container` interface. Some of them are described in the following table:

Name of class	Description
`BeanItemContainer<BEANTYPE>`	An in-memory container for JavaBeans. Uses the beans themselves as identifiers.
`BeanContainer<IDTYPE,BEANTYPE>`	An in-memory container for JavaBeans. The item IDs do not have to be the beans themselves. The container can be used either with explicit item IDs or the item IDs can be generated when adding beans.
`IndexedContainer`	Used for indexing, ordering, sorting and filtering an item.
`FilesystemContainer`	A hierarchical container wrapper for a filesystem.
`SQLContainer`	Container using the `QueryDelegate` interface for database transactions.

See also

- More information about the `Container` is described in the Vaadin book available at `https://vaadin.com/book/vaadin7/-/page/datamodel.container.html`
- API of the `Container` interface is available at `https://vaadin.com/api/7.0.0/com/vaadin/data/Container.html`
- API of the `BeanItemContainer` class is available at `https://vaadin.com/api/7.0.0/com/vaadin/data/util/BeanItemContainer.html`

Creating a complex table – CRUD II

In this recipe, we will build on the previous one. Again, we will create a table. However, this time, we will do it with more complex functions. We will create a **CRUD** (**create, read, update, delete**) application. It will be similar to the *Creating a CRUD form* recipe in *Chapter 7, Working with Forms* but we will do it a little differently. It will be possible to change the width of the table using the mouse. The form will be viewed next to the table and both functions `Add` and `Delete` will be integrated as a context menu to the table.

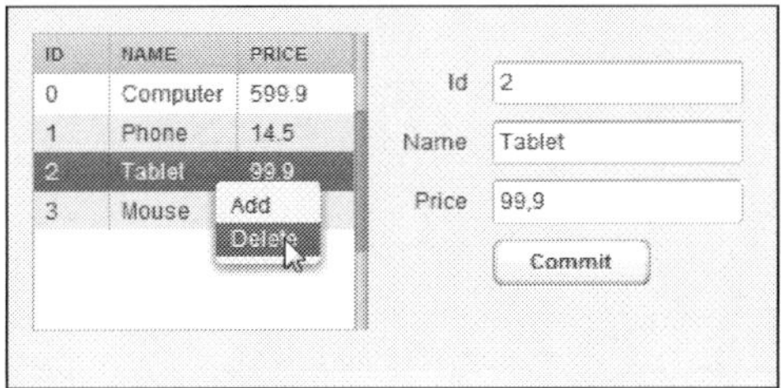

How to do it...

Carry out the following steps to create a CRUD application with complex table:

1. Create a Vaadin project with a **topmost** class called `Demo`:

   ```
   public class Demo extends UI {…}
   ```

2. First, we need a `Product` bean. It's the same bean as used in the previous recipe.
3. Next, we create a class called `CRUD` that is based on the horizontal split panel.

   ```
   public class CRUD extends HorizontalSplitPanel {…}
   ```

4. At the beginning, we create instance for two actions: `Add` and `Delete`. Next, we initialize variable id and create an instance of the `BeanItemContainer` class that will store the `Product` beans.

   ```
   private final static Action
     ACTION_ADD = new Action("Add");
   private final static Action
     ACTION_DELETE = new Action("Delete");
   private int id = 0;
   private BeanItemContainer<Product> products =
           new BeanItemContainer<>(Product.class);
   ```

5. In the constructor, we fill in the container by some `Product` objects and insert the table to the left panel in the main layout.

```
public CRUD() {
  fillContainer(products);
  setFirstComponent(createTable(products));
}
```

6. The table will be created according to the data in the container. Setting full size of table enables that user to change the width of the table using panel separator. Furthermore, we enable selecting rows and we add a mouse click listener to the items. On the click event in this listener, we build and insert a new form into the right side of the main panel.

```
private Table createTable(Container container) {
  final Table table = new Table(null, container);
  table.setSelectable(true);
  table.setSizeFull();
  table.addItemClickListener(new ItemClickListener() {
    @Override
    public void itemClick(ItemClickEvent event) {
      if (MouseButton.LEFT.getName().equals
        (event.getButtonName())) {
        setSecondComponent
          (createForm(event.getItem()));
      }
    }
  });
  ...
```

7. Next, we add a handler for the actions. Actions can be bound to shortcut keys or used in the context menus. Using the shortcuts is described in the *Customizing shortcuts* recipe in *Chapter 5, Events*. We have to override the `handleAction()` and `getActions()` methods. In the first one, we handle an action for the given target. The second method gets the array of actions applicable to this handler. These two actions will appear as a context menu in the table as we can see in the following screenshot:

```
  table.addActionHandler(new Handler() {
    @Override
    public void handleAction
      (Action action, Object sender, Object target) {
```

```
          if (ACTION_DELETE == action) {
            products.removeItem(target);
          }
          if (ACTION_ADD == action) {
            products.addBean(new Product(id++, "", 0));
          }
        }

        @Override
        public Action[] getActions
          (Object target, Object sender) {
          return new Action[]
            { ACTION_ADD, ACTION_DELETE };
        }
      });
      return table;
    }
```

8. The form will be generated according to the selected table item. We use `FormLayout` with enabled spacing and margin around the table. By the `FieldGroup`, we bind each property of the selected item with the generated field.

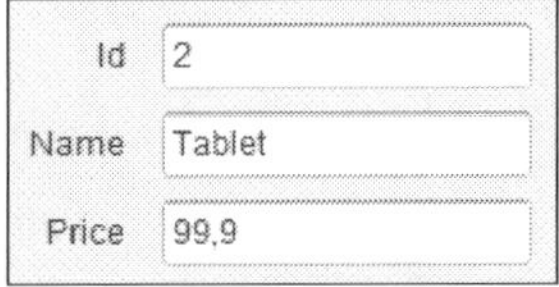


```
    private Layout createForm(Item item) {
      FormLayout layout = new FormLayout();
      layout.setSpacing(true);
      layout.setMargin(true);
      final FieldGroup group = new FieldGroup(item);
      for (Object propertyId :
        group.getUnboundPropertyIds()){
        layout.addComponent
          (group.buildAndBind(propertyId));
      }
      ...
```

9. Next, we add a button for commit values. The values of the text fields are transferred to the item's properties after calling the `FieldGroup.commit()` method. Therefore, we will call this method on the click event in the button's listener.

```
      Button button = new Button("Commmit");
      button.addClickListener(new ClickListener() {
        @Override
```

```
        public void buttonClick(ClickEvent event) {
          try {
            group.commit();
          } catch (CommitException e) {
            Notification.show(e.getCause().getMessage(),
                         Type.ERROR_MESSAGE);
          }
        }
      });
      layout.addComponent(button);
      return layout;
    }
```

10. At the end, we fill the container with some data.

```
    private void fillContainer(Container container) {
      container.addItem
        (new Product(id++, "Computer",599.90));
      container.addItem(new Product(id++, "Phone", 14.5));
      container.addItem(new Product
        (id++, "Tablet", 99.90));
      container.addItem(new Product(id++, "Mouse", 0.99));
    }
```

11. That is all. Now we can use our CRUD class in the main UI class `Demo`.

```
  public class Demo extends UI {
    @Override
    protected void init(VaadinRequest request) {
      setContent(new CRUD());
    }
  }
```

We run the server and open the application in the web browser.

How it works...

`Table` is used for representing data or components in a scrollable and selectable table. Scalability of the `Table` is largely dictated by the container. A table does not have a limit for the number of items and is just as fast with hundreds of thousands of items as with just a few. The current GWT implementation with scrolling however limits the number of rows to around 500,000, depending on the browser and the pixel height of rows. It's never good to show that many rows at a time since no human will want to scroll through that amount of rows.

In Vaadin 7, `Table` was updated. Some constants and methods are deprecated and replaced by new ones. For example, constants `Table.ALIGN_XXX` (`XXX` means `LEFT`, `CENTER`, or `RIGHT`) were replaced by enumerator `Table.Align.XXX`. Constants for header `Table.COLUMN_HEADER_MODE_XXX` (for example, `EXPLICIT` and `HIDDEN`) were replaced by `Table.ColumnHeaderMode.XXX`. Methods for adding listener `table.addListener(XXX listener)` were replaced by `table.addXXXListener(XXX listener)`. And there are other minor changes. These changes are described in the Table's API on the web link mentioned in the following section.

See also

- More information about the `Table` is described in the Vaadin book at `https://vaadin.com/book/vaadin7/-/page/components.table.html`
- API of the `Table` class is available at `https://vaadin.com/api/7.0.0/com/vaadin/ui/Table.html`

Filtering data in the table

When we want to filter data in the table, we have to bind this table with the container that implements the `Container.Filterable` interface. With this kind of container, we can filter the rows, for example, by strings or by numbers. Vaadin provides several built-in filters. Some of them are described in the *There's more...* section at the end of this recipe. Values may be equal, or may be greater, smaller, or may contain a part of the substring. We can also create our own filter. In this recipe, we will create a simple table with custom filter. We will filter two values by string and ID value by the greater one. Our filter will be placed on the top of the table as shown in the following screenshot:

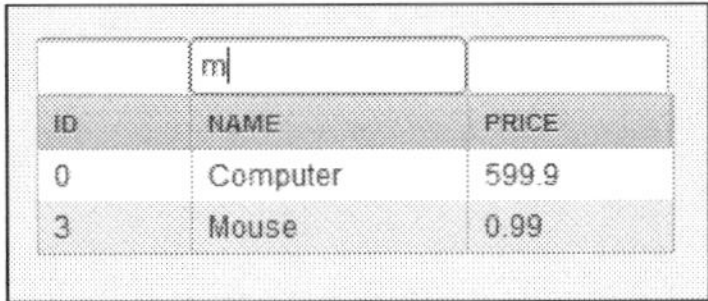

How to do it...

Carry out the following steps to create a table with filter:

1. Create a Vaadin project with a **topmost** class called `Demo`.

   ```
   public class Demo extends UI {…}
   ```

2. First, we need a `Product` bean. It's the same bean as used in the *Binding a container to a component* recipe.

3. Our filtered table will extend `CustomComponent` that provides simple implementation of the `Component` interface for the creation of new UI components by composition of existing components.

   ```
   public class FilteredTable extends CustomComponent {…}
   ```

4. At the beginning, we initialize the container that will store `Product` objects. Names of the columns are kept in the array of column IDs and the width of each column is kept in an array of integer values. `COLUMN_SPACE` constant is used to set the proper width of the fields. It is the width of the free space on the left and right side in the cell of the table.

   ```
   private BeanItemContainer<Product> container =
           new BeanItemContainer<>(Product.class);
   private Object[] COLUMN_IDS = new Object[]
     { "id", "name", "price" };
   private int[] COLUMN_WIDTHS = { 50, 100, 70 };
   private static final int COLUMN_SPACE = 13;
   ```

5. In the constructor, we create table, text field filters, and insert them into the vertical layout. Using the `setCompositionRoot()` method, we set the composite root that can contain more components, but their interfaces are hidden from the users.

   ```
   public FilteredTable() {
     VerticalLayout layout = new VerticalLayout();
     setCompositionRoot(layout);

     Table table = new Table();
     layout.addComponent(createFilters(table));

     fillContainer(container);
     table.setPageLength(table.size());
     table.setContainerDataSource(container);
     layout.addComponent(table);
   }
   ```

6. Filters consist of three text fields. These fields are built according to column IDs. We set the same width for the columns and for the appropriate text fields. The field that filters IDs of `Product` has set the validation of integer values. We do it by setting the converter. On each field, we add text change listener. On the event in this listener, we will set the filter according to the value in the field.

   ```
   rivate HorizontalLayout createFilters
     (final Table table) {
     HorizontalLayout filtersLayout = new
       HorizontalLayout();
     int i = 0;
     for (final Object columnID : COLUMN_IDS) {
   ```

```
        int columnWidth = COLUMN_WIDTHS[i++];
        table.setColumnWidth(columnID, columnWidth);
        final TextField field = new TextField();
        field.setWidth(columnWidth + COLUMN_SPACE,
          Unit.PIXELS);
        if ("id".equals(columnID)) {
          field.setConverter(Integer.class);
        }
        field.addTextChangeListener
          (new TextChangeListener() {
          @Override
          public void textChange(TextChangeEvent event) {
            filterTable(table, columnID, event.getText());
          }
        });

        filtersLayout.addComponent(field);
      }
      return filtersLayout;
    }
```

7. Filtering table is performed in the separate method. First, we remove the old filter and then we set appropriate filter in the container. The IDs of `Product` are filtered by the values greater than the input. Other values are filtered by string.

```
    private void filterTable(Table table,
      Object columnID, String value) {
      container.removeContainerFilters(columnID);

      if ("id".equals(columnID)) {
        try {
          Filter greater = new Greater
            (columnID, new Integer(value));
          container.addContainerFilter(greater);
        } catch (NumberFormatException e) {
          if (!value.isEmpty()) {
            Notification.show("Cannot filter by value: " +
            value);
          }
        }
      } else {
        container.addContainerFilter
          (columnID, value, true, false);
      }
    }
```

8. At the end, we fill the container with some values.

   ```
   private void fillContainer
     (BeanItemContainer<Product> container) {
     int id = 0;
     container.addItem(new Product
       (id++, "Computer", 599.90));
     container.addItem(new Product(id++, "Phone", 14.5));
     container.addItem(new Product(id++, "Tablet",
       99.90));
     container.addItem(new Product(id++, "Mouse", 0.99));
   }
   ```

9. That is all. Now we can use our created `FilteredTable` in the main UI `Demo` class.

   ```
   public class Demo extends UI {
     @Override
     protected void init(VaadinRequest request) {
       setContent(new FilteredTable());
     }
   }
   ```

We run the server and open the application in a web browser.

How it works...

Filters implement the `Filter` interface and we add them to a filterable container with the `addContainerFilter()` method. Container items that pass the filter condition are kept and shown in the filterable component. If multiple filters are added to a container, they are evaluated using the logical `AND` operator, so that only items that are passed by all the filters are kept.

There's more...

In Vaadin, we can find some built-in filter types:

Name of filter	Description
`SimpleStringFilter`	Passes items where the specified property that must be of `String` type, contains the given filter `String` as a substring.
`Equal`, `Greater`, `Less`, `GreaterOrEqual`, `LessOrEqual`	The comparison filter implementations compare the specified property value to the given constant and pass items for which the comparison result is true.
`And`, `Or`	These logical operator filters are composite filters that combine multiple other filters.
`Not`	The logical unary operator filter negates which items are passed by the filter given as the parameter.

See also

- More information about filtering containers is described in the Vaadin book at `https://vaadin.com/book/vaadin7/-/page/datamodel.container.html`
- API of the `Container.Filterable` interface is available at `https://vaadin.com/api/7.0.0/com/vaadin/data/Container.Filterable.html`

Using converters

Converters are a completely new feature in Vaadin 7. They are used to convert between the UI and the data model type. For example, we can convert `String` to some other types such as `Date`, `Integer`, `Boolean`, or we can convert `Date` to `Long` type or we can create custom converter. They are also used as an initial validator. In this recipe, we will create a converter that converts Roman numerals to integer numbers. We will create both conversions, Roman to integer and vice versa. It will consist of text field for the Roman numeral, one button, and one label for converted value as shown in the following screenshot:

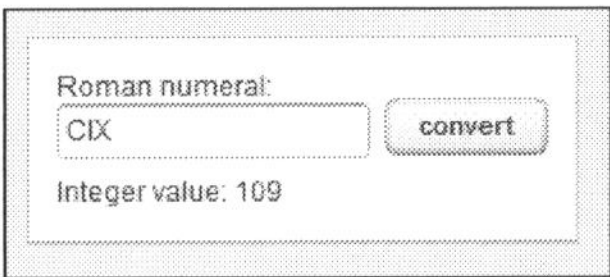

How to do it...

1. Create a Vaadin project with a main UI class called `Demo`.

   ```
   public class Demo extends UI {…}
   ```

2. We start with the creation of the converter class. This class has to implement the `Converter` interface.

   ```
   public class RomanToIntegerConverter implements
     Converter<String, Integer> {…}
   ```

3. We need three maps. The first two maps are used for conversion from Roman numerals to integer and the third map is used for conversion from integer to Roman. The `romanChars` map contains the Roman numeral as a key and integer values. The second map is for values that will be subtracted. For example, Roman numeral IV means 4. In the first step of our algorithm, we add values of 1 (I) and 5 (V), which is 6. Therefore, we must subtract 2 to get the value of 4 (IV).

   ```
     private Map<Character, Integer>
       romanChars = new LinkedHashMap<>();
     private Map<String, Integer>
   ```

```
    subtractedValues = new LinkedHashMap<>();

  private Map<String, Integer>
    romanNumerals = new LinkedHashMap<>();
```

4. We fill these maps by values in the constructor.

```
  public RomanToIntegerConverter() {
    romanChars.put('M', 1000);
    romanChars.put('D', 500);
    romanChars.put('C', 100);
    romanChars.put('L', 50);
    romanChars.put('X', 10);
    romanChars.put('V', 5);
    romanChars.put('I', 1);

    subtractedValues.put("IV", 2);
    subtractedValues.put("IX", 2);
    subtractedValues.put("XL", 20);
    subtractedValues.put("XC", 20);
    subtractedValues.put("CD", 200);
    subtractedValues.put("CM", 200);

    romanNumerals.put("M", 1000);
    romanNumerals.put("CM", 900);
    romanNumerals.put("D", 500);
    romanNumerals.put("CD", 400);
    romanNumerals.put("C", 100);
    romanNumerals.put("XC", 90);
    romanNumerals.put("L", 50);
    romanNumerals.put("XL", 40);
    romanNumerals.put("X", 10);
    romanNumerals.put("IX", 9);
    romanNumerals.put("V", 5);
    romanNumerals.put("IV", 4);
    romanNumerals.put("I", 1);
  }
```

5. Then we create a method that converts Roman numerals to integer values. We put our algorithm into the overridden `convertToModel()` method. In the first `for-loop`, we add all known values from the input string. If we find an unknown character, we throw a conversion exception. In the second `for-loop`, we subtract values found in the `subtractedValues` map.

```
  @ Override
  public Integer convertToModel
    (String romanInput, Locale locale)
```

```
  throws ConversionException {
    int intOutput = 0;
    for (int x = 0; x < romanInput.length(); x++) {
      Integer integer = romanChars.get
        (romanInput.charAt(x));
      if (integer == null) {
        throw new ConversionException();
      }
      intOutput += integer;
    }

    romanInput = romanInput.toUpperCase();
    for (String substract : subtractedValues.keySet()) {
      if (romanInput.contains(substract)) {
        intOutput -= subtractedValues.get(substract);
      }
    }

    return intOutput;
  }
```

6. The next method from the `Converter` interface is `convertToPresentation()`. It converts the given integer input to Roman numeral. In the outer loop we go through all known Roman numerals. And in the inner loop we gradually subtract the value of the given Roman numeral from the input integer. Each such Roman numeral is added to the `romanOutput` string.

```
@ Override
public String convertToPresentation
  (Integer intInput, Locale locale)
throws ConversionException {
  String romanOutput = "";
  for (String romanKey : romanNumerals.keySet()) {
    int romanValue = romanNumerals.get(romanKey);
    while (intInput >= romanValue) {
      intInput -= romanValue;
      romanOutput += romanKey;
    }
  }
  return romanOutput;
}
```

7. The `getModelType()` method returns the type of the result after conversion.

```
@Override
public Class<Integer> getModelType() {
  return Integer.class;
}
```

8. The `getPresentationType()` method returns the type of the converted value.

    ```
    @Override
    public Class<String> getPresentationType() {
      return String.class;
    }
    ```

9. Now we create a UI for our Roman numeral converter.

    ```
    public class RomanNumeralPanel extends Panel {…}
    ```

10. We need one constant for the label.

    ```
    private static final String
        INTEGER_LABEL = "Integer value: ";
    ```

11. We will create all components in the constructor. At first we define a grid layout.

    ```
    public RomanNumeralPanel() {
      GridLayout layout = new GridLayout(2, 2);
      layout.setMargin(true);
      layout.setSpacing(true);
      setContent(layout);
      setSizeUndefined();
      …
    ```

12. Then we create a label for the integer value and text field for the input value of the Roman numeral.

    ```
    final Label integerLabel = new Label(INTEGER_LABEL);
    final TextField romanField = new TextField
      ("Roman numeral:");
    romanField.setConverter
      (new RomanToIntegerConverter());
    …
    ```

13. Next, we create a button that will call converter. We bind it with the `Enter` shortcut.

    ```
    Button convertButton = new Button("convert");
    convertButton.setClickShortcut(KeyCode.ENTER, null);
    …
    ```

14. The converter will be called in the event on the button's click listener. Here we call the `getConvertedValue()` method on the input text field. If the method throws an exception, we set `integerLabel` to `n/a` (not available).

    ```
    convertButton.addClickListener(new ClickListener() {
      @Override
      public void buttonClick(ClickEvent event) {
        String convertedValue;
        try {
    ```

```
            Integer value = (Integer)
              romanField.getConvertedValue();
            convertedValue = value.toString();
          } catch (ConversionException e) {
            convertedValue = "n/a";
          }
          integerLabel.setValue
            (INTEGER_LABEL + convertedValue);
        }
      });
      ...
```

15. At the end, we add all created components to the layout. The button is aligned to the left side on the layout, because we want to have it close to the text field.

```
      layout.addComponent(romanField);
      layout.addComponent(convertButton);
      layout.addComponent(integerLabel);

      layout.setComponentAlignment
        (convertButton, Alignment.BOTTOM_LEFT);
    }
```

16. That is all. We can use our converter in the main `Demo` class.

```
public class Demo extends UI {
  @Override
  protected void init(VaadinRequest request) {
    setContent(new RomanNumeralPanel());
  }
}
```

We run the server and open the application in the web browser.

See also

- More information about converters is described in the Vaadin book at `https://vaadin.com/book/vaadin7/-/page/datamodel.properties.html`
- API of the `Converter` interface is available at `https://vaadin.com/api/7.0.0/com/vaadin/data/util/converter/Converter.html`

Storing the last selected tab name in cookies

Cookies are small pieces of data that are stored in the user's web browser. They can be considered as a small database. Each cookie is defined by a name and value of `String`. Cookies have many uses. Perhaps the most common use is user authentication.

In this recipe, we will show how to store information about the last selected tab name. This example is based on the *Binding tabs with a hard URL* recipe in *Chapter 2, Layouts*. We will continue on the same implementation. We add two new methods for read and for write cookie. In the original application, if the user entered the URL without the tab name after the hash-tag #, the first tab was selected. In this new version, the last opened tab will be selected again.

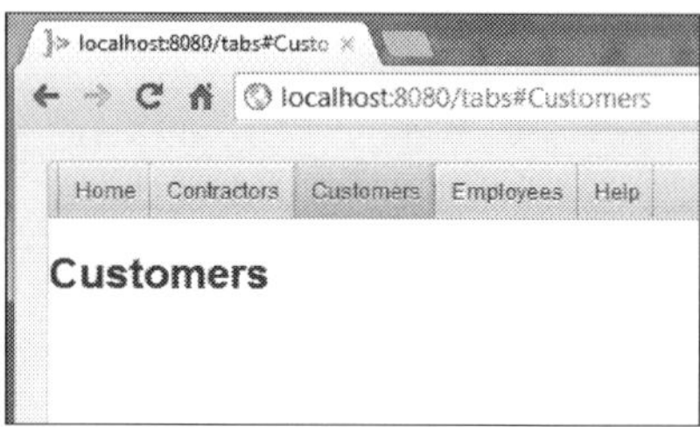

Getting ready

Create application described in the *Binding tabs with a hard URL* recipe in *Chapter 2, Layouts*.

How to do it...

1. We will continue on the previous implementation. First, we add two constants. The first is for the name of the cookie and second is for the path of the application. By this value, we say when cookies are to be used. For example, if we run our application on `http://localhost:8080/data` then the path value is `/data`.

```
private static final String LAST_TAB_COOKIE_NAME =
  "vaadin_last_tab_name";
private static final String PATH = "/data";
```

2. Then we insert two new methods. First is for writing the tab name to the cookie. Here we create a new instance of the `Cookie` class with the parameter's name and value. And we also set the path for this cookie. If we want to add this cookie to the web browser, we have to get the current Vaadin response. We'll do it using the static `VaadinService. getCurrentResponse()` method.

```
private void setLastTabNameToCookies(String tabName) {
  Cookie lastTabCookie = new Cookie
```

```
        (LAST_TAB_COOKIE_NAME, tabName);
            lastTabCookie.setPath(PATH);
            VaadinServletResponse response =
      (VaadinServletResponse)
        VaadinService.getCurrentResponse();
        response.addCookie(lastTabCookie);
}
```

3. Next we add a method for reading the last selected tab name from the cookies. At first we get an array of current cookies in the browser related to our path. In the loop, we try to find our cookie according to cookie name. If there isn't a cookie with our searched name, then we return an empty string. In that case the first tab will be selected.

```
private String getLastTabNameFromCookies() {
  Cookie[] cookies = ((VaadinServletRequest)
  VaadinService.getCurrentRequest()).getCookies();
  for (Cookie cookie : cookies) {
    if (LAST_TAB_COOKIE_NAME.equals(cookie.getName())){
      return cookie.getValue();
    }
  }
  return "";
}
```

4. The last modification is in the `selectTab()` method. We'll change the rule for selecting tab when the user doesn't enter the name of the tab in the URL. It means that if the fragment will be null, then we select the tab with name stored in the cookie. Take a look at the following lines of code:

```
    setSelectedTab(0);
    return;
```

We replace the previous lines of code with the following line of code:

```
    fragment = getLastTabNameFromCookies();
```

5. This is our change in the context of the `selectTab()` method.

```
public void selectTab(){
  String fragment =
    UI.getCurrent().getPage().getUriFragment();
    if (fragment == null) {
      fragment = getLastTabNameFromCookies();
    }
    Iterator<Component> iterator =
      getComponentIterator();
    ...
```

That is all. We run the server and open the application in a web browser. At the beginning, we select some tab and close the web page. If we open it again without entering a name after the hash-tag, our last selected tab will be open.

How it works...

In Vaadin 7, cookies are handled by the `VaadinService` class. We can read them using the `getCurrentRequest()` method. We get the `VaadinServletRequest` class that extends `javax.servlet.http.HttpServletRequestWrapper`. On this wrapper, the `getCookies()` method returns array of `javax.servlet.http.Cookie`.

If we want to write some values to the cookie, we have to get the current response by the `VaadinService.getCurrentResponse()` method. Then, we can add our cookie using the `addCookie()` method in the `VaadinServletResponse` class.

See also

- More information about the API of the `Cookie` class is available at `http://docs.oracle.com/javaee/6/api/javax/servlet/http/Cookie.html`

10
Architecture and Performance

In this chapter, we will cover:

- Building the core
- Login form with Model View Presenter
- Model View Presenter for a view with two panels
- Unit testing in an MVP pattern
- Improving the application's startup time
- Avoiding sluggish UI – lazy loaded table
- Avoiding sluggish UI – paged table
- Optimizing Vaadin applications for search engines

Introduction

Rich Internet Applications are web applications that have the features and the functionalities of desktop applications. In Vaadin, we can create whole applications just using server-side code written in Java. That brings a completely different approach to web application development. We create Vaadin applications as a composition of Vaadin components, instead of making HTML pages that redirect between themselves. We will see one way of designing composition of Vaadin components and building an application.

Model View Presenter (**MVP**) design pattern seems to be the perfect choice for Vaadin applications, because it separates an application into layers and thus provides good basics for making testable architecture. We will explore MVP in three recipes.

At the beginning, we make a simple login feature. The recipe will be as easy as possible, so we can concentrate on the principles behind MVP instead of complex code. Then we create a more complex application with two layouts. The last recipe, which will be related to MVP, will be showing how to write unit tests inside an application that is built on top of the MVP design pattern.

Then we will explore a few areas that we need to keep in mind, so that we develop well-performing Vaadin applications.

The last recipe from this chapter shows you how to make Vaadin applications visible for search engines.

Building the core

We will build an application with one of the "standard" layout compositions, which will consist of a header, a body, and a footer.

Before we start coding, we need to make a prototype of the application, so we clarify what exactly we are going to build. A prototype can be done as a set of simple drawings on paper where we pretend the application is working. This recipe is not about prototyping, but it is mentioned here because the power of prototyping is underestimated and it is an important part of the software creation process. More about prototyping can be found on the following link: `http://en.wikipedia.org/wiki/Software_prototyping`.

We will draw the basic layout of the application. In the layout sketch, we concentrate on the static and dynamic parts. The static blocks will be the blocks that might be referenced from our UI class. The dynamic blocks are going to be the parts that are going to be loaded during the application's execution based on user interaction. The following image describes the static blocks (gray boxes) and dynamic (white box) and helps us to make a good composition of layouts:

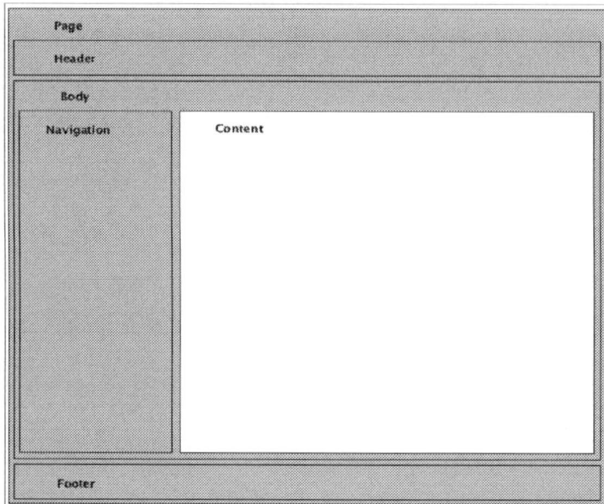

Now we can turn the layout sketch into a more concrete proposal, where we make up the class names. We will follow this approach: if the component we extend is a layout, the postfix is `Layout` (for example, `PageLayout`). If the component is going to extend `Tree`, then we name the class as, for example, `NavigationTree`.

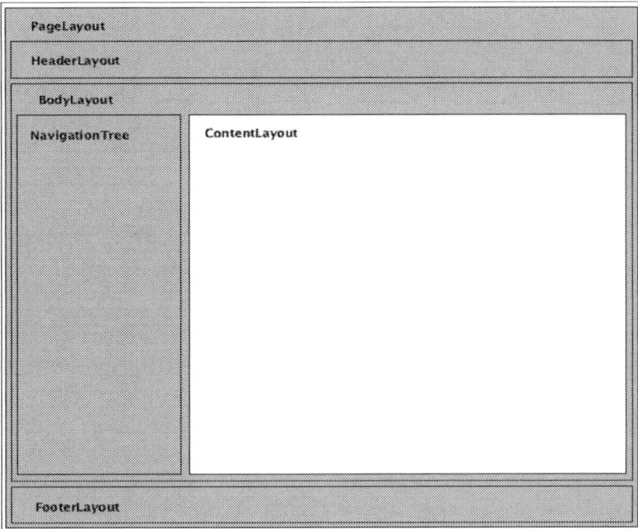

There will be only one dynamic block in the application. The content of the dynamic block will depend on the selection in the navigation tree. When we select an item in the navigation tree, the content inside `ContentLayout` will be changed accordingly. The following screenshot shows how the application will look:

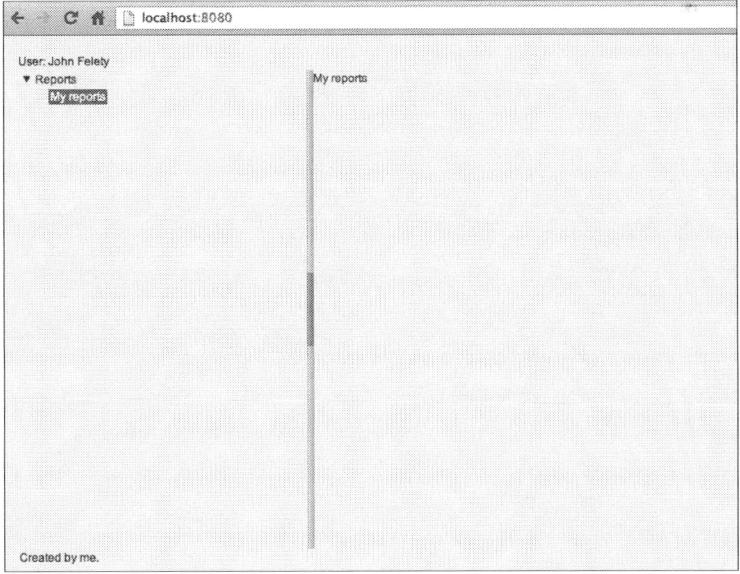

Getting ready

First, we create a class diagram showing relationships between the classes representing the basic structure of the user interface. The diagram can be read from the bottom to the top, starting at `MyVaadinUI` (`MyVaadinUI` contains `PageLayout`). `PageLayout` has `HeaderLayout`, `BodyLayout`, and so forth. `NavigationTreeListener` creates instances of two layouts that are going to be placed inside `ContentLayout`.

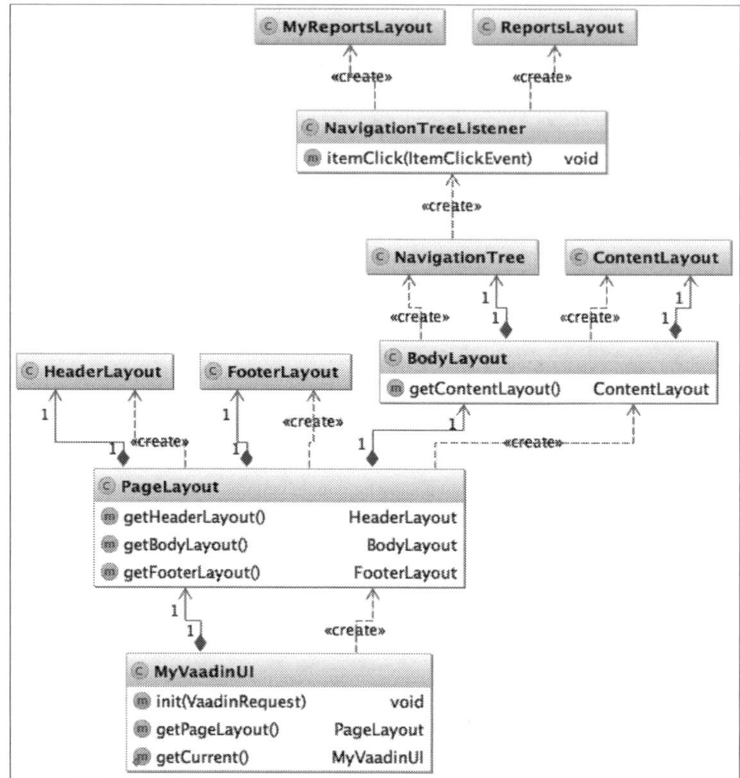

How to do it...

Perform the following steps:

1. Create the `MyVaadinUI` class, which has a reference to `PageLayout`. Create a new instance of `PageLayout` as the content of our UI class. Then we create a static method `getCurrent` that returns the current UI casted to the `MyVaadinUI` type:

```
public class MyVaadinUI extends UI {

    private PageLayout pageLayout;
```

```
    @Override
    protected void init(VaadinRequest request) {
        pageLayout = new PageLayout();
        setContent(pageLayout);
    }

    public PageLayout getPageLayout() {
        return pageLayout;
    }

    public static MyVaadinUI getCurrent() {
        return (MyVaadinUI) UI.getCurrent();
    }
}
```

2. The static blocks should be accessible from every place of the application. Therefore, we reference header, body, and footer layouts from the page layout:

```
public class PageLayout extends VerticalLayout {

    private HeaderLayout headerLayout;
    private BodyLayout bodyLayout;
    private FooterLayout footerLayout;

    public PageLayout() {
        setMargin(true);

        headerLayout = new HeaderLayout();
        addComponent(headerLayout);

        bodyLayout = new BodyLayout();
        addComponent(bodyLayout);

        footerLayout = new FooterLayout();
        addComponent(footerLayout);
    }

    public HeaderLayout getHeaderLayout() {
        return headerLayout;
    }

    public BodyLayout getBodyLayout() {
        return bodyLayout;
    }

    public FooterLayout getFooterLayout() {
        return footerLayout;
    }
}
```

3. Here is an example of how we will access the body layout from any place in the application code:

```
MyVaadinUI ui = MyVaadinUI.getCurrent();
BodyLayout layout = ui.getPageLayout().getBodyLayout();
```

4. Now, we can create the classes that represent the header and footer layouts. Both these classes will contain just a dummy content; two labels in our case:

```
public class HeaderLayout extends HorizontalLayout {

    public HeaderLayout() {
        Label label = new Label("User: John Felety");
        addComponent(label);
    }
}
public class FooterLayout extends HorizontalLayout {

    public FooterLayout() {
        Label label = new Label("Created by me.");
        addComponent(label);
    }
}
```

5. Create the class representing the body layout, which contains the navigation tree and the content layout:

```
public class BodyLayout extends HorizontalSplitPanel {

    private NavigationTree navigationTree;
    private ContentLayout contentLayout;

    public BodyLayout() {
        setHeight("500px");
        setSplitPosition(300, Unit.PIXELS);

        navigationTree = new NavigationTree();
        setFirstComponent(navigationTree);

        contentLayout = new ContentLayout();
        setSecondComponent(contentLayout);
    }

    public ContentLayout getContentLayout() {
        return contentLayout;
    }
}
```

6. It is time to create the remaining static blocks that will be used for adding the content. `NavigationTree` will be a kind of a tree menu that will invoke setting of the dynamic layout on `ContentLayout`. `ContentLayout` will just act as a placeholder, which will be re-used for placing the dynamic layouts.

```
public class NavigationTree extends Tree {

    public static final String REPORTS_LABEL = "Reports";
    public static final String MY_REPORTS_LABEL = "My reports";

    public NavigationTree() {
        setCaption("Navigation");

        addItem(REPORTS_LABEL);
        setChildrenAllowed(REPORTS_LABEL, true);

        addItem(MY_REPORTS_LABEL);
        setParent(MY_REPORTS_LABEL, REPORTS_LABEL);
        setChildrenAllowed(MY_REPORTS_LABEL, false);

        expandItemsRecursively(REPORTS_LABEL);
        setNullSelectionAllowed(false);

        NavigationTreeListener listener = new
NavigationTreeListener();
        addItemClickListener(listener);
    }
}

public class ContentLayout extends VerticalLayout {
}
```

7. Now we create the `NavigationTreeListener` class, which will handle click events from the navigation tree. We remove all the components from the content layout and display `ReportsLayout` or `MyReportsLayout`, depending on user's choice.

```
public class NavigationTreeListener implements ItemClickEvent.
ItemClickListener {

    @Override
    public void itemClick(ItemClickEvent event) {

        Object value = event.getItemId();
        MyVaadinUI current = MyVaadinUI.getCurrent();

        ContentLayout contentLayout = current.getPageLayout().
getBodyLayout().getContentLayout();
        contentLayout.removeAllComponents();
```

```
            if (NavigationTree.REPORTS_LABEL.equals(value)) {
                ReportsLayout layout = new ReportsLayout();
                contentLayout.addComponent(layout);
            } else if (NavigationTree.MY_REPORTS_LABEL.equals(value))
    {
                MyReportsLayout layout = new MyReportsLayout();
                contentLayout.addComponent(layout);
            }
        }
    }
```

8. Next, we create two classes that represent the dynamic layout, which will be placed into `ContentLayout`:

```
public class ReportsLayout extends VerticalLayout {

    public ReportsLayout() {
        Label lbl = new Label("Reports");
        addComponent(lbl);
    }
}
public class MyReportsLayout extends VerticalLayout {

    public MyReportsLayout() {
        Label lbl = new Label("My reports");
        addComponent(lbl);
    }
}
```

9. Run the application and see how the dynamic part of the application changes when we select an item in the navigation tree.

How it works...

We have demonstrated one of the many ways to build Vaadin applications.

At the beginning of this recipe, we designed the basic layout composition. Then we turned the layout names into their corresponding classes and created the class diagram. The class diagram shows the relationships between the Vaadin layouts and the components we have extended.

Simply put, we made a skeleton application, which we can fill in with the content. The skeleton is represented by classes: `PageLayout`, `HeaderLayout`, `BodyLayout`, `HeaderLayout`, `ContentLayout`, `NavigatorTree`, and `NavigatorTreeListener`. Two classes—`ReportsLayout` and `MyReportsLayout`—represent the content.

When we click on the tree, `NavigatorTreeListener` is notified and appropriate content is shown on the content layout.

The Login form with Model View Presenter

In this recipe, we will implement a login form using the Model View Presenter (MVP) pattern.

We want to introduce a Vaadin application applying the MVP pattern in this recipe and therefore the login form will be of low complexity. The login form will consist of two text fields and a `login` button. When a user clicks on the `login` button, the request is forwarded to the presenter. The presenter calls the service in order to fetch a user from the database. Then the presenter notifies the user interface about the success or the failure.

> Basic information about Model View Presenter pattern can be found on Wikipedia at `http://en.wikipedia.org/wiki/Model-view-presenter`.
>
> More detailed description of MVP pattern is available at `http://martinfowler.com/eaaDev/ModelViewPresenter.html`.

Getting ready

Before we start, we create a simple class diagram. Start reading the class diagram from the `MyVaadinUI` class. `MyVaadinUI` creates all the three MVP layers; view, presenter, and model (model is represented by `UserService`).

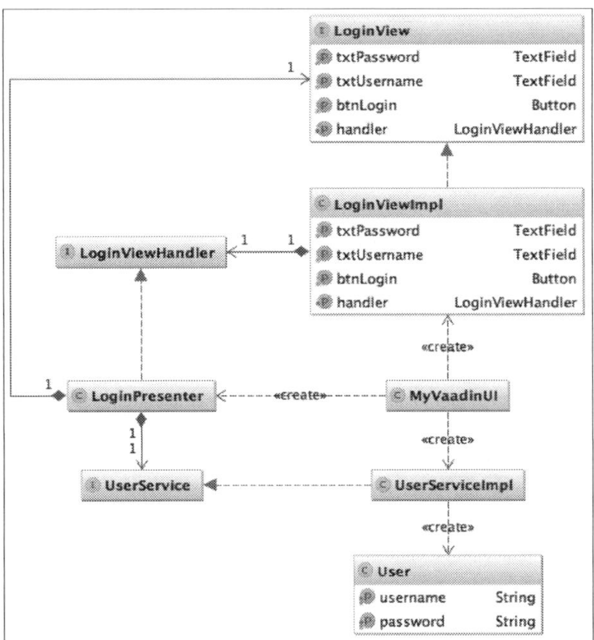

How to do it...

Perform the following steps:

1. Create the model layer, which is represented by `UserService` interface and classes `UserServiceDummy` and `User`. Also, create an exception named `ServiceException` that will be used for the service layer.

```
public interface UserService {
  User login(String username, String password) throws
ServiceException;
}

public class UserServiceDummy implements UserService {
  @Override
  public User login(String username, String password) throws
ServiceException {
    return new User(username, password);
  }
}

public class User {
  private String username;
  private String password;
  // generate constructor and getters and setters
}

public class ServiceException extends Exception {
}
```

2. Create the `LoginView` interface, which defines all the needed methods for the view layer. The presenter will communicate with the view layer via this interface.

```
public interface LoginView extends View {

    void setHandler(LoginViewHandler handler);
    void init();

    TextField getTxtUsername();

    TextField getTxtPassword();
    Button getBtnLogin();

    void afterSuccessfulLogin();
}
```

3. Create the `LoginViewHandler` interface. The presenter will implement this interface and the `login()` method will be called from the view layer when a user clicks on the `login` button.

```
public interface LoginViewHandler {
    void login();
}
```

4. Now we can implement the `LoginView` interface, lay out the components, and decide what should happen after a successful login:

```
public class LoginViewImpl extends VerticalLayout implements
LoginView {

    private LoginViewHandler handler;

    private TextField txtUsername;
    private TextField txtPassword;

    private Button btnLogin;

    @Override
    public void setHandler(LoginViewHandler handler) {
        this.handler = handler;
    }

    @Override
    public void init() {
        txtUsername = new TextField("Username:");
        addComponent(txtUsername);
        txtPassword = new TextField("Password:");
        addComponent(txtPassword);

        btnLogin = new Button("Login");
        addComponent(btnLogin);
        btnLogin.addClickListener(new Button.ClickListener() {
            @Override
            public void buttonClick(Button.ClickEvent event) {
                handler.login();
            }
        });
    }

    @Override
    public TextField getTxtUsername() {
        return txtUsername;
    }
```

```
    @Override
    public TextField getTxtPassword() {
        return txtPassword;
    }

    @Override
    public void enter(ViewChangeListener.ViewChangeEvent event) {
    }

    @Override
    public Button getBtnLogin() {
        return btnLogin;
    }

    @Override
    public void afterSuccessfulLogin() {
        UI.getCurrent().getNavigator().navigateTo("only-for-
signed-in-users");
    }
}
```

5. The presenter implements `LoginViewHandler`, which defines the `login()` method. The `login()` method is called after a user clicks on the `login` button.

```
public class LoginPresenter implements LoginViewHandler {

    private LoginView view;
    private UserService service;

    public LoginPresenter(LoginView view, UserService service) {
        this.view = view;
        this.service = service;
    }

    @Override
    public void login() {
        TextField txtUsername = view.getTxtUsername();
        TextField txtPassword = view.getTxtPassword();

        String username = txtUsername.getValue();
        String password = txtPassword.getValue();

        try {
            service.login(username, password);

            view.afterSuccessfulLogin();
        } catch (ServiceException e) {
            // TODO: log exception
```

```
                // TODO: notify view about failure
            }
        }
    }
```

6. The last steps are used to bind the login view with the user service via the login presenter, add the login view to the navigator, and navigate a user to the login view:

```
public class MyVaadinUI extends UI {

    @Override
    protected void init(VaadinRequest request) {
        Navigator navigator = new Navigator(this, this);

        LoginView loginView = new LoginViewImpl();
        LoginPresenter loginPresenter = new
LoginPresenter(loginView, new UserServiceDummy());
        loginView.setHandler(loginPresenter);
        loginView.init();
        navigator.addView("", loginView);

        setNavigator(navigator);
        navigator.navigateTo("");
    }
}
```

7. Run the application and test the `login` button. It now redirects users to a new view. The next step would be to implement the other view.

How it works...

In this example, we used the MVP pattern to separate the application into three layers: model, view, and presenter. Now we will see how we did it and what benefits we get from using the MVP pattern.

The service layer is basically represented by the `UserService` interface, which defines the `login()` method, and which is used in the presenter. `UserServiceDummy` is just a dummy service always returning a new user when the `login()` method is called. In a real project, the dummy service should be replaced by a real service fetching a user from a data source.

The login presenter knows just the interfaces to the service and the view layers. Because the `LoginPresenter` presenter contains references to the `LoginView` and the `UserService` interfaces, we can easily mock these two interfaces and write unit tests covering the logic of the login presenter. We will show you how to make unit tests for the MVP pattern in the *Unit testing in an MVP pattern* recipe.

The view layer redirects all the user's actions and needs for the communication with the service layer to the presenter. We added a new click listener to the `login` button. Inside the `buttonClicked` method, we call the `login()` method from the presenter. Which means the presenter is notified when a user clicks on the `login` button, the presenter calls the service and propagates the response to the view by calling the `afterSuccessfulLogin` method from the `LoginView` interface.

There's more...

In the `LoginPresenter` presenter's `login()` method, there is a `try-catch` block. When the login operation is successful, the `afterSuccessfulLogin` method from the `LoginView` interface is called and the user is notified about success of the login operation. In our example, we redirect a user to the other view, which is accessible only to the logged users.

We also need to take care about alternative scenarios, for example, when the user is not found in a database or fetching of a user fails when, for example, the database is offline:

```
try {
    User user = service.login(username, password);
    if (user != null) {
        view.afterSuccessfulLogin();
    } else {
        view.afterFailedLogin();
    }
} catch (ServiceException e) {
    log.error(e);
    view.afterServiceException();
}
```

Model View Presenter for a view with two panels

This recipe is the continuation of the previous *Login form with Model View Presenter* recipe. In this recipe, we will create a complex view, which will consist of two panels. The first panel will be used for adding new items and the second for showing the list of items.

The application will be about adding tags to the database and showing the list of all the tags from a database. The layout of the user interface is as follows:

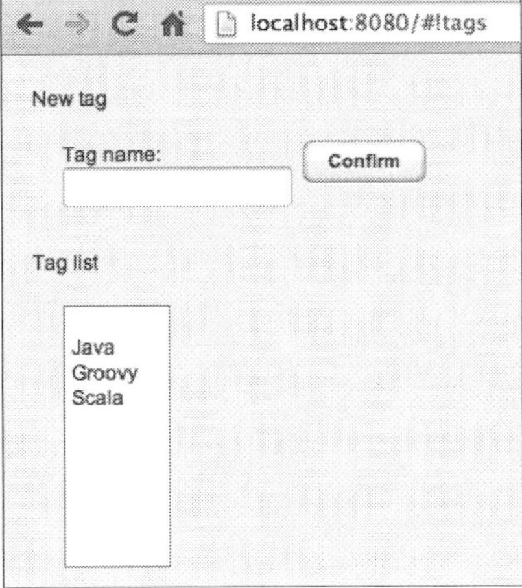

Getting ready

Before we start, we create a simplified class diagram of the application we are going to develop. Start reading the class diagram from the `MyVaadinUI` class. `MyVaadinUI` creates the tag view, tag presenter, and the tag service. The implementation of the `TagView` interface, the `TagViewImpl` class, contains two layouts, the first one for creating new tags and the second to display the list of the tags. `TagService` provides and saves the instances of the `Tag` class. `TagPresenter` binds view and service layer together via the interfaces `TagView` and `TagService`.

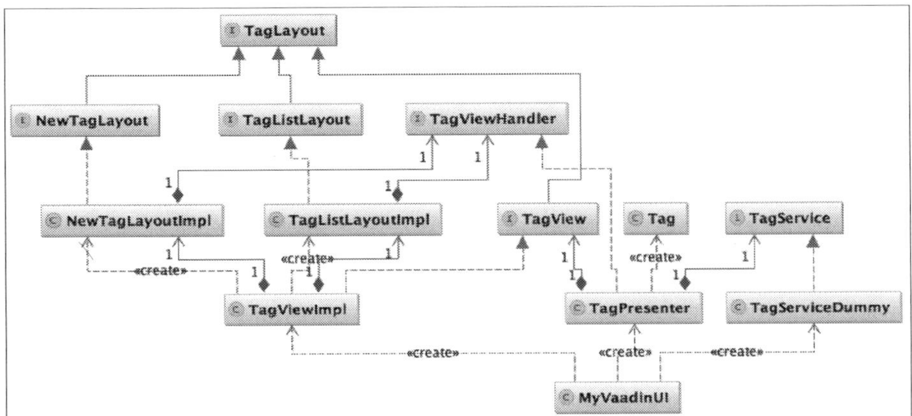

We need to decide where to put our classes. See the following screenshot, which shows the packaging structure for our example:

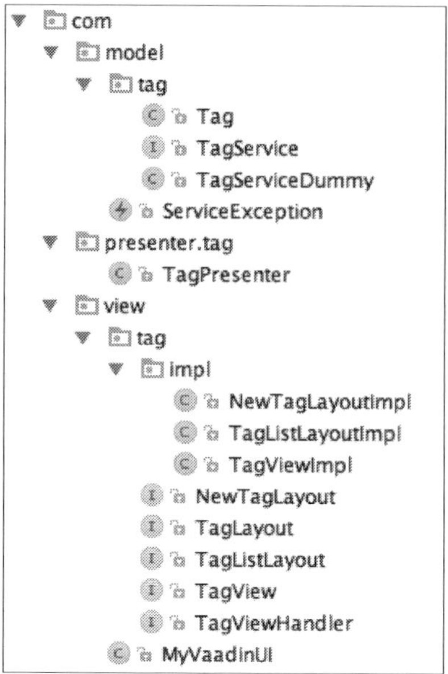

How to do it...

Perform the following steps:

1. Create the interface for the service layer, which takes care of fetching and saving tags. Also create an exception named `ServiceException` for the service layer.

```
public interface TagService {
    List<Tag> findAll() throws ServiceException;
    void save(Tag tag) throws ServiceException;
}
public class ServiceException extends Exception {
}
```

2. Make a dummy service, which implements the methods from `TagService`. `TagServiceDummy` just pretends to be a service that fetches data from a data source. The dummy class can be used from the beginning of development and should be replaced by a real service that fetches data from a data source.

```
public class TagServiceDummy implements TagService {

    ArrayList<Tag> tags = new ArrayList<Tag>();

    public TagServiceDummy() {
```

```
        Tag java = new Tag("Java");
        Tag groovy = new Tag("Groovy");
        Tag scala = new Tag("Scala");
        tags.add(java);
        tags.add(groovy);
        tags.add(scala);
    }

    @Override
    public List<Tag> findAll() {
        return tags;
    }

    @Override
    public void save(Tag tag) {
        tags.add(tag);
    }
}
```

3. Create the `Tag` class, which contains the name of a tag. The `Tag` class can be expanded with other fields, such as `creationDate`, `author`, and so on. Generate getters, setters, and the constructor for the `name` field:

```
public class Tag {
    private String name;
    // generate constructor, getter and setter for name field
}
```

4. Create an interface that defines common methods for all the layouts inside the tag view.

```
public interface TagLayout {
    void setHandler(TagViewHandler handler);
    void init();
}
```

5. Create an interface for the tag view and define two getters—`getNewTagLayout`, which returns reference to the layout that contains components for adding of a new tag and `getTagListLayout`, which returns a reference to the layout that shows the list of tags.

```
import com.vaadin.navigator.View;

public interface TagView extends View, TagLayout {
    NewTagLayout getNewTagLayout();
    TagListLayout getTagListLayout();
}
```

6. Create the `NewTagLayout` interface, which defines methods that are required to handle adding of a new tag:

```
public interface NewTagLayout extends TagLayout {
    TextField getTxtTagName();
    void afterSuccessfulSave();
}
```

7. Create `TagListLayout` that defines the `afterSuccessfulFetch` method, which will be called from the tag presenter after the tags are received from a data source:

```
public interface TagListLayout extends TagLayout {
    void afterSuccessfulFetch(List<Tag> tags);
}
```

8. Now, we need to create an interface, which connects the view with a presenter. Create `TagViewHandler`, which defines the `addTag()` and `showTagList()` methods. These two methods will be called from the view layer. The presenter will implement them.

```
public interface TagViewHandler {
    void addTag();
    void showTagList();
}
```

9. Next, implement the `NewTagLayout` interface, which extends `HorizontalLayout`, creates, and lays out text field and button components. Add to the button a new click listener that just calls the `addTag()` method from the `TagViewHandler` interface:

```
public class NewTagLayoutImpl extends HorizontalLayout implements 
NewTagLayout {

    private TextField txtTagName;
    private TagViewHandler handler;
    private Button btnConfirm;

    @Override
    public void setHandler(TagViewHandler handler) {
        this.handler = handler;
    }

    @Override
    public void init() {
        setCaption("New tag");
        setSpacing(true);
        setMargin(true);

        txtTagName = new TextField("Tag name:");
        addComponent(txtTagName);
```

```
        btnConfirm = new Button("Confirm");
        btnConfirm.addClickListener(new Button.ClickListener() {
            @Override
            public void buttonClick(Button.ClickEvent clickEvent)
{
                handler.addTag();
            }
        });
        addComponent(btnConfirm);
    }

    public Button getBtnConfirm() {
        return btnConfirm;
    }

    public TextField getTxtTagName() {
        return txtTagName;
    }

    @Override
    public void afterSuccessfulSave() {
        txtTagName.setValue("");
        txtTagName.focus();
    }
}
```

10. Implementation of `TagListLayout` will contain a `ListSelect` component for showing the list of tags. We call the `showTagList()` method from `TagViewHandler`, inside the `init()` method, so the tags are fetched when the layout is initialized. Then we implement the `afterSuccessfulFetch()` method from the `TagListLayout` interface, which is called after the successful fetch of the tag list.

```
public class TagListLayoutImpl extends HorizontalLayout implements
TagListLayout {

    private ListSelect tagList;
    private TagViewHandler handler;

    @Override
    public void init() {
        setCaption("Tag list");
        setSpacing(true);
        setMargin(true);

        tagList = new ListSelect();
        tagList.setItemCaptionPropertyId("name");
```

```
        addComponent(tagList);

        handler.showTagList();
    }

    @Override
    public void setHandler(TagViewHandler handler) {
        this.handler = handler;
    }

    @Override
    public void afterSuccessfulFetch(List<Tag> tags) {
        tagList.setContainerDataSource(new
BeanItemContainer<Tag>(Tag.class, tags));
    }
}
```

11. Implement `TagViewImpl` that consists of `NewTagLayoutImpl` and `TagListLayoutImpl`. We initialize these two layouts and implement the `setHandler()` method, which delegates the handler setting to the `setHandler()` method from `NewTagLayout` and `TagListLayout`.

```
public class TagViewImpl extends VerticalLayout implements TagView
{

    private NewTagLayoutImpl newTagLayout;
    private TagListLayoutImpl tagListLayout;

    @Override
    public void enter(ViewChangeListener.ViewChangeEvent e) {
    }

    @Override
    public NewTagLayoutImpl getNewTagLayout() {
        return newTagLayout;
    }

    @Override
    public TagListLayoutImpl getTagListLayout() {
        return tagListLayout;
    }

    @Override
    public void setHandler(TagViewHandler handler) {
        newTagLayout.setHandler(handler);
        tagListLayout.setHandler(handler);
    }
```

```
    @Override
    public void init() {
        setSpacing(true);
        setMargin(true);

        newTagLayout = new NewTagLayoutImpl();
        addComponent(newTagLayout);
        tagListLayout = new TagListLayoutImpl();
        addComponent(tagListLayout);
    }
}
```

12. Now we create `TagPresenter`, which implements the methods that are called from the view—the `TagViewHandler` interface. `TagPresenter` needs to have access to the tag view and tag service, in order to handle the `addTag()` and `showTagList()` methods. Therefore we create a constructor into which we have to pass implementations of the `TagView` and `TagService` interfaces:

```
public class TagPresenter implements TagViewHandler {

    private TagView tagView;
    private TagService tagService;

    public TagPresenter(TagView view, TagService service) {
        this.tagView = view;
        this.tagService = service;
    }

    @Override
    public void addTag() {
        NewTagLayout layout = tagView.getNewTagLayout();
        TextField txtTagName = layout.getTxtTagName();
        String value = txtTagName.getValue();

        try {
            Tag tag = new Tag(value);
            tagService.save(tag);

            layout.afterSuccessfulSave();
            showTagList();
        } catch (ServiceException e) {
            // TODO: log the exception
            // TODO: notify view about failure
        }
    }
```

```
    @Override
    public void showTagList() {
        try {
            TagListLayout layout = tagView.getTagListLayout();
            layout.afterSuccessfulFetch(tags);
        } catch (ServiceException e) {
            // TODO: log the exception
            // TODO: notify view about failure
        }
    }
}
```

13. Now we create the `MyVaadinUI` class, where we put together all the classes we have made. First we create and initialize the tag view. Then we make the dummy service, which we pass, together with the view, to the tag presenter. Then we set the handler to the view, so the handler is passed to the layouts that are responsible for the tag creation and showing the tag list.

```
public class MyVaadinUI extends UI {

    @Override
    protected void init(VaadinRequest request) {
        Navigator navigator = new Navigator(this, this);

        TagView view = new TagViewImpl();
        view.init();

        TagService service = new TagServiceDummy();
        TagPresenter handler = new TagPresenter(view, service);
        view.setHandler(handler);

        view.getNewTagLayout().init();
        view.getTagListLayout().init();

        navigator.addView("tags", view);

        setNavigator(navigator);
        navigator.navigateTo("tags");
    }
}
```

How it works...

In this recipe, we saw one way to implement MVP for more complex layouts. We need to keep in mind that we always have to consider proper implementation of the MVP pattern for our project and that the way, which we have described in this recipe, is not applicable for all the cases.

Now let's clearly state which classes represent which layers from the Model View Presenter pattern.

`Tag`, `TagService`, `TagServiceDummy`, and `ServiceException` classes represent the model.

`TagLayout`, `TagView`, `TagViewHandler`, `NewTagLayout`, `TagListLayout`, `TagViewImpl`, `TagListLayoutImpl`, and `NewTagLayoutImpl` represent the view layer.

And just one class, `TagPresenter`, represents the presenter layer.

There's more...

The service layer in this recipe is used only for loading and saving of items. But we might place some logic inside the service layer. If we do that, we could consider moving database operations, such as database queries, to a Data Access Object (DAO) pattern that could be used by the service layer.

More information about the Data Access Object (DAO) pattern can be found at `http://www.oracle.com/technetwork/java/dataaccessobject-138824.html`.

See also

We have put little focus on the service layer because the service layer can be implemented in many ways depending on many technical decisions. Describing the service layer in all the details is a big task, which is beyond the scope of this recipe and book. To give you a hint, we can implement the service layer in the Spring framework. The detailed tutorial how to get started with the service layer in Spring can be found at the following link:

- `http://blog.springsource.org/2011/01/07/green-beans-getting-started-with-spring-in-your-service-tier`

Unit testing in an MVP pattern

Unit tests are testing code without any outside dependencies. The outside dependencies are usually mocked by framework such as, in this recipe, **Mockito** (`https://code.google.com/p/mockito`).

In this recipe, we will demonstrate testability of the MVP pattern, so we will write unit tests for the presenter and view. We will utilize the `LoginPresenter`, `UserService`, `LoginView`, `LoginViewHandler`, and `LoginViewImpl` classes from the *Login form with Model View Presenter* recipe.

Getting ready

Get the code from the *Login form with Model View Presenter* recipe.

How to do it...

Perform the following steps:

1. Create the `LoginViewImplTest` class inside the test folder:

   ```
   public class LoginViewImplTest { }
   ```

2. Before we start testing, we need to set up the environment for running a unit test. Put the following code inside the `LoginViewImplTest` class:

   ```
   private LoginView view;
   private LoginViewHandler handler;

   @Before
   public void setUp() {
       view = new LoginViewImpl();
       handler = mock(LoginViewHandler.class);
       view.setHandler(handler);
       view.init();
   }
   ```

3. Write the first test, which verifies that the `login()` method is called after the user clicks the `login` button:

   ```
   @Test
   public void isLoginWorkingWhenLoginButtonIsClicked() {
       view.getBtnLogin().click();

       verify(handler, times(1)).login();
   }
   ```

4. We also want to test the login presenter. Create a new class named `LoginPresenterTest`.

   ```
   public class LoginPresenterTest { }
   ```

5. Set up the environment for the unit test. Mock the `LoginView` and `UserService` classes:

   ```
   private LoginView view;
   private UserService service;
   private LoginPresenter presenter;

   @Before
   ```

```
    public void setUp() throws Exception {
        view = mock(LoginView.class);

        service = mock(UserService.class);
        presenter = new LoginPresenter(view, service);
    }
```

6. Write a test, which verifies that the `login()` method from `LoginPresenter` is working properly, in case the username and password were filled in.

```
    @Test
    public void isLoginWorking() throws Exception {
        when(view.getTxtUsername()).thenReturn(new
TextField("Jimmy"));
        when(view.getTxtPassword()).thenReturn(new
TextField("Jimmy123"));

        presenter.login();

        Mockito.verify(service, times(1)).login(anyString(),
anyString());
        Mockito.verify(view, times(1)).afterSuccessfulLogin();
    }
```

7. Run the tests from IDE, or from Maven `mvn test`.

How it works...

This recipe shows how easy it is to write unit tests for Vaadin applications, which are written on top of the Model View Presenter pattern.

Let's describe how we have tested the login view and presenter.

Inside the `LoginViewImplTest` class, we created two methods. The method `isLoginWorkingWhenLoginButtonIsClicked()` with the `@Test` annotation is a unit test, checking whether the `login()` method from the login presenter is called exactly one time, after the `login` button was clicked. The `setUp()` method with the `@Before` annotation, is executed before each unit test, so a new instance of `LoginViewImpl` and a new mock of `LoginViewHandler` are created before the unit test execution. That way we ensure that each unit test will be executed on the same conditions.

In the `setUp` method from the `LoginPresenterTest` class, we created mocks of the `LoginView` and `UserService` interfaces. We are not using the implementations of `LoginView` and `UserService` interfaces, because the unit tests need to test the code without any outside dependencies.

Inside the `isLoginWorking` unit test, we test the following scenario: when the `login()` method from the login presenter is called, the username and password are provided, then the `login()` method from `UserService` and the `afterSuccessfulLogin` method are called.

There's more...

Another test could verify whether the empty inputs are ignored, so the user service is not called and the `afterFailedLogin` method from the view is called. Inside the `afterFailedLogin` method, we can implement notification about a failed login attempt, like so:

```
@Test
public void isLoginAttemptIgnoredForEmptyInputs() throws Exception {
  when(view.getTxtUsername()).thenReturn(new TextField(""));
  when(view.getTxtPassword()).thenReturn(new TextField(""));

  presenter.login();

  Mockito.verify(service, times(0)).login(anyString(), anyString());
  Mockito.verify(view, times(1)).afterFailedLogin();
}
```

See also

The complete implementation of the MVP pattern along with the tests is available on the following Github repository:

- `https://github.com/ondrej-kvasnovsky/vaadin-model-view-presenter`

Improving the application's startup time

In this recipe, we will show how to optimize widget set loading strategies. We will show how to speed up the starting of a Vaadin application by reducing the number of widgets that are initially downloaded from the server. A widget is a client-side implementation of a component, which needs to be downloaded to the client browser.

First, we will create a simple UI class, which we are going to optimize:

```
public class MyVaadinUI extends UI {

    @Override
    protected void init(VaadinRequest request) {
        new WidgetSetOptimizer().extend(this);

        final VerticalLayout layout = new VerticalLayout();
        layout.setMargin(true);
```

```
        setContent(layout);

        Button button = new Button("Click Me");
        button.addClickListener(new Button.ClickListener() {
            public void buttonClick(ClickEvent event) {
                layout.addComponent(new Label("Thank you for
clicking"));
            }
        });
        layout.addComponent(button);
    }
}
```

The preceding application code uses `UI`, `VerticalLayout`, and the `Button` components. Only the client-side implementations for these three components should be loaded during the application startup.

In a real-life scenario, we might have many components on the initial view and it might be difficult to get the list of components that should be loaded at the startup. There is an add-on called **Widget Set Optimizer**, which helps us with optimization of widget loading. We will use it in this recipe.

Getting ready

Add the dependency to the Widget Set Optimizer add-on of the project and then recompile the widget set. The JAR file can be downloaded from `https://vaadin.com/directory#addon/widget-set-optimizer`.

Because Maven dependency was not present on the add-on home page, I have added it to my Maven repository. Do check the Widget Set Optimizer add-on page for any updates or up-to-date Maven dependency. If the Maven dependency is not there, you can use the following:

```
<repository>
    <id>qiiip-repo</id>
    <url>http://qiiip.org/mavenRepo</url>
</repository>
<dependency>
    <groupId>org.vaadin.addons</groupId>
    <artifactId>widgetsetoptimizer</artifactId>
    <version>0.1.0</version>
</dependency>
```

How to do it...

Perform the following steps:

1. Add the following line into the `init` method inside the `MyVaadinUI` class:

   ```
   new WidgetSetOptimizer().extend(this);
   ```

2. Run the application and open it with the `?debug` parameter in URL, as shown here:

   ```
   http://localhost:8080/?debug
   ```

3. In order to see what widgets are currently loaded, click on the **SU** button. A list of component connectors appears in the debug window:

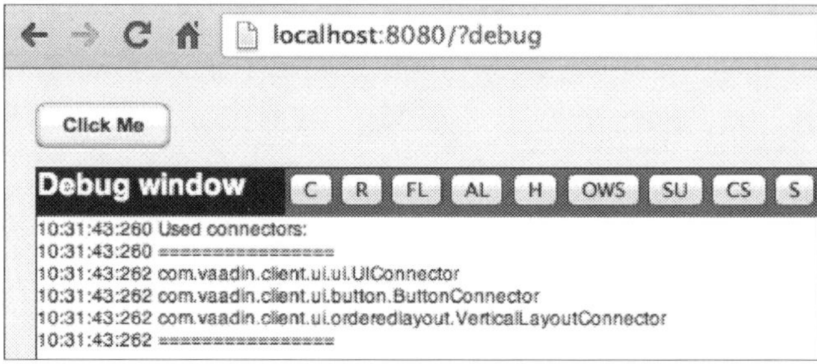

4. Click on the **OWS** button that generates optimization code in the server console:

```
Debug window  C R FL AL H OWS SU CS S
10:43:04:640 Variable burst to be sent to server:
10:43:04:641   4 (class com.vaadin.client.ui.ui.UIConnector) :
10:43:04:641         com.vaadin.shared.ui.ui.UIServerRpc.resize([480, 859, 859, 480])
10:43:04:642   5 (class org.vaadin.artur.widgetsetoptimizer.client.widgetsetoptimizer.WidgetSetOptimizerConnector) :
10:43:04:642         org.vaadin.artur.widgetsetoptimizer.client.widgetsetoptimizer.WidgetSetOptimizerServerRpc.generateOptimizedWidgetSe
10:43:04:645 Making UIDL Request with params: 235baed0-e67c-47f9-a701-34a8d24eb2bd[["4","com.vaadin.shared.ui.ui.UIServerRpc","re
10:43:04:651 Server visit took 6ms
10:43:04:652 JSON parsing took 0ms
10:43:04:652 Handling message from server
10:43:04:652  * Handling resources from server
10:43:04:652  * Handling type inheritance map from server
10:43:04:654 Handling type ma
10:43:04:654 Handling resource
10:43:04:654  * Handling locale
10:43:04:654  * Handling meta i
10:43:04:654  * Creating conne
10:43:04:654  * Updating connector states
Optimized widgetset configuration files output to server console
```

5. Go to the server console and follow the instructions that have been printed out:

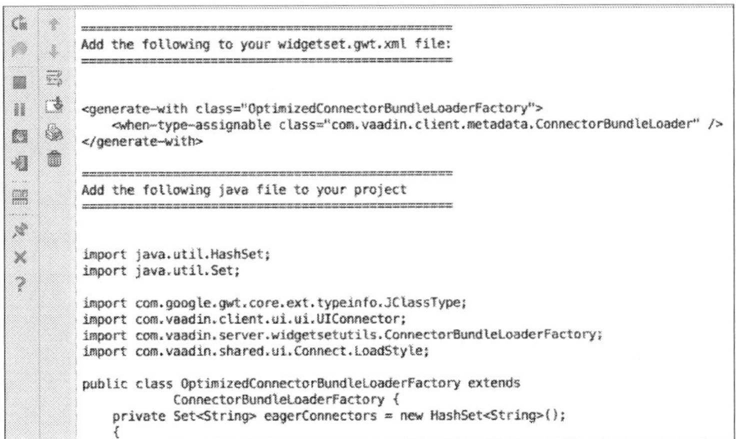

6. Create the `OptimizedConnectorBundleLoaderFactory` class, copy and paste the generated code from the server console and fix the imports:

```
package com;

import com.google.gwt.core.ext.typeinfo.JClassType;
import com.vaadin.server.widgetsetutils.
ConnectorBundleLoaderFactory;
import com.vaadin.shared.ui.Connect;
import com.vaadin.ui.*;

import java.util.*;

public class OptimizedConnectorBundleLoaderFactory extends
        ConnectorBundleLoaderFactory {
  private Set<String> eagerConnectors = new HashSet<String>();

  {
      eagerConnectors.add(com.vaadin.client.ui.orderedlayout.
VerticalLayoutConnector.class.getName());
      eagerConnectors.add(com.vaadin.client.ui.button.
ButtonConnector.class.getName());
      eagerConnectors.add(com.vaadin.client.ui.ui.UIConnector.
class.getName());
  }

  @Override
  protected Connect.LoadStyle getLoadStyle(JClassType
connectorType) {
```

```
        if (eagerConnectors.contains(connectorType.
getQualifiedBinaryName())) {
          return Connect.LoadStyle.EAGER;
        } else {
          return Connect.LoadStyle.DEFERRED;
        }
      }
    }
```

7. Add the generated XML from the server console into the `AppWidgetSet.gwt.xml` file. Do not forget to update the full class name of `OptimizedConnectorBundleLoaderFactory` inside the `class` parameter:

```
<module>
  <generate-with class="com.OptimizedConnectorBundleLoaderFactory">
    <when-type-assignable class="com.vaadin.client.metadata.
ConnectorBundleLoader"/>
  </generate-with>
```

8. Recompile the widget set.

How it works...

When the Vaadin application is starting up, the default widget set is uploading all the available components from the server to the client browser. All the available components are downloaded, because Vaadin does not know which components are going to be used on the startup page. Therefore, we need to always optimize the widget download strategy.

There are three strategies for widget downloading:

- **Eager**: Widget is downloaded during the initial payload
- **Deferred**: Widget is downloaded right after the initial rendering of an application is done
- **Lazy**: Widget is downloaded when the component is going to be rendered, which can slow down the rendering speed

The Widget Set Optimizer add-on uses the eager and deferred strategies. All the components that will be eagerly loaded are inserted into the `eagerConnectors` collection. The `getLoadStyle` method is called for each connector type. The other components, which are not in the `eagerConnectors` collection, will be uploaded after the application is rendered.

Avoid sluggish UI – lazy loaded tables

A Table is probably one of the most used and complex components in Vaadin. We need to keep the following points in mind when using a table from Vaadin, so that our applications do not become sluggish:

- Use lazy loaded container to obtain data from a database
- Don't use heavy layouts in generated columns (use `CssLayout` instead)
- Try to avoid complex forms inside table cells
- Turn on lazy loading of rows from server to client
- Optimize caching with the `setCacheRate` function

The first point is very likely the most time consuming one in case we have large data to be shown in the table. We must not fetch all the data from the database and put it to the table. We will have a look at how to create a standard table that fetches data from a database lazily.

It is important to understand how a Vaadin table works. There are two types of lazy loading. The first one is done when a client renders the table. In that moment, the table lazily fetches data from the server to the client. That means even if you add 1000 items into the table in Java server code, only a few (for example, 15 items) are going to be actually transferred to the client.

The second type of lazy loading can be implemented on a container level. The containers are responsible for providing data to tables and therefore we will hook there and do the lazy loading from a database.

We will extend `BeanContainer` in this example. You might pick up some other container as well. However, we want to utilize `BeanItem` to easily get values from a domain class.

How is the lazy loading going to work in the bean container? When the table is displayed for the first time, the container tries to fetch rows between certain indexes depending on the `cacheRate` value (for instance, start index at `0`, end index at `46`).

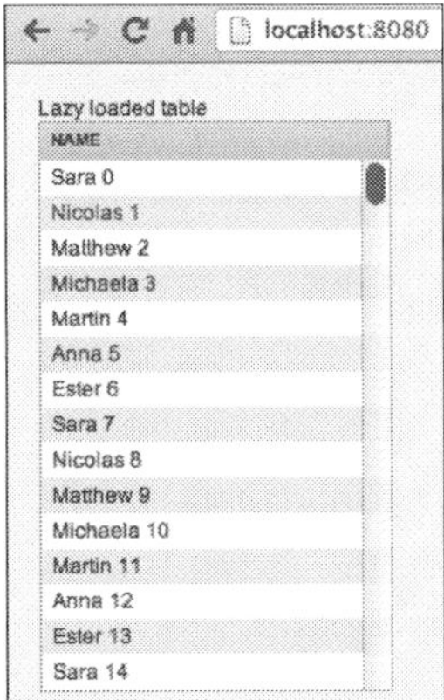

When we scroll down in the table, the bean container just fetches the items that are going to be shown. So the table fetches data, for example, from these ranges with a start index of `149` and an end index of `224` (depending on where we have scrolled to):

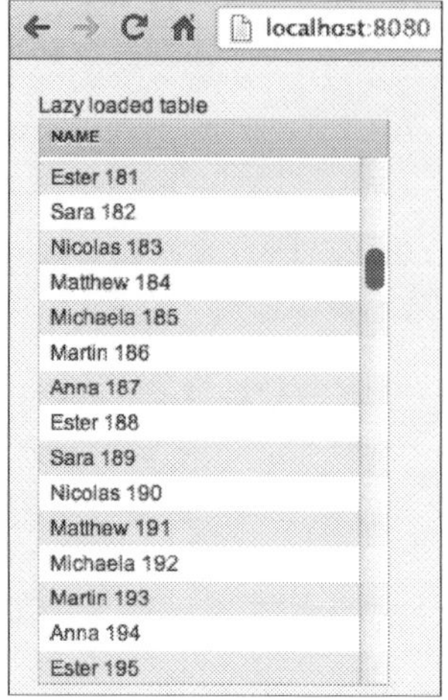

Getting ready

There are no external dependencies needed. We can just create a new Vaadin project and go ahead.

How to do it...

Perform the following steps:

1. First, we create a UI class where we use `VerticalLayout` on which we place the table. We need to create two instances. The first one is the table and the second is the container. The container will be implemented in the next step.

```
public class MyVaadinUI extends UI {

    @Override
    protected void init(VaadinRequest request) {
        final VerticalLayout layout = new VerticalLayout();
        layout.setMargin(true);
        setContent(layout);

        Table table = new Table("Lazy loaded table");
        table.setWidth("200px");

        LazyLoadedContainer container = new
LazyLoadedContainer(User.class);
```

```
        table.setContainerDataSource(container);
        layout.addComponent(table);
    }
}
```

2. The container extends `BeanContainer` because we want to expose fields from our domain class `User` automatically. In order to make it lazy loaded, we need to override three methods. The `size()` method needs to return count from the database (how many records can be fetched into the table). The `getItem(objectId)` method just wraps domain object into `BeanItem`. And the most important method, `getItemIds`, returns items for a specific range that is requested from the client.

3. We are using `UserService` that returns faked data from an in-memory collection. We should replace `userService` by a real service that fetches data from a database in a real project. In the `getItemIds` method, we print out (for learning reasons) the index range from which the table requests the rows for rendering:

```
class LazyLoadedContainer extends BeanContainer {

    private UserService userService = new UserService();

    public LazyLoadedContainer(Class type) {
        super(type);
    }

    @Override
    public int size() {
        return userService.size();
    }

    @Override
    public BeanItem getItem(Object itemId) {
        return new BeanItem((User) itemId);
    }

    @Override
    public List getItemIds(int startIndex, int numberOfIds) {
        int endIndex = startIndex + numberOfIds;
        System.out.println("startIndex: " + startIndex + ",
endIndex: " + endIndex);
        List<User> list = userService.list(startIndex, endIndex);
        return list;
    }
}
```

4. In `UserService`, we create faked users and put them into the collection:

```
public class UserService {

    private List<User> dbFake = new ArrayList<User>();

    public UserService() {
        for (int i = 0; i < 1000; i++) {
            dbFake.add(new User("Sara " + i++));
            dbFake.add(new User("Nicolas " + i++));
            dbFake.add(new User("Matthew " + i++));
            dbFake.add(new User("Michaela " + i++));
            dbFake.add(new User("Martin " + i++));
            dbFake.add(new User("Anna " + i++));
            dbFake.add(new User("Ester " + i));
        }
    }

    public int size() {
        return dbFake.size();
    }

    public List<User> list(int startIndex, int endIndex) {
        List<User> users = dbFake.subList(startIndex, endIndex);
        return users;
    }
}
```

5. Now we create a domain class called `User`. Make sure there are getters and setters for all the fields that should be visible in the table. Otherwise, `BeanItem` will not help and display any columns.

```
public class User {

    private String name;

    public User(String name) {
        this.name = name;
    }

    public String getName() {
        return name;
    }

    public void setName(String name) {
        this.name = name;
    }
}
```

6. Run the application, test the scrolling, and check the output in the server console, which has been generated from the `getItemIds` method.

How it works...

When a user scrolls in the table that is displayed in the client's browser, then the client asks the server for data in a specific range. We then make a query to the database and get the items from the requested range.

There's more...

Maybe you noticed that the table is fetching some items twice or multiple times. That can be avoided by setting the cache rate.

What happens when we set the cache rate to `0`, like so:

```
table.setCacheRate(0);
```

When we set the cache rate to `0` and then scroll in the table, we get data from these indexes:

```
startIndex: 0, endIndex: 15
startIndex: 14, endIndex: 30
startIndex: 29, endIndex: 45
startIndex: 45, endIndex: 60
startIndex: 45, endIndex: 61
startIndex: 62, endIndex: 77
startIndex: 62, endIndex: 78
```

We actually say that we don't want to fetch data up front and therefore when a user scrolls he or she will see a white area in the table because no data was cached.

However, if we leave the default value of the cache rate, the calls will look something like this:

```
startIndex: 0, endIndex: 15
startIndex: 0, endIndex: 46
startIndex: 0, endIndex: 61
startIndex: 1, endIndex: 77
startIndex: 19, endIndex: 95
startIndex: 35, endIndex: 111
startIndex: 52, endIndex: 128
```

Scrolling becomes smoother but there will be also bigger traffic to the database.

We could also try to set the cache rate to `10`. The calls, then, will become something like this:

```
startIndex: 0, endIndex: 15
startIndex: 0, endIndex: 166
startIndex: 0, endIndex: 219
startIndex: 0, endIndex: 264
```

Scrolling in the table is very smooth and also there are not that many calls to database.

Maybe we should try to set the cache rate to `50`:

```
startIndex: 0, endIndex: 15
startIndex: 0, endIndex: 766
```

Only two calls have been made. That might look more efficient but we somehow feel it is not perfect. When we scroll down to the table, it calls another fetch and a lot of database records are fetched again.

```
startIndex: 236, endIndex: 1001
```

If we need to have a standard, scrollable Vaadin table, then we need to accept this lazy loaded approach or we can use some caching framework to cache items from a database and lower the traffic. Alternatively, we can use the **PagedTable** add-on that makes fetching the data from different ranges much more straightforward. The PagedTable add-on is explained in the next recipe.

See also

There are many implementations of the lazy loaded container. If you don't want to make your own lazy container, have a look at the following implementations:

- `https://vaadin.com/directory#addon/lazy-query-container`
- `https://vaadin.com/directory#addon/vaadin-jpacontainer`
- `https://vaadin.com/directory#addon/vaadin-sqlcontainer`
- `https://vaadin.com/directory#addon/jpa-criteria-lazy-container`
- `https://vaadin.com/directory#addon/lucenecontainer`
- `https://vaadin.com/directory#addon/transactional-container`
- `https://github.com/ondrej-kvasnovsky/lazy-container`

Avoid sluggish UI – paged tables

The standard Vaadin table might not be good enough for some scenarios. In case we display thousands of rows, it becomes difficult to actually find a specific row by scrolling up and down. In that case, we would rather use the classical paged table. Up-to-date info about the PagedTable add-on can be found at `https://vaadin.com/directory#addon/pagedtable`.

In this recipe, we will use the paged table from the repository at `https://github.com/ondrej-kvasnovsky/PagedTable`. It is a forked paged table, which is enhanced and contains a few fixes.

We are going to implement a paged table, as shown in the following screenshot:

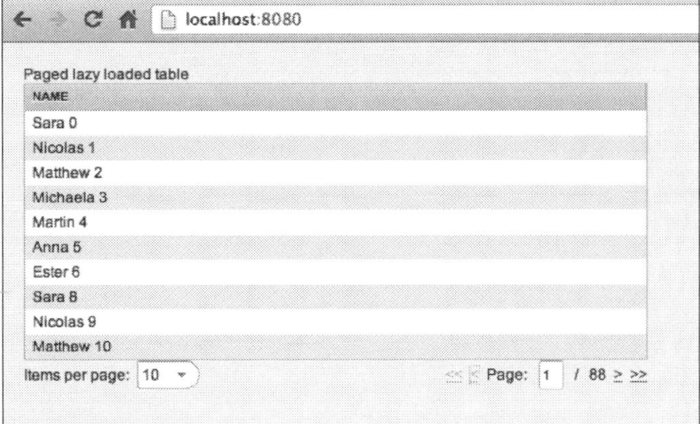

Getting ready

Create a project in Maven or some other tool that handles dependencies easily. We are going to use the PagedTable add-on and so dependency management might be handy.

How to do it...

Perform the following steps:

1. Add the following repository and dependency to `pom.xml` or download the JAR file and place it in the `WEB-INF\lib` folder:

```
<repository>
   <id>qiiip-repo</id>
   <url>http://qiiip.org/mavenRepo</url>
</repository>
<dependency>
   <groupId>org.vaadin.addons</groupId>
   <artifactId>pagedtable</artifactId>
   <version>0.6.7</version>
</dependency>
```

2. The paged table is divided into two parts. The first one is the `PagedTable` itself and the second is `ControlLayout` that contains buttons and a combo-box for controlling the table:

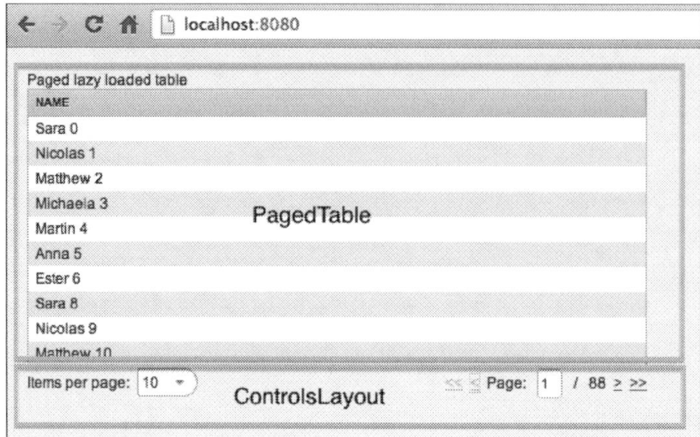

3. Create new UI class with `VerticalLayout` set as the content. Then create the paged table and the corresponding lazy loaded container. We also need to create controls for controlling the table:

```
public class MyVaadinUI extends UI {

    @Override
    protected void init(VaadinRequest request) {
        final VerticalLayout layout = new VerticalLayout();
        layout.setMargin(true);
        setContent(layout);

        PagedTable table = new PagedTable("Paged lazy loaded 
table");
        table.setWidth("500px");

        LazyLoadedContainer container = new 
LazyLoadedContainer(User.class);
        table.setContainerDataSource(container);
        layout.addComponent(table);

        ControlsLayout controls = table.createControls();
        controls.setWidth("500px");
        layout.addComponent(controls);
    }
}
```

4. Now extend `BeanContainer` and create a container that is lazily fetching data from `UserService`.

```
class LazyLoadedContainer extends BeanContainer {

    private UserService userService = new UserService();

    public LazyLoadedContainer(Class type) {
        super(type);
    }

    @Override
    public int size() {
        return userService.size();
    }

    @Override
    public BeanItem getItem(Object itemId) {
        return new BeanItem((User) itemId);
    }

    @Override
    public List getItemIds(int startIndex, int numberOfIds) {
        int endIndex = startIndex + numberOfIds;
        List list = userService.list(startIndex, endIndex);
        return list;
    }
}
```

5. We will put the data-fetching logic into the service class. We will just fake the database and will get the users just from a collection. Note that the `size()` method should return data by using a database `COUNT` operation (and not by calling `size()` on the collection of fetched items):

```
public class UserService {

    private List<User> dbFake = new ArrayList<User>();

    public UserService() {
        for (int i = 0; i < 1000; i++) {
            dbFake.add(new User("Sara " + i++));
            dbFake.add(new User("Nicolas " + i++));
            dbFake.add(new User("Matthew " + i++));
            dbFake.add(new User("Michaela " + i++));
            dbFake.add(new User("Martin " + i++));
            dbFake.add(new User("Anna " + i++));
            dbFake.add(new User("Ester " + i));
        }
```

```
        }

        public int size() {
            return dbFake.size();
        }

        public List<User> list(int startIndex, int endIndex) {
            List<User> users = dbFake.subList(startIndex, endIndex);
            return users;
        }
    }
```

6. The last step is to create the `User` domain class that represents a user that is fetched from a database and displayed in the paged table:

```
public class User {

    private String name;

    // generate constructor, getter and setter for name field
}
```

7. Run the application and try to click on the next page button or change the number of displayed items.

How it works...

The PagedTable add-on strictly separates pages and therefore the paging in the database can be done in a much more efficient way than for a table with scrollbars. We only fetch the rows from the range that is going to be shown.

`ControlsLayout` contains all the control components (buttons, text field, and a combo-box). There are also public getters for these control components and therefore we can change them. For example, we can localize the labels or add our custom icons to the navigation buttons, like so:

```
controlsLayout.getItemsPerPageLabel().setValue("Nr. Of Items:")
controlsLayout.getPageLabel().setValue("Current Page:")
```

See also

In this recipe, we have shown a simplified usage of PagedTable. A more complex example with an in-memory database is available at `https://github.com/ondrej-kvasnovsky/lazy-loaded-paged-table`.

Optimizing Vaadin applications for search engines

Vaadin is a RIA framework that should be used for building business applications (for example, an online accountant application). Vaadin is not meant for building web pages that should be searchable on the Internet.

Search engines can see only what a text browser can see when crawling our web pages. A Vaadin application is actually a JavaScript application that is handling rendering and communication with the server. A full explanation of this problem can be found at `https://developers.google.com/webmasters/ajax-crawling`.

If we want to make our Vaadin application searchable on the Internet, we need to provide an HTML snapshot that could be processed by search engine robots.

We can easily test what is returned to the search engine when we add `_escaped_fragment_` into the URL.

In this recipe, we are going to implement a simple application that will be visible for crawling. There will be two views implemented. The first will be a classic Vaadin application, as shown in the following screenshot:

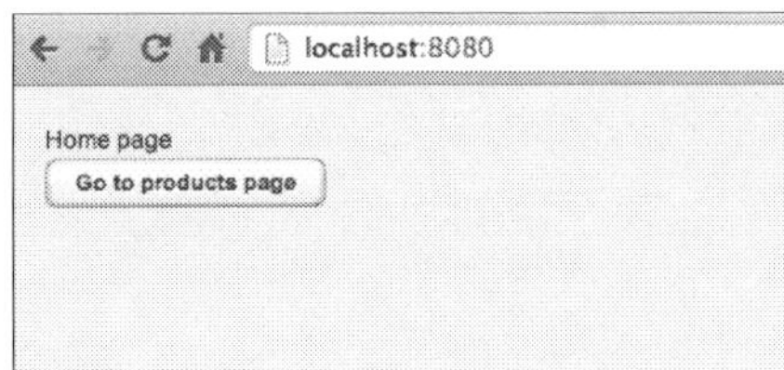

The second view will be an HTML page without any fancy design that will be readable for search engines robots:

We are going to provide an easy recipe on how to achieve that.

Getting ready

Just create a new Vaadin project and follow the steps given.

How to do it...

Perform the following steps:

1. Register a new filter in the `web.xml` file:

```
<filter>
   <filter-name>seo-filter</filter-name>
   <filter-class>com.app.SeoFilter</filter-class>
</filter>
<filter-mapping>
   <filter-name>seo-filter</filter-name>
   <url-pattern>/*</url-pattern>
</filter-mapping>
```

2. Create a new filter named `SeoFilter`. This filter checks whether there is a `_escaped_fragment_` string passed as a parameter. If yes, then it renders a pure HTML page we have prepared. If no, then it forwards filtering to the next filter in the chain.

```
import javax.servlet.*;
import java.io.*;

public class SeoFilter implements Filter {

    @Override
    public void init(FilterConfig filterConfig) throws
ServletException {
    }

    @Override
    public void doFilter(ServletRequest request, ServletResponse
response, FilterChain chain) throws IOException, ServletException
{
        Object searchEngineFlag = request.getParameter("_escaped_
fragment_");
        if (searchEngineFlag != null) {
InputStream in = getClass().getResourceAsStream("index_for_seo.
html");
            ServletOutputStream out = response.getOutputStream();
            byte[] buffer = new byte[1024];
            int len;
```

```
                while ((len = in.read(buffer)) != -1) {
                    out.write(buffer, 0, len);
                }
                in.close();

            } else {
                chain.doFilter(request, response);
            }
        }

        @Override
        public void destroy() {
        }
    }
```

3. Now we create a new HTML file that will be a snapshot of our application and that we show to the search engine robots. Create the `index_for_seo.html` file and save it in the `src/main/resources/com/app` folder:

```
<html>
    <body>
        <h2>My Vaadin application</h2>
        <ul>
            <li><a href="http://localhost:8080/#!home">Home</a></
li>
            <li><a href="http://localhost:8080/#!products">Produc
ts</a></li>
        </ul>
    </body>
</html>
```

4. Next, we create a new UI class where we just set up the navigator. So that the links from the HTML web page work properly:

```
@PreserveOnRefresh
public class MyVaadinUI extends UI {

    @Override
    protected void init(VaadinRequest request) {
        Navigator navigator = new Navigator(this, this);
        navigator.addView("", HomeView.class);
        navigator.addView("home", HomeView.class);
        navigator.addView("products", ProductsView.class);
    }
}
```

5. Now we create the view for the **Home** page and the **Products** page. These two pages are here just to simulate some content on the page and make the example appear more realistic; we can place whatever components we want there.

```
public class HomeView extends VerticalLayout implements View {

    public HomeView() {
        Label lblHome = new Label("Home page");
        addComponent(lblHome);

        Button btnProducts = new Button("Go to products page");
        btnProducts.addClickListener(new Button.ClickListener() {
            @Override
            public void buttonClick(Button.ClickEvent event) {
                UI.getCurrent().getNavigator().
navigateTo("products");
            }
        });
        addComponent(btnProducts);

        setMargin(true);
    }

    @Override
    public void enter(ViewChangeListener.ViewChangeEvent event) {
    }
}

public class ProductsView extends VerticalLayout implements View {

    public ProductsView() {
        Label lblHome = new Label("Products page");
        addComponent(lblHome);

        setMargin(true);
    }

    @Override
    public void enter(ViewChangeListener.ViewChangeEvent event) {
    }
}
```

6. Run the application and try out the two links. The first one is `http://localhost:8080` and second is `http://localhost:8080/?_escaped_fragment_`.

How it works...

`SeoFilter` catches all the requests that contain the `_escaped_fragment_` string. When `_escaped_fragment_` is contained, it writes the content of the HTML file to the response.

When it is a normal request without the `_escaped_fragment_` string, `SeoFilter` redirects the flow to the next filter in the filter chain and the Vaadin application is going to be returned.

There's more...

We should generate HTML for the search engine robots from the database instead of providing a static HTML page. The reason behind this is, that we should always provide up-to-date data to the search engines.

11
Facilitating Development

In this chapter, we will cover:

- Basics of test-driven development in Vaadin
- Basics of mocking in Vaadin
- Testing table with a container
- Testing the UI with TestBench
- Recompiling widgetsets in Maven
- Auto-reloading changes in Maven
- Blocking uncatched exceptions in the production mode

Introduction

This chapter will discuss testing, recompilation of widgetsets, auto-reloading changes on classpath in Maven, and will give a tip on how to handle uncatched exceptions in the production mode.

Simply put, day-to-day coding in Vaadin consists of working in Java source code, recompilation of the source codes, and refreshing the browser so that we can see the result of our work. Let's have a look at each activity separately.

Because Vaadin's application code is written in an object-oriented programming (OOP) language, such as Java, we can easily create cool object structures following OOP principles (basically encapsulation, inheritance, and abstraction).

The most important stuff to keep in mind is to define clear responsibilities for our Vaadin project components. Therefore we keep our application components separated from each other so that they can become easily testable (a component is represented by a class or a set of classes). Doing this, we will be well on our way to making a testable architecture of our application.

Basically, we can, and should, divide the application into small pieces of code that will be easy to test. Then, we can write the unit tests for these small pieces of code.

In this chapter, we will show how to write tests for a login form, how to use the mocking frameworks, and how to test more complicated components such as a Vaadin table with a container.

When we start making unit tests for our Vaadin code, we start exploring the Vaadin architecture and this will become part of our learning path, because we start thinking about the code behind the Vaadin components.

We would like to recommend trying out test-driven development, which should help us with making the better code. Using the test-driven development approach, we first write a unit test for the code we want to implement. Then we implement the code required by the unit and see the result of the unit test, instead of reloading the changes in the browser.

When we write code in a Java-based language, we need to compile this code into byte code, which can be run on a Java Virtual Machine (JVM). Permanent recompilation after every change of the source codes is necessary and time consuming. There are at least two ways to defeat this recompilation. Either use **JRebel**, which makes it possible to instantly see any changes in code without redeploying or configure auto-redeploys for web server, which is what we are going to do in this chapter.

There is no recipe for JRebel in this book, but all the needed information is accessible from `http://zeroturnaround.com/software/jrebel` (note that JRebel is paid for commercial use).

The basics of test-driven development in Vaadin

In this recipe, we will use the **Test-driven Development** (**TDD**) approach. It means we first write tests that fail and then we implement the code, which will be required by the tests. We will explore how we can test Vaadin applications with pure JUnit tests without any mocking frameworks.

We will create a simple login form. The login form will be kept quite simple in this example, so we can easily absorb the idea of developing Vaadin applications with unit tests.

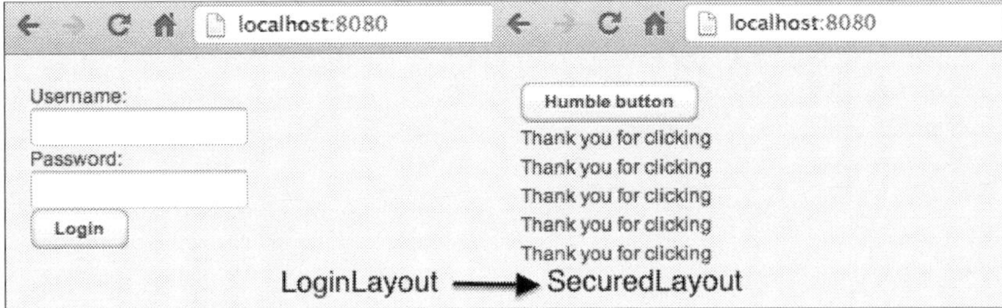

A simple login screen is as follows:

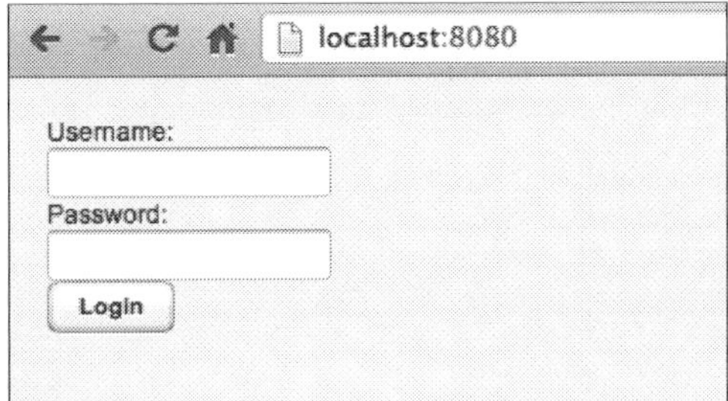

Getting ready

First, we create a new Maven project. Inside the project, create a source folder for tests, as `src/test/java`.

The project structure will be as follows:

Add JUnit dependency into the pom.xml file. The latest version of JUnit is available at https://github.com/junit-team/junit.

```
<dependency>
  <groupId>junit</groupId>
  <artifactId>junit</artifactId>
  <version>4.9</version>
</dependency>
```

How to do it...

Perform the following steps:

1. Create a new test named MyVaadinUITest inside the test folder. We want LoginForm to be set as the content of UI after the init method is called:

```
import com.vaadin.ui.Component;
import org.junit.Assert;
import org.junit.Before;
import org.junit.Test;

public class MyVaadinUITest {

    private MyVaadinUI ui;

    @Before
    public void setUp() {
        ui = new MyVaadinUI();
        ui.init(null);
    }

    @Test
    public void isContentLoginLayout() throws Exception {
        Component content = ui.getContent();
        Assert.assertTrue(content instanceof LoginLayout);
    }
}
```

2. Create LoginLayout, which we are referencing from the test. The good thing on test-driven development is that we usually write only the minimum code needed. So, there shouldn't be any additional and useless code.

```
public class LoginLayout extends VerticalLayout {
}
```

3. Now we need `MyVaadinUI`, which extends Vaadin's `UI` class:

```
public class MyVaadinUI extends UI {

    @Override
    protected void init(VaadinRequest request) {
    }
}
```

4. The code is now compilable and we can run the test. Run the test from the command line by using `mvn test`, or from the IDE as shown in the following screenshot:

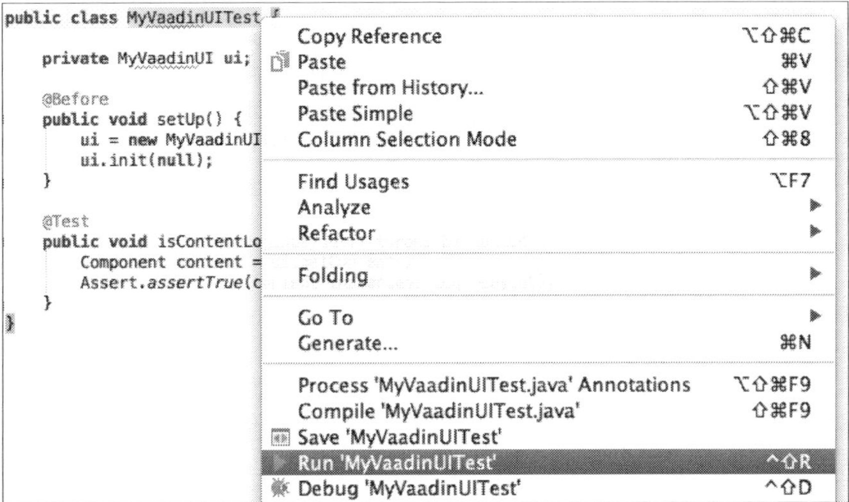

5. We will find that the test fails, with the following error message. That is the proper starting point in a test-driven development.

```
java.lang.AssertionError
  at org.junit.Assert.fail(Assert.java:92)
  at org.junit.Assert.assertTrue(Assert.java:43)
  at org.junit.Assert.assertTrue(Assert.java:54)
  at com.app.MyVaadinUITest.isContentLoginLayout(MyVaadinUITest.
java:21)
```

6. Implement the content of the `init` method that we expect to work:

```
protected void init(VaadinRequest request) {
    LoginLayout loginLayout = new LoginLayout();
    setContent(loginLayout);
}
```

7. Run the test again. The test should end up with success now. If not, go to `MyVaadinUI` and check the code you have implemented in the `init` method.

8. We have created `MyVaadinUI` with `LoginLayout` set as content. Now we can move to the implementation of `LoginLayout`. Let's create test class named `LoginLayoutTest`. We want to implement the following scenario: a user fills in his or her username and password, clicks on the `login` button, and is logged into the application. `LoginLayout` needs to contain a text field for username, a text field for password, and a button to start up the login action. We will create a test only for the `login` button (the remaining tests for the text fields will be similar and therefore we skip them in this recipe).

```
public class LoginLayoutTest {

    private LoginLayout loginLayout;

    @Before
    public void setUp() throws Exception {
        loginLayout = new LoginLayout();
        loginLayout.init();
    }

    @Test
    public void isLoginButtonPresent() {
        Button btnLogin = loginLayout.getBtnLogin();
        int index = loginLayout.getComponentIndex(btnLogin);

        Component component = loginLayout.getComponent(index);
        Assert.assertEquals(btnLogin, component);
    }

    @Test
    public void isLoginWorking() {
        TextField txtUsername = loginLayout.getTxtUsername();
        txtUsername.setValue("myusername");
        TextField txtPassword = loginLayout.getTxtPassword();
        txtPassword.setValue("mypassword");
        Button btnLogin = loginLayout.getBtnLogin();
        btnLogin.click();

        User user = (User) UI.getCurrent().getData();
        Assert.assertNotNull(user);
    }
}
```

9. When we try to run the test, we notice that `UI.getCurrent()` returns `null`. We need to set an instance of `MyVaadinUI` as the current UI, so the test can proceed. We just add the following line into the `setUp()` method, which is called before each test execution:

```
UI.setCurrent(new MyVaadinUI());
```

10. `LoginLayout` needs to access a database in order to get the user's data. We postpone the implementation of the classes that handle database to a later phase of development. We create the `UserService` interface that defines a method for the login and returns an instance of the type `User`. That will be enough for the testing of `LoginLayout`. Also, we create the `User` class, which represents a user of the application:

```
public interface UserService {
    User login(String username, String password);
}
public class User {
}
```

11. The following code shows one of the many ways by which the `LoginLayout` class could be implemented:

```
public class LoginLayout extends VerticalLayout {

  private Button btnLogin = new Button("Login");
  private TextField txtUsername = new TextField("Username:");
  private TextField txtPassword = new TextField("Password:");

  private UserService userService;

  public void init() {
    setMargin(true);
    addComponent(txtUsername);
    addComponent(txtPassword);
    addComponent(btnLogin);
    btnLogin.addClickListener(new Button.ClickListener() {

      @Override
      public void buttonClick(Button.ClickEvent clickEvent) {
        String username = txtUsername.getValue();
        String password = txtPassword.getValue();
        User user = userService.login(username, password);
        UI.getCurrent().setData(user);
      }
    });
  }

  public Button getBtnLogin() {
    return btnLogin;
  }

  public TextField getTxtUsername() {
    return txtUsername;
  }
```

```
    public TextField getTxtPassword() {
      return txtPassword;
    }

    public void setUserService(UserService userService) {
      this.userService = userService;
    }
  }
```

12. We are using `userService` in `LoginLayout`, but it is not set anywhere. We need to fake the service in the unit test. Therefore we add the following code in the `setUp()` method:

```
loginLayout.setUserService(new UserService() {
  @Override
  public User login(String username, String password) {
    return new User();
  }
});
```

13. We can run the tests again. The tests are successful this time around:

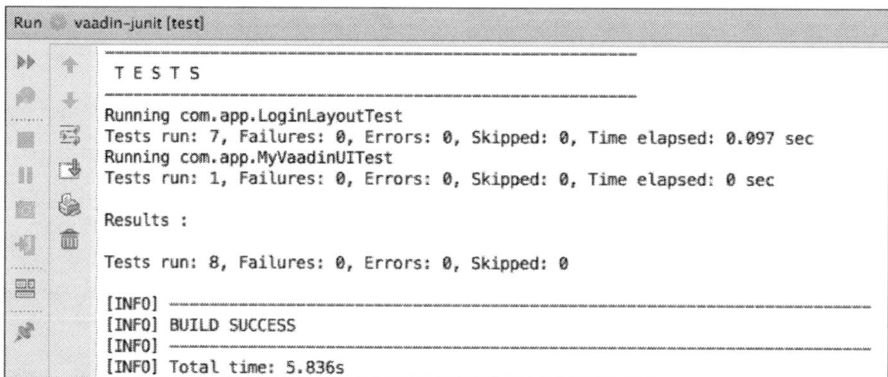

How it works...

Test-driven development offers the other way of doing programming. First we specify what we need by writing a unit test (so we are forced to think about what needs to be implemented in quite a practical way). Then we implement what is required by the test we wrote. After the test is green, we know the work is done.

We faked the application in the unit tests a few times. We don't work with an instance of `VaadinRequest` in the `init` method, so we could pass a `null` value there without any problem:

```
ui.init(null);
```

If we need to work with an instance of `VaadinRequest`, we can make a mock from the `VaadinRequest` interface. Mocking is shown in the next recipe.

We needed to set an instance of `UI` as the current UI, so `UI.getCurrent()` doesn't return `null`. We created a new instance of `MyVaadinUI` and set it as the current UI:

```
UI.setCurrent(new MyVaadinUI());
```

We then defined `UserService` as an interface, which is basically good practice to code against interfaces. It keeps a good level of abstraction between the Vaadin components and the service layer. Creating interfaces also makes it easier to follow test-driven development. In our case, we can easily create a new implementation of `UserService` in the `setUp()` method and return whatever we need:

```
loginLayout.setUserService(new UserService() {
  @Override
  public User login(String username, String password) {
    return new User();
  }
});
```

Notice that we have put all the initialization of the login layout into the `init()` method. We could create a test that makes sure the login layout is initialized after the `init` method from the `MyVaadinUI` class is called. Then we need to call `loginLayout.init()` in the `init` method of the `MyVaadinUI` class.

```
loginLayout.init();
```

The basics of mocking in Vaadin

In this recipe, we will show how to write a test for code which is not designed for easy unit testing. For example, we are forced to use an external class, which contains only a static method returning the status of a system. We just return a plain and hardcoded string "Online" in this example. But the class could, for example, return a status of a system, which is fetched from a web service.

```
public class SystemStatusService {

    public static String getValue() {
        return "Offline";
    }
}
```

We create a horizontal layout on which we place a label that contains a system status we get from the service:

```
public class SystemStatusLayout extends HorizontalLayout {

    private Label lblSystemStatus;

    public SystemStatusLayout() {
        String value = SystemStatusService.getValue();
        lblSystemStatus = new Label(value);
        addComponent(lblSystemStatus);
    }

    public Label getLblSystemStatus() {
        return lblSystemStatus;
    }
}
```

Some developers might say "It is not possible to test it, because we call the external service, which is in the constructor of the `SystemStatusLayout` class and the service is fetching data from the web service via a static method". Another good example of a class which is not easy to test is the data access object that fetches values from a database. We simply need to isolate the classes that communicate with external sources, so the unit test can be run anytime.

There is a way to test the preceding code. We can use some great frameworks, which help us with the mocking of static methods (generally, with mocking of everything). We will use PowerMock together with Mockito (the combination of the PowerMock and Mockito frameworks is called **PowerMockito**).

Getting ready

First, we create a new Maven project and create a new test source folder namely, `src/test/java` inside the project.

Add dependencies to JUnit, PowerMock, and PowerMockito:

```
<dependency>
   <groupId>junit</groupId>
   <artifactId>junit</artifactId>
   <version>4.9</version>
</dependency>
<dependency>
   <groupId>org.powermock</groupId>
   <artifactId>powermock-module-junit4</artifactId>
   <version>1.5</version>
   <scope>test</scope>
```

```
</dependency>
<dependency>
   <groupId>org.powermock</groupId>
   <artifactId>powermock-api-mockito</artifactId>
   <version>1.5</version>
   <scope>test</scope>
</dependency>
```

How to do it...

Perform the following steps:

1. Create a new class named `SystemStatusLayoutTest` in the test source folder:

```
import com.vaadin.ui.Label;
import junit.framework.Assert;
import org.junit.Before;
import org.junit.Test;
import org.junit.runner.RunWith;
import org.mockito.Mockito;
import org.powermock.api.mockito.PowerMockito;
import org.powermock.core.classloader.annotations.PrepareForTest;
import org.powermock.modules.junit4.PowerMockRunner;

@RunWith(PowerMockRunner.class)
@PrepareForTest({SystemStatusService.class})
public class SystemStatusLayoutTest {

  private SystemStatusLayout layout;

  @Before
  public void setUp() throws Exception {
    PowerMockito.mockStatic(SystemStatusService.class);
    Mockito.when(SystemStatusService.getValue()).
thenReturn("Online");

    layout = new SystemStatusLayout();
  }

  @Test
  public void isSystemStatusShown() {
    Label lblSystemStatus = layout.getLblSystemStatus();
    String value = lblSystemStatus.getValue();

    Assert.assertEquals("Online", value);
  }
}
```

2. Run the test and check whether the test has passed:

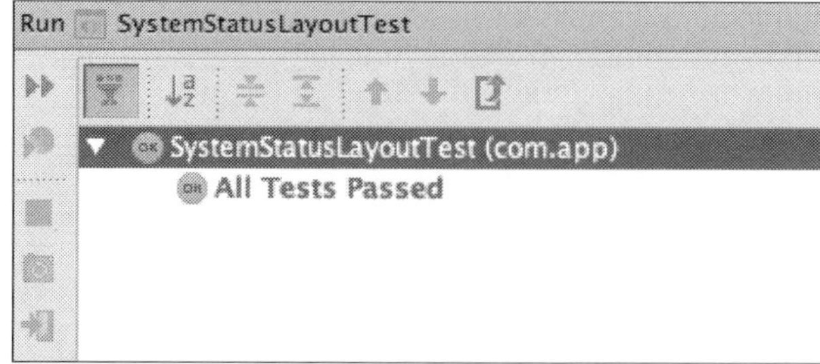

How it works...

We have to do four things in order to mock a static method. First, define the runner for JUnit tests. We need to set `PowerMockRunner` into the `@RunWith` annotation, so that JUnit will use specific runners for running the tests:

```
@RunWith(PowerMockRunner.class)
```

Then, we need to prepare the classes that contain static stuff by passing these classes to the `@PrepareForTest` annotation:

```
@PrepareForTest( { SystemStatusService.class, AnotherStatic.class })
```

The third step is to mock the static class. In case we need to mock only a specific method; we can use the `PowerMockito.spy()` method for this purpose:

```
PowerMockito.mockStatic(SystemStatusService.class);
```

The last step is to define what should be returned when the static `getValue()` method is called:

```
Mockito.when(SystemStatusService.getValue()).thenReturn("Online");
```

See also

There is a lot more to learn about mocking and we really recommend learning materials that can be found on the following links:

- `http://code.google.com/p/mockito`
- `http://code.google.com/p/powermock`
- `http://code.google.com/p/powermock/wiki/MockitoUsage13`

Testing a table with a container

What if we need to test more complicated components? One of the most complex components in Vaadin is the `Table`. Let's see a short example on how to verify that the items are properly shown without starting the Internet browser.

Before we start, let's introduce the code that we are going to test.

The domain model is going to be represented by the `User` class that will be shown in the table.

```
public class User {

    private String name;

    public User(String name) {
        this.name = name;
    }
    // getters and setters
}
```

The `UserService` class simulates a database call just by creating the list of users and returning it back. The content of the `findAll()` method can be replaced by a real database query from a real-world project.

```
public class UserService {

    public List<User> findAll() {
        List<User> res = new ArrayList<User>();
        res.add(new User("Jaromir Jagr"));
        res.add(new User("Wayne Gretzky"));
        res.add(new User("David Vyborny"));
        res.add(new User("Jari Kurri"));
        res.add(new User("Martin Straka"));
        res.add(new User("Patrik Elias"));
        res.add(new User("Sidney Crosby"));
        return res;
    }
}
```

`TableLayout` consists of a table, which shows data from a container. The container is fetching data from `UserService`. In this recipe, we are going to write a test for this class.

```
public class TableLayout extends VerticalLayout {

    private Table table = new Table();
```

```
    private UserService userService = new UserService();

    public void init() {
        BeanItemContainer<User> container = getContainer();
        table.setContainerDataSource(container);

        addComponent(table);
    }

    public Table getTable() {
        return table;
    }

    BeanItemContainer<User> getContainer() {
        BeanItemContainer<User> container = new
          BeanItemContainer<User>(User.class);

        List<User> all = userService.findAll();
        for (User user : all) {
            container.addBean(user);
        }
        return container;
    }

    void setUserService(UserService service) {
        this.userService = service;
    }
}
```

The table will contain names of some great hockey players and it is going to look like the following:

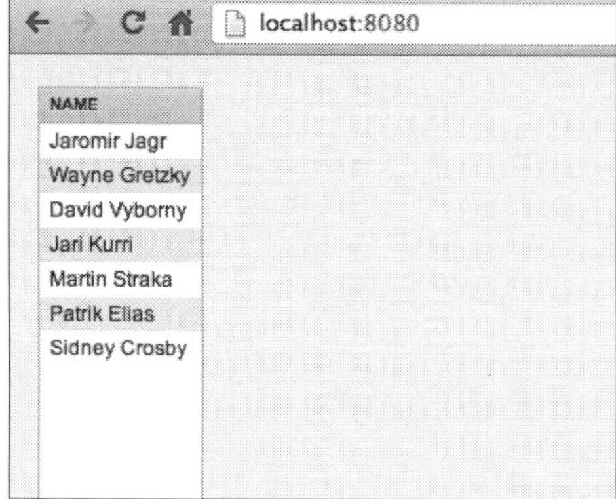

Getting ready

First, we create a new Maven project and create a new test source folder as `src/test/java` inside the project.

We need to add Maven dependencies for JUnit, PowerMock, and PowerMockito in `pom.xml`, as shown here:

```
<dependency>
  <groupId>junit</groupId>
  <artifactId>junit</artifactId>
  <version>4.9</version>
</dependency>
<dependency>
  <groupId>org.powermock</groupId>
  <artifactId>powermock-module-junit4</artifactId>
  <version>1.5</version>
  <scope>test</scope>
</dependency>
<dependency>
  <groupId>org.powermock</groupId>
  <artifactId>powermock-api-mockito</artifactId>
  <version>1.5</version>
  <scope>test</scope>
</dependency>
```

How to do it...

Perform the following steps:

1. Create the `TableLayoutTest` class in the test source folder and implement the `setUp` method where we just create a new instance of `TableLayout`:

```
public class TableLayoutTest {

  private TableLayout tableLayout;

  @Before
  public void setUp() throws Exception {
    tableLayout = new TableLayout();
  }
}
```

2. Create a test method that checks if the table contains items that are fetched from `UserService`:

```
@Test
public void doesTableContainItems() {
    List<User> fakeUsers = new ArrayList<User>();
    User wayneGretzky = new User("Wayne Gretzky");
    fakeUsers.add(wayneGretzky);
    User jaromirJagr = new User("Jaromir Jagr");
    fakeUsers.add(jaromirJagr);
    User sidneyCrosby = new User("Sidney Crosby");
    fakeUsers.add(sidneyCrosby);
    UserService mockedUserService = Mockito.mock(UserService.
class);
    Mockito.when(mockedUserService.findAll()).
thenReturn(fakeUsers);
    tableLayout.setUserService(mockedUserService);

    tableLayout.init();
    Table table = tableLayout.getTable();
    List<User> itemIds = (List<User>) table.getItemIds();

    Assert.assertEquals(3, itemIds.size());
    Assert.assertEquals(wayneGretzky, itemIds.get(0));
    Assert.assertEquals(jaromirJagr, itemIds.get(1));
    Assert.assertEquals(sidneyCrosby, itemIds.get(2));
}
```

3. Run the test and see whether the test has ended up with success. Now we can run the application server and see the table in the browser.

How it works...

In this test, we created a collection of users that will replace the data from the database, which is returned from `UserService`. Then we mocked `UserService`, because we want `UserService` to be independent from any database connection. The last step was to mock the `findAll()` method, so that the method returns the collection of users we have made.

Then we call the `init()` method on the instance of `TableLayout`. The `init()` method creates the container and fetches data from `UserService`.

We have got the items' IDs from the table (which represents data that is going to be shown in the browser) and asserted them against the collection of users.

Testing the UI with TestBench

TestBench is a paid add-on that enables automatic testing of the user interface in the Internet browser.

TestBench uses Selenium and JUnit for the test's execution. We can write TestBench tests manually in JUnit or we can let the TestBench Firefox plugin generate JUnit tests for us.

We will explore the latter method. It means we will install the TestBench plugin into Firefox. Then we run the Vaadin application in the browser, record the test scenario, and export the recorded test scenario to a `.java` JUnit file.

Getting ready

Create a new Maven project from the Vaadin archetype and create a new test source folder named `src/test/java` inside the project.

Download **TestBench** (ZIP file) from `https://vaadin.com/directory#addon/vaadin-testbench`. Unzip the file and open Firefox's **Add-ons** window from the **Tools** menu option:

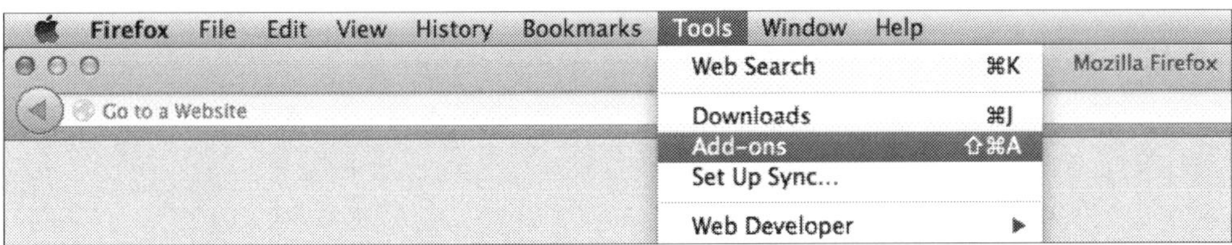

Click on **Install Add-on From File...** and choose a file with a `.xpi` extension from the unzipped folder, for example, `vaadin-testbench-recorder-3.0.4.xpi`.

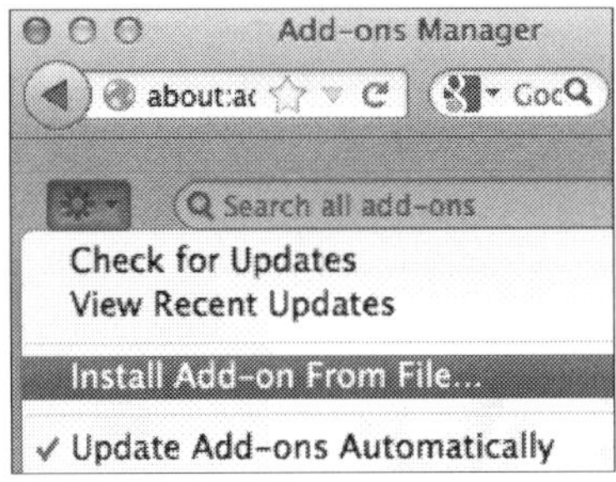

Confirm the add-on installation in order to proceed:

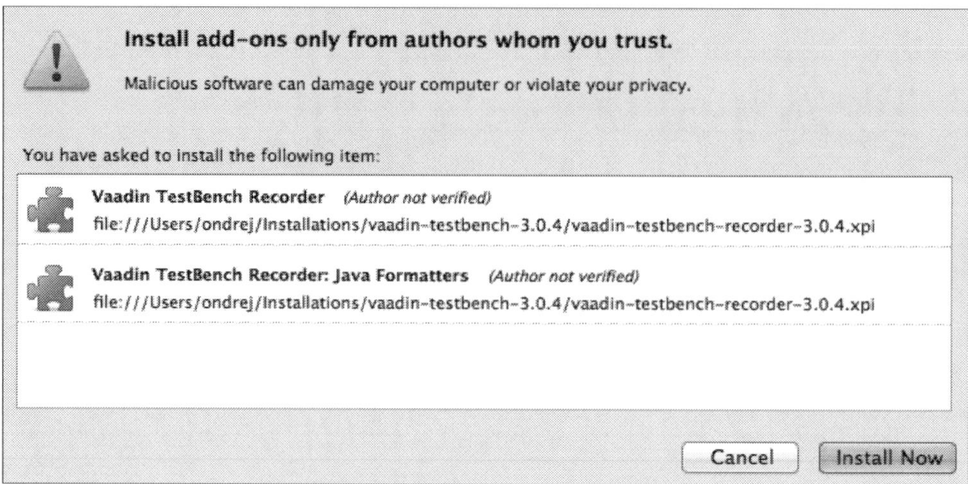

The next thing we need to do is add the TestBench dependency to our project. We can just add the Maven dependency that can be found on the TestBench add-on's page or we can drop JAR files into the `WEB-INF/lib` folder (in case we don't have a Maven project).

Before we start testing, we need a Vaadin application. Here is the code we are going to use in this recipe. It is going to be a really simple calculator.

```
public class MyVaadinUI extends UI {

    HorizontalLayout layout = new HorizontalLayout();
    TextField txtNr1 = new TextField("Number:");
    ComboBox cmbOperand = new ComboBox("Operand:");
    TextField txtNr2 = new TextField("Number:");
    TextField txtResult = new TextField("Result:");
    Button btnCalculate = new Button("Calculate");

    @Override
    protected void init(VaadinRequest request) {
        layout.setMargin(true);
        layout.setSpacing(true);
        setContent(layout);

        txtNr1.setId("txtNr1");
        txtNr1.setImmediate(true);
        layout.addComponent(txtNr1);

        cmbOperand.setId("cmbOperand");
        cmbOperand.addItem("+");
```

```
        cmbOperand.addItem("-");
        cmbOperand.select("+");
        cmbOperand.setNullSelectionAllowed(false);
        layout.addComponent(cmbOperand);

        txtNr2.setId("txtNr2");
        txtNr2.setImmediate(true);
        layout.addComponent(txtNr2);

        txtResult.setId("txtResult");
        txtResult.setImmediate(true);
        layout.addComponent(txtResult);
        layout.setComponentAlignment(txtResult, Alignment.BOTTOM_
RIGHT);

        btnCalculate.setId("btnCalculate");
        btnCalculate.addClickListener(new Button.ClickListener() {
            public void buttonClick(ClickEvent event) {
                System.out.println("User clicked!");

                String nr1 = txtNr1.getValue();
                String operand = cmbOperand.getValue().toString();
                String nr2 = txtNr2.getValue();

                Integer result = 0;

                if ("".equals(nr1) || "".equals(nr2)) {
                    // warn user he has inserted wrong input
                } else {
                    Integer i1 = Integer.valueOf(nr1);
                    Integer i2 = Integer.valueOf(nr2);
                    if ("+".equals(operand)) {
                        result = i1 + i2;
                    } else if ("-".equals(operand)) {
                        result = i1 - i2;
                    }
                }
                txtResult.setValue(result.toString());
            }
        });
        layout.addComponent(btnCalculate);
        layout.setComponentAlignment(btnCalculate, Alignment.BOTTOM_
RIGHT);
    }
}
```

The following screenshot shows the application that we are going to test:

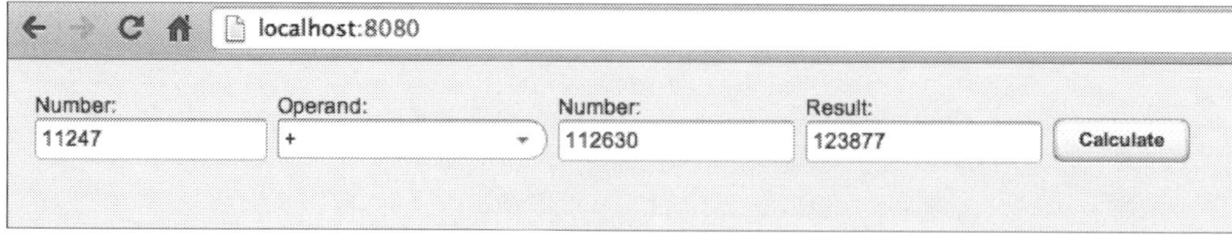

We are now done with the preparation work and can now start the creation of the test.

How to do it...

Perform the following steps:

1. Open the application we want to test in Firefox by using `http://localhost:8080/?restartApplication`. Start **Vaadin TestBench Recorder** from the Firefox menu. When we start the recorder, it automatically starts recording whatever we do in the application.

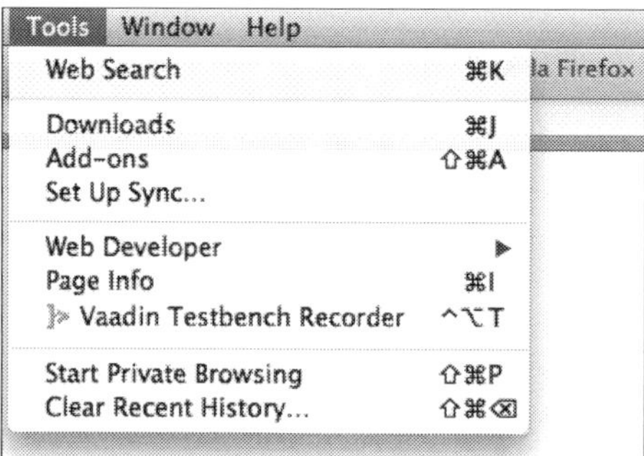

2. Fill in some values inside the text fields and press the **Calculate** button. See how the user's actions are reflected in the recorder. For each action in the application, there is one record that maps what the user has done.
3. The last step is to right-click on the **Result** text field and select the **verifyValue** option that adds a new assert to the test. It tests whether the output value inside **the Result** text field is 25.

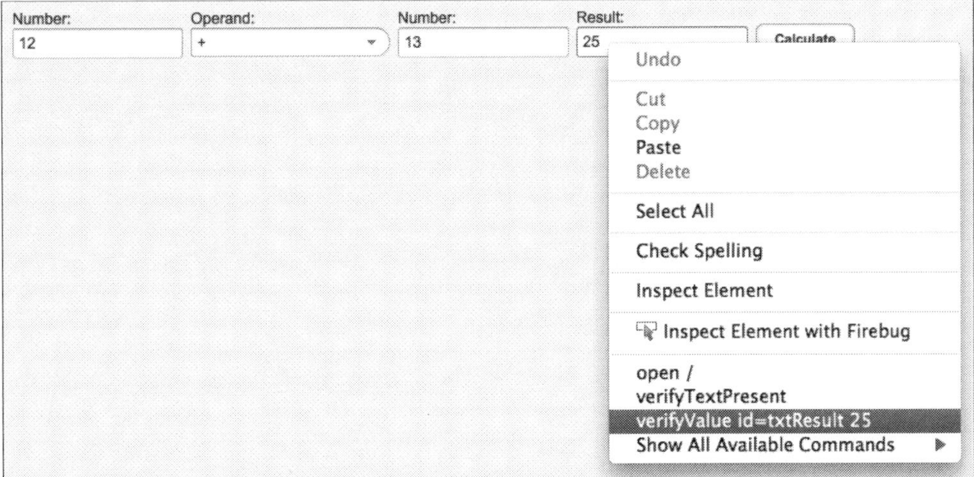

4. After we are done with the test case, we can generate the JUnit test and save it inside the test folder in our project:

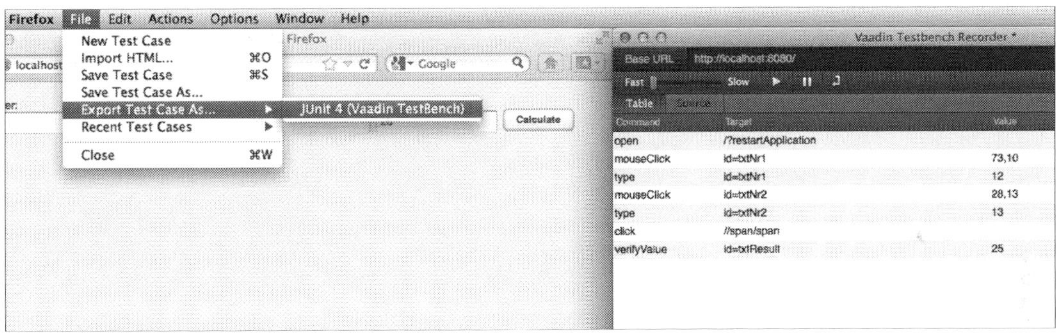

5. Then we need to go to the test and correct the package location. We can change the default name of the package in the TestBench plugin's options. This is how our test will most likely look:

```
@Test
public void testSimplePlus() throws Exception {
  driver.get(concatUrl(baseUrl, "/?restartApplication"));
    testBenchElement(driver.findElement(By.id("txtNr1"))).
click(73,10);
  driver.findElement(By.id("txtNr1")).clear();
  driver.findElement(By.id("txtNr1")).sendKeys("12");
    testBenchElement(driver.findElement(By.id("txtNr2"))).
click(28,13);
  driver.findElement(By.id("txtNr2")).clear();
  driver.findElement(By.id("txtNr2")).sendKeys("13");
```

```
    driver.findElement(By.xpath("//span/span")).click();
    try {
      assertEquals("25", driver.findElement(By.id("txtResult")).
getAttribute("value"));
    } catch (Error e) {
      verificationErrors.append(e.toString());
    }
  }
```

6. Now we can run the test that we have created. We just start the Jetty server and then run the test, for example, from our IDE.

How it works...

TestBench is running JUnit tests and all the testing is done in the browser. That means we can create these tests just in the code without clicking in the browser if we want to.

When we decide to use the generated tests, note that it is recommended to refactor the generated tests, so they are more readable and well prepared for any upcoming changes.

There's more...

We need to install additional drivers in case we need to test in other browsers. These drivers can be downloaded from `http://code.google.com/p/selenium/downloads/list` or `http://code.google.com/p/chromedriver/downloads/list`.

Recompiling widgetsets in Maven

When we add a client-side add-on into our project, we need to recompile the widgetset. In this recipe, we will explore how to recompile widgetsets in the new Maven plugin for Vaadin.

Getting ready

Create a new Vaadin project in Maven.

How to do it...

When we change the client-side components, we just run the following command in the project root where the `pom.xml` file is located. Then the recompilation of the widgetset is started.

```
mvn vaadin:compile
```

In case we want to just update a widgetset after adding an add-on, we run the following Maven target in the command line:

```
mvn vaadin:update-widgetset
```

How it works...

Maven plugin for Vaadin takes care of the widgetset compilation, which makes the widget compilation much easier than it was in Vaadin 6.

Java widget code is compiled to JavaScript during the widgetset's compilation. If you wish to know more about that, then follow the tutorial at `https://developers.google.com/web-toolkit/doc/latest/tutorial/gettingstarted`.

The widgetset compilation result is written under `webapp/VAADIN/widgetsets`. We can speed up widgetset compilation by specifying only certain browsers in the `.gwt.xml` file. If we use Firefox for development, we add there the following line:

```
<set-property name="user.agent" value="gecko1_8"/>
```

There's more...

A list of all the available Maven targets provided by the Vaadin plugin can be found, for example, in IntelliJ IDEA Maven Project window:

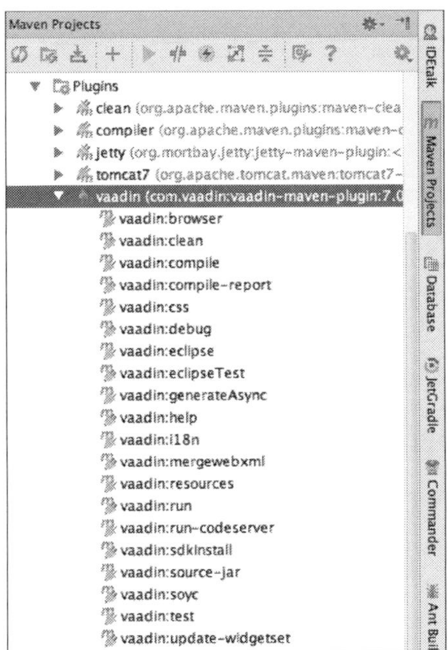

When we create a new Maven project, we need to run the `mvn package` goal that compiles the widgetset for us.

Or we can remove the `AppWidgetSet.gwt.xml` file from the project, together with `init-param` from the `web.xml` file. The default widgetset will be used instead of `AppWidgetSet`:

```
<init-param>
  <description>Application widgetset</description>
  <param-name>widgetset</param-name>
  <param-value>com.app.AppWidgetSet</param-value>
</init-param>
```

If we want to force `mvn package` to run the widgetset compilation, we need to run `mvn vaadin:clean`.

Auto-reloading changes in Maven

We need to do many changes in the code during development and it is really annoying when we have to restart the server after every little change.

We will explore ways of enabling auto-reloading in a Maven project when we use the Jetty web server. Why Jetty? It is because Jetty is lightweight and a quick container that is just perfect for application development.

How to do it...

We add the `scanIntervalSeconds` configuration element that defines the number of seconds after Jetty checks for the changes in the classpath:

```
<plugin>
  <groupId>org.mortbay.jetty</groupId>
  <artifactId>jetty-maven-plugin</artifactId>
  <configuration>
    <scanIntervalSeconds>2</scanIntervalSeconds>
  </configuration>
</plugin>
```

Alternatively, we just define we want to use the Jetty plugin and can set the scan interval in the Maven command when starting up the Jetty web server:

```
mvn -Djetty.reload=automatic -Djetty.scanIntervalSeconds=2 jetty:run
```

How it works...

Scanning for changes in the classpath happens after a specified period (two seconds in our case). That means that Jetty checks whether there was a change in the classpath every two seconds. Therefore, we have to enable auto-recompiling in our IDE or we have to recompile the project when we want to see the changes.

Blocking uncaught exceptions in the production mode

The client's browser is always informed whenever something bad happens on the server and an uncatched exception is thrown.

We can simulate that quite easily. Just create a new application and add the following code there:

```
protected void init(VaadinRequest request) {
   VaadinService service = request.getService();
   DeploymentConfiguration deploymentConfiguration = service.
getDeploymentConfiguration();
   boolean productionMode = deploymentConfiguration.
isProductionMode();
   if (productionMode) {
      ProductionErrorHandler errorHandler = new
ProductionErrorHandler();
      setErrorHandler(errorHandler);
   }

   final VerticalLayout layout = new VerticalLayout();
   layout.setMargin(true);
   setContent(layout);

   Button button = new Button("Throw an error please");
   button.addClickListener(new Button.ClickListener() {
   public void buttonClick(ClickEvent event) {
   layout.addComponent(new Label("Click and bang!"));
      throw new RuntimeException("I am the runtime exception and I
shouldn't be shown to the clients in production.");
     }
  });
  layout.addComponent(button);
}
```

When the user clicks on the button, `RuntimeException` is thrown and the user is informed about that:

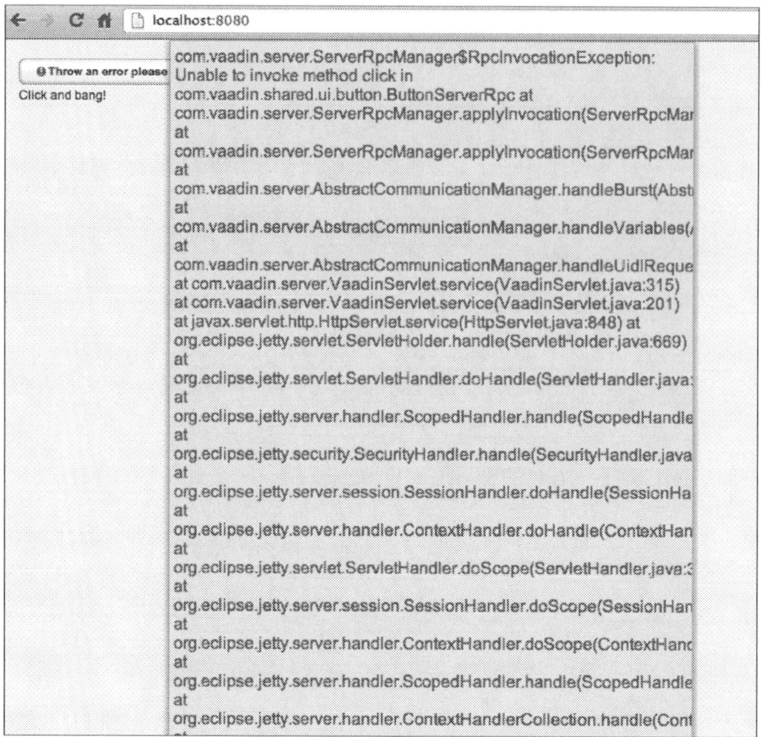

It might be clever to inform users immediately about errors that happened on the server in Internet browser (as shown in the preceding screenshot) while doing development or testing. However, we should handle these errors in the production run. We can log them to a file, if we want, we can send them by e-mails so developers are informed about errors in production, or we can send them to our ticketing system, so the production errors get fixed.

Information about the current production environment must be set in `web.xml` (it is set to `false` by default). We are going to change `productionMode` to `true` in order to simulate the production environment:

```
<context-param>
   <description>Vaadin production mode</description>
   <param-name>productionMode</param-name>
   <param-value>true</param-value>
</context-param>
```

Still the errors are propagated to the browser window. Let's say that we don't want to show these errors to the users. We just want to log them when `productionMode` is set to `true`.

How to do it...

Perform the following steps to do so:

1. Create a new class named `ProductionErrorHandler` that extends `ErrorHandler` from Vaadin:

```
public class ProductionErrorHandler implements ErrorHandler {

  private static final Logger log = Logger.getLogger(ProductionErr
orHandler.class.getName());

  @Override
  public void error(com.vaadin.server.ErrorEvent errorEvent) {
    Throwable throwable = errorEvent.getThrowable();
    log.log(Level.SEVERE, "UI error occurred.", throwable);
  }
}
```

2. Create a new instance of `ProductionErrorHandler` and set it as the error handler for the current UI in the `init` method of our `UI` class:

```
protected void init(VaadinRequest request) {
  VaadinService service = request.getService();
  DeploymentConfiguration deploymentConf = service.
getDeploymentConfiguration();
  boolean productionMode = deploymentConf.isProductionMode();
  if (productionMode) {
    ProductionErrorHandler errorHandler = new
ProductionErrorHandler();
    setErrorHandler(errorHandler);
  }
}
```

3. Now when we click on the button, the error is just logged in the console and nothing is shown to the user:

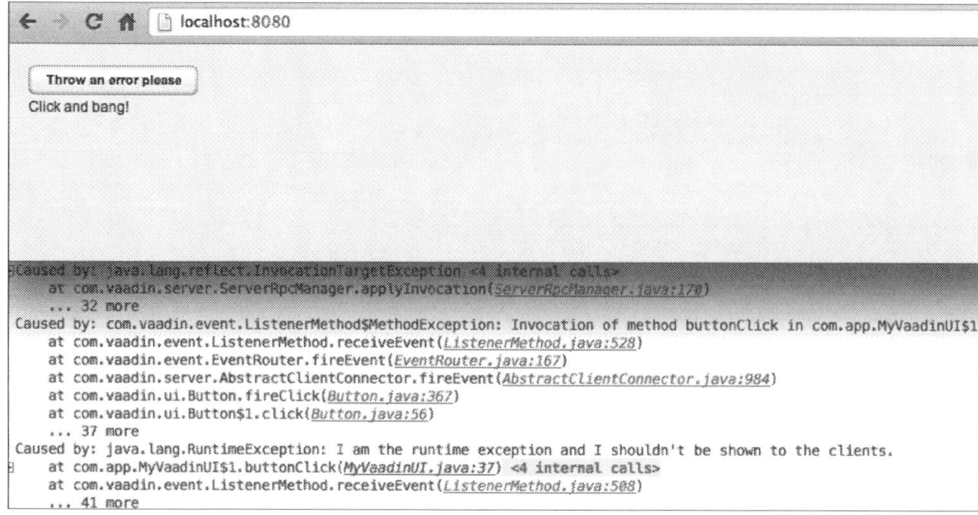

How it works...

Information about the production mode is fetched from `web.xml` (deployment descriptor, which is located in the `webapp/WEB-INF` folder). Information about the production mode is stored in an instance of `DeploymentConfiguration` that is accessible from `VaadinService`, which can be obtained from `VaadinRequest` or `VaadinSession`. Just because we were in the `init` method, we got the reference to the deployment descriptor from `VaadinRequest`.

Then we created a new instance of `ProductionErrorHandler` that we have set to the current instance of our UI class named `MyVaadinUI`. That means we have overridden the default behavior of adding a component error to the components.

12
Fun

In this chapter, we will cover:

- Magic trick
- Can you raed tihs?
- Goodbye, world!

Introduction

This is the last chapter of our book. It is a good opportunity for a little fun. We will describe three fun-oriented recipes. In the first one, we will learn the good old magic card trick and create it as a web application. Next, we will use two text areas to create a nice optical effect with letters inside the words. Finally, we will learn how to alert the user before closing the web page.

Magic tricks

In this recipe, we will describe how to create a magic card trick as a web application. It is called the **Princess Card trick**. American magician Henry Hardin created it in 1905. The Princess Card trick is a well-known mentalist effect.

The effect: A small deck of cards (about five) is shown to a spectator. The spectator remembers one card. Then, the cards are shuffled and again shown. One card disappears! And it's the spectator's thought card.

The trick's explanation: The main essence of the trick is that we replace the original deck of card with a deck of similar cards during the shuffling of cards. Because the user will think of his/her card, he/she will not exactly remember the other cards. However, visually the user will have a feeling that we are still using the same cards.

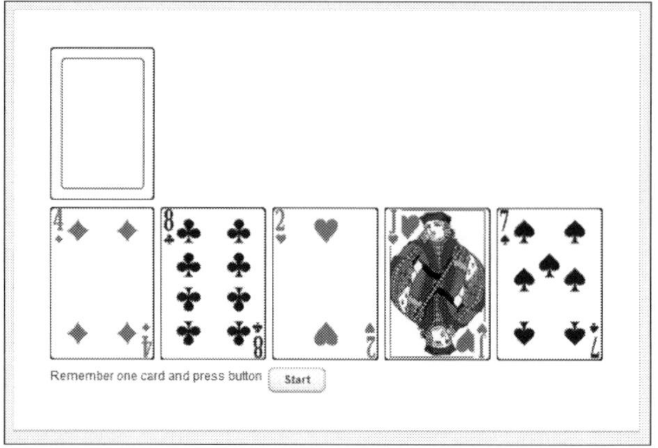

Getting ready

1. Create a Vaadin project with a main UI class named `MagicTrick` as follows:

```
public class MagicTrick extends UI {…}
```

2. We will use two add-ons—**Refresher** (author Henrik Paul) and **PlayingCards** (author Artur Signell). We can download them or add Maven dependencies according to the respective instructions on the following web pages:
   - **Refresher**: `http://vaadin.com/addon/refresher`
   - **PlayingCards**: `http://vaadin.com/addon/playingcards`

3. Then, we recompile the widgetset to include the add-ons' widgets. In the Eclipse IDE, we can do it by pressing *Ctrl* + *6* or by clicking on the button with the **Compile Vaadin widgets** tooltip in the top toolbar.

How to do it...

Perform the following steps to create a magic trick as a web application.

We start with the `MyCard` class as follows:

1. We'll need instances of the `Card` class with the methods `hashCode()` and `equals()`, because we'll work with them in the collections. Therefore, we create our `MyCard` class that extends the `Card` class from the `PlayingCards` add-on.

```
public class MyCard extends Card {…}
```

2. First, we add the `hashCode()` method that returns a hash code value for the `Card` object. This value is computed by the rank and suite of the card.

```
@Override
public int hashCode() {
  final int prime = 31;
  int result = 1;
  result = prime * result + getRank();
  result = prime * result +
      ((getSuite() == null) ? 0 : getSuite().hashCode());
  return result;
}
```

3. Next, we add the `equals()` method that indicates whether some other object is "equal to" this one. It also uses the rank and suite values of the card.

```
@Override
public boolean equals(Object obj) {
  if (this == obj)
    return true;
  if (obj == null)
    return false;
  if (getClass() != obj.getClass())
    return false;
  MyCard other = (MyCard) obj;
  if (getRank() != other.getRank())
    return false;
  if (getSuite() != other.getSuite())
    return false;
  return true;
}
```

Now we create the the `PrincessCardTrick` class as follows:

1. We can begin with the main class `PrincessCardTrick`.

```
public class PrincessCardTrick extends VerticalLayout {…}
```

2. We need some global variables. The `actionNumber` variable defines the number of actions that will be performed after clicking on `nextActionButton`. `Piles` are used as placeholders for cards on the web page. The `deck` object is used to show the collection of cards. It's placed above the line of cards at the top-left corner. The `HelpDeck` object is only used for initializing the original and their corresponding similar cards. In this card trick, we need two lists of cards. The first list consists of random cards. We'll call it `originCards`. The second list consists of similar cards to the original cards. We'll call it `similarCards`. Through the `message` label, we pass the user instructions. The `refresher` object is used for the continuous repainting of the web page.

```
private static final int NUMBER_PILES = 5;
private static final String INITIAL_BUTTON_NAME = "Start";
```

```
private int actionNumber = 0;
private final List<CardPile> piles;
private Deck deck = new Deck();
private List<MyCard> helpDeck;
private List<MyCard> originCards;
private List<MyCard> similarCards;
private Label message = new Label();
private Button nextActionButton =
                  new Button(INITIAL_BUTTON_NAME);
private Refresher refresher = new Refresher();
```

3. In the constructor, we set the `refresher` object's interval in milliseconds. It specifies how often the page is repainted. We need it for animating the cards. Next, we call methods for creating layouts and we initialize decks of cards using the `initCards()` method:

```
public PrincessCardTrick() {
  setMargin(true);
  setSpacing(true);

  refresher.setRefreshInterval(500);
  addExtension(refresher);

  addComponent(deck);

  Layout cardLayout = createCardLayout();
  addComponent(cardLayout);

  piles = createPiles(NUMBER_PILES, cardLayout);
  addComponent(createMessageLayout());

  initCards();
}
```

4. Through the `createCardLayout()` method, we create the layout of the card piles:

```
private Layout createCardLayout() {
  HorizontalLayout cardLayout = new HorizontalLayout();
  cardLayout.setSpacing(true);
  return cardLayout;
}
```

5. Through the `createMessageLayout()` method, we create the layout for the user instructions. It consists of a label and a button. The button is used to call the next set of actions:

```
private Layout createMessageLayout() {
  HorizontalLayout messageLayout = new HorizontalLayout();
  messageLayout.setSpacing(true);
```

```
    messageLayout.setSizeFull();

    nextActionButton.addClickListener(new ClickListener() {

      @Override
      public void buttonClick(ClickEvent event) {
        nextAction();
      }
    });

    messageLayout.addComponent(message);
    messageLayout.addComponent(nextActionButton);
    return messageLayout;
  }
```

6. The `nextAction()` method switches between two actions. The first action creates and runs the thread animation. The second action reinitializes the magic trick.

```
  private void nextAction() {
    actionNumber++;
    switch (actionNumber) {
    case 1:
      message.setValue("Shuffling cards...");
      Thread animation = new Thread(
                 new Animation(originCards, similarCards,
                 piles, deck, message, nextActionButton));
      animation.start();
      nextActionButton.setVisible(false);
      break;
    case 2:
      actionNumber = 0;
      nextActionButton.setCaption(INITIAL_BUTTON_NAME);
      initCards();
      break;
    }
  }
```

7. Through the `createPiles()` method, we create card piles and insert them into the given layout:

```
  private List<CardPile> createPiles(
                               int number, Layout layout) {
    List<CardPile> piles = new ArrayList<CardPile>();
    for (int i = 0; i < number; i++) {
      CardPile pile = new CardPile();
      piles.add(pile);
      layout.addComponent(pile);
```

```
    }
    return piles;
}
```

8. Next, we add a method to initialize the cards. At the beginning, we remove all cards from the piles. Then, we create a new `helpDeck` object and clean the main deck. We prepare two lists—one for each original and similar cards. Original cards are placed into the card piles. We also set the default message text.

```
private void initCards() {
  for (CardPile pile : piles) {
    pile.removeAllCards();
  }
  helpDeck = createHelpDeck();
  cleanDeck(deck);
  originCards = new ArrayList<MyCard>();
  similarCards = new ArrayList<MyCard>();
  for (int i = 0; i < NUMBER_PILES; i++) {
    addOriginAndSimilarCard();
    CardPile pile = piles.get(i);
    pile.addCard(originCards.get(i));
  }
  message.setValue("Remember one card and press
                     button");
}
```

9. Next, we create a method that adds original and similar cards to the appropriate lists. It starts by shuffling `helpDeck`. From this `helpDeck`, we remove the first card and try to find a similar card to this one. If we don't find one (because it was already removed by the previous step), we return the original card back to the `helpDeck` object and call this method again recursively. Therefore, we again shuffle `helpDeck`, remove the first card, and try to find a similar card until we find two similar cards.

```
private void addOriginAndSimilarCard() {
  Collections.shuffle(helpDeck);
  MyCard originCard = helpDeck.remove(0);
  MyCard similarCard = findSimilarCard(originCard);
  if (helpDeck.remove(similarCard)) {
    originCards.add(originCard);
    similarCards.add(similarCard);
  } else {
    helpDeck.add(originCard);
    addOriginAndSimilarCard();
  }
}
```

10. Now we add the key method of this magic trick. It's called `findSimilarCard()`. By the list of similar cards, we create an illusion that we still work with the same original cards, but the user's card isn't there. The similar card has the same color but belongs to a different type of suite. For example, if our card is the hearts, a similar card will be diamonds. We also reduce the rank of the card. Because we cannot reduce rank of the ace, we raise it to the value two. And because we are looking for the similar card we can't reduce rank of Jack to value ten. The Jack and the Ten cards are visually different. So we raise it to the King.

```
private MyCard findSimilarCard(Card originCard) {
  Suite suite = originCard.getSuite();
  Suite similarSuite = null;
  switch (suite) {
  case HEARTS:
    similarSuite = Suite.DIAMONDS;
    break;
  case DIAMONDS:
    similarSuite = Suite.HEARTS;
    break;
  case CLUBS:
    similarSuite = Suite.SPADES;
    break;
  case SPADES:
    similarSuite = Suite.CLUBS;
    break;
  }
  int rank = originCard.getRank() - 1;
  if (rank < 0) {
    rank = 2;
  }
  if (rank == 10) {
    rank = 13;
  }
  return new MyCard(similarSuite, rank);
}
```

11. Next, we add a method to create the help deck. The `HelpDeck` object has a list of 52 `MyCard` objects.

```
private List<MyCard> createHelpDeck() {
  List<MyCard> cards = new ArrayList<MyCard>();
  for (Suite suite : Suite.values()) {
    for (int i = 1; i <= 13; i++) {
      MyCard card = new MyCard(suite, i);
      cards.add(card);
    }
```

```
    }
    return cards;
  }
```

12. We also need a method that cleans the deck of cards:

```
private void cleanDeck(Deck deck) {
  int size = deck.size();
  for (int i = 0; i < size; i++) {
    deck.removeTopCard();
  }
}
```

Now we create the `Animation` class as follows:

1. We create a class that handles animations. It will run in a separate thread, so we have to implement the `Runnable` interface:

   ```
   public class Animation implements Runnable {…}
   ```

2. First, we need some global variables—a list of the original and their similar cards, a list of piles for cards, and a list of numbers used for the random collection and deployment of cards to the piles. We also need a reference to the `message` label and the `nextActionButton` object. In the `ui` object we'll keep a reference to the current UI. We'll need it to get the lock of the main UI thread. When the UI is updated from a background thread, we have to lock the application appropriately by using the session lock. The delay between the steps of animation is set to `500` milliseconds.

   ```
   private List<MyCard> originCards;
   private List<MyCard> similarCards;
   private List<Integer> numbers = new ArrayList<Integer>();
   private List<CardPile> piles;
   private Deck deck;
   private Label message;
   private Button nextActionButton;
   private UI ui;
   private static final long DELAY = 500;
   ```

3. In the constructor, we pass references of objects and prepare the list of numbers:

   ```
   public Animation(
               List<MyCard> originCards,
               List<MyCard> similarCards,
               List<CardPile> piles,
               Deck deck, Label message,
               Button nextActionButton) {
     this.originCards = originCards;
     this.similarCards = similarCards;
     this.piles = piles;
   ```

```
    this.deck = deck;
    this.message = message;
    this.nextActionButton = nextActionButton;
    prepareNumbers();
  }
```

4. Next, we add the `run()` method. This method is called by the `animation.start()` method in the `PrincessCardTrick` class. Here we do some animation actions. We inform the user that the cards are shuffled. We randomly turn the entire cards backside up. Then we randomly collect all cards and put them on the deck. In the next step, we deploy similar cards on the piles. Then one random card disappears and all other cards are turned front side up. As we mentioned just now, during an update of the components the main UI is locked.

```
  public void run() {
    turnOriginCardsBacksideUp();
    collectOriginCards();
    deploySimilarCards();
    disappearOneCard();
    turnSimilarCardsFrontsideUp();

    ui.getSession().getLockInstance().lock();
    nextActionButton.setCaption("Play again");
    nextActionButton.setVisible(true);
    ui.getSession().getLockInstance().unlock();
  }
```

5. Now we add the first animation action. This action turns the original cards backside up on the piles. Here we use the numbers list. It is a collection of integer numbers. By shuffling this collection, we get a list of non-repeating random numbers in a given range. After each turn of a card, we put the thread to sleep for a few milliseconds (and again during an update of the components, the main UI is locked).

```
  private void turnOriginCardsBacksideUp() {
    Collections.shuffle(numbers);
    for (Integer number : numbers) {
      ui.getSession().getLockInstance().lock();
      originCards.get(number).setBacksideUp(true);
      piles.get(number).requestRepaint();
      ui.getSession().getLockInstance().unlock();
      sleep(DELAY);
    }
    sleep(DELAY);
  }
```

6. The next animation action collects all the original cards in one deck. All cards from the piles are removed and added to the deck:

```
private void collectOriginCards() {
  Collections.shuffle(numbers);
  for (Integer number : numbers) {
    ui.getSession().getLockInstance().lock();
    Card card = piles.get(number).removeTopCard();
    deck.addCard(card);
    ui.getSession().getLockInstance().unlock();
    sleep(DELAY);
  }
  sleep(DELAY);
}
```

7. In the next animation, we switch from the list of original cards to the list of similar cards. We deploy them backside up on the piles.

```
private void deploySimilarCards() {
  Collections.shuffle(similarCards);
  for (Integer number : numbers) {
    ui.getSession().getLockInstance().lock();
    deck.removeTopCard();
    Card card = similarCards.get(number);
    card.setBacksideUp(true);
    piles.get(number).addCard(card);
    piles.get(number).requestRepaint();
    ui.getSession().getLockInstance().unlock();
    sleep(DELAY);
  }
}
```

8. Through the `disappearOneCard()` method, we choose one random pile and remove one card from this pile:

```
private void disappearOneCard() {
  sleep(DELAY * 8);
  ui.getSession().getLockInstance().lock();
  message.setValue("Your thought of card DISAPPEARS!");
  Collections.shuffle(numbers);
  piles.get(numbers.get(0)).removeTopCard();
  ui.getSession().getLockInstance().unlock();
  sleep(DELAY * 8);
}
```

9. In the last animation, we turn the rest of the cards front side up on the piles:

   ```
   private void turnSimilarCardsFrontsideUp() {
     for (int i = 0; i < piles.size(); i++) {
       ui.getSession().getLockInstance().lock();
       similarCards.get(i).setBacksideUp(false);
       piles.get(i).requestRepaint();
       ui.getSession().getLockInstance().lock();
       sleep(DELAY);
     }
   }
   ```

10. At the end, we add two helper methods. The first one prepares the list of numbers. This list is used by other methods to get non-repeating random numbers in a given range (from `0` to the number of piles).

    ```
    private void prepareNumbers() {
      for (int i = 0; i < piles.size(); i++) {
        numbers.add(i);
      }
    }
    ```

11. A second helper method causes the currently executing thread to sleep for a specified number of milliseconds:

    ```
    private void sleep(long millis) {
      try {
        Thread.sleep(millis);
      } catch (InterruptedException e) {
        e.printStackTrace();
      }
    }
    ```

12. That's all. Now we can use our created `PrincesCardTrick` class in the main UI `MagicTrick` class:

    ```
    public class MagicTrick extends UI {

      @Override
      protected void init(VaadinRequest request) {
        setContent(new PrincessCardTrick());
      }

    }
    ```

We can now run the server and open our application in the web browser.

How it works...

In this recipe, we used the Refresher add-on. How to work with this add-on is described in *Chapter 5, Events* in the *Updating the noticeboard using the Refresher add-on* recipe.

Using threads per user in a web application should be normally avoided. This is just a demonstration of a simple animated web application. When we want to use animation in the production system, we can use, for example, the **Animator** add-on (`http://vaadin.com/addon/animator`), which can animate any component, even sub-windows with a small set of usable animations. Or we can create our own client-side animation. The creation of client-side widgets is described in *Chapter 4, Custom Widgets*.

See also

Add-ons used in this recipe:

- Refresher, created by Henrik Paul: `http://vaadin.com/addon/refresher`
- PlayingCards, created by Artur Signell: `http://vaadin.com/addon/playingcards`

Vaadin help:

- Using directory: `http://vaadin.com/directory/help/using-vaadin-add-ons/`
- Using add-ons: `http://vaadin.com/directory/help/using-vaadin-add-ons/`

Can you raed tihs?

It's quite common between friends and colleagues to send some funny e-mails. For example, like this:

"Aoccdrnig to a rscheearch at Cmabrigde Uinervtisy, it deosn't mttaer in waht oredr the ltteers in a wrod are, the olny iprmoatnt tihng is taht the frist and lsat ltteers be at the rghit pclae. The rset can be a toatl mses and you can sitll raed it wouthit porbelm. Tihs is bcuseae the huamn mnid deos not raed ervey lteter by istlef, but the wrod as a wlohe."

In this recipe, we will create an application that transforms text according to the mentioned rules. Then, we can also send a similar e-mail to our friends with our text ☺.

How to do it...

Perform the following steps to create two editors that will transform the text:

1. Create a Vaadin project with a main UI class named `Demo`:

```
public class Demo extends UI {…}
```

2. We create a class named `ReadIt` that is based on `HorizontalLlayout`:

```
public class ReadIt extends HorizontalLayout {…}
```

3. We will use two text areas. The first one is for the editor. Here, the user inserts the original text. The second area is for the viewer. Here, the user gets the transformed text. The size of these areas is defined by width and height constants. We also add a constant for minimal word length. Words with less than `4` characters don't need to be transformed.

```
private TextArea editor;
private TextArea viewer;
private static final int WIDTH = 400;
private static final int HEIGHT = 200;
private static final int MIN_WORD_LENGTH = 4;
```

4. In the constructor, we create and add editor and viewer components to the main horizontal layout:

```
public ReadIt() {
  setMargin(true);
  setSpacing(true);
  editor = createEditor();
  viewer = createViewer();
  addComponent(editor);
  addComponent(viewer);
}
```

5. The editor area is created through a separate method. Here we set the name, size, and the text change listener. We add this listener because we want to transform the original text immediately after each change in the editor area.

```
private TextArea createEditor() {
  TextArea editor = new TextArea("Original");
  editor.setWidth(WIDTH, Unit.PIXELS);
  editor.setHeight(HEIGHT, Unit.PIXELS);
  editor.setImmediate(true);
    editor.setTextChangeEventMode(
                             TextChangeEventMode.EAGER);
  editor.addTextChangeListener(new TextChangeListener() {
    @Override
    public void textChange(TextChangeEvent event) {
      viewer.setValue(transformText(event.getText()));
    }
  });
  return editor;
}
```

6. The viewer is a simple text area with a set name and size properties:

```
private TextArea createViewer() {
  TextArea view = new TextArea("Transformed");
  view.setWidth(WIDTH, Unit.PIXELS);
  view.setHeight(HEIGHT, Unit.PIXELS);
  return view;
}
```

7. Now we add a method that transforms the original text to text with shuffled inner characters. First, we get an array of words by splitting the input text. If the length of the word is less than the minimal word length or all inner characters are the same, then the resulting word will be the same as the input word. Otherwise, we transform this word by shuffling the inner characters:

```
private String transformText(String text) {
  String result = "";
  String words[] = text.split(" ");
  for (String word : words) {
    if (word.length() < MIN_WORD_LENGTH
                          || areAllInnerCharsSame(word)) {
      result += word + " ";
    } else {
      result += shuffleChars(word) + " ";
    }
  }
  return result;
}
```

8. Next, we add a method that shuffles inner characters of the word. It ignores the first and the last character. Inner characters are moved into the list, shuffled in this list, and then joined to the result world. At the end, we check if the word was shuffled. If not, then the `shuffleChars()` method is again called recursively:

```
private String shuffleChars(String word) {
  String result = "";
  result += word.charAt(0);
  List<Character> characters = new ArrayList<>();
  for (int i = 1; i < word.length() - 1; i++) {
    characters.add(word.charAt(i));
  }
  Collections.shuffle(characters);

for (char character : characters) {
    result += character;
  }

  result += word.charAt(word.length() - 1);
  if (word.equals(result)) {
    result = shuffleChars(word);
  }
  return result;
}
```

9. At the end, we add a helper method that checks whether all inner characters are the same:

```
private boolean areAllInnerCharsSame(String word) {
  Character firstChar = word.charAt(1);
  for (int i = 2; i < word.length() - 1; i++) {
    if (!firstChar.equals(word.charAt(i))) {
      return false;
    }
  }
  return true;
}
```

10. That's all, now we can use our created `ReadIt` class in the main UI `Demo` class:

```
public class Demo extends UI {

  @Override
  public void init(VaadinRequest request) {
    setContent(new ReadIt());
  }
}
```

We can now run the server and open our application in the web browser.

How it works...

The system of reading text with shuffled letters inside the word is described in the introduction. From Vaadin's components, we used only the text area. How to work with events in the text area is described in *Chapter 5, Events* in the *Responding immediately on an event in TextArea* recipe.

See also

This recipe is inspired by an article in `FoxNews.com` named *If You Can Raed Tihs, You Msut Be Raelly Smrat*. See the article yourself at `http://www.foxnews.com/story/0,2933,511177,00.html`.

Goodbye, world!

Ok, it's time to say Goodbye. This is the last recipe of our book. In every book that describes some new software technology, we can find the famous "Hello, world!" example. But there is never a "Goodbye, world!" program. That's the reason why we have added one such recipe ☺. We will see how to handle the closing application. Sometimes users close the application before saving some important settings. In that case, we can alert users to stay on the page. We'll do it by using native JavaScript code, which will be added as a component to the Vaadin application.

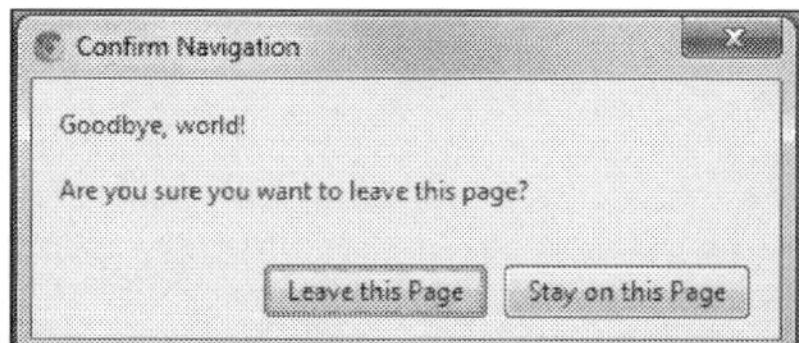

How to do it...

Perform the following steps to add a JavaScript component to the Vaadin application that will be called before closing the web page:

1. Create a Vaadin project with a main UI class called `Demo`:

   ```
   public class Demo extends UI {…}
   ```

2. We create a class named `GoodbyeWorld`. This class is based on the `AbstractJavaScriptComponent` class. By the `@JavaScript` annotation, we define which JavaScript file will be loaded with our annotated class:

   ```
   @JavaScript({ "goodbye_world.js" })
   public class GoodbyeWorld extends AbstractJavaScriptComponent  {…}
   ```

3. Next, we create a JavaScript file named `goodbye_world.js`. We place this file in the same path as the `GoodbyeWorld` class. JavaScript contains a function that will be called before a page unload.

```
com_packtpub_vaadin_close_GoodbyeWorld = function() {
  window.onbeforeunload = function() {
    return ('Goodbye, world!');
  };
};
```

4. That's all. We can add the `GoodbyeWorld` class to the main UI `Demo` class. Because our created class is empty, we can add some label on the page to identify our page.

```
public class Demo extends UI {

  @Override
  public void init(VaadinRequest request) {
    VerticalLayout layout = new VerticalLayout();
    setContent(layout);
      layout.addComponent(new Label("Vaadin application"));
    layout.addComponent(new GoodbyeWorld());
  }

}
```

We run the server and open our application in the web browser. To test our functionality we close the page. We will see the pop-up confirmation dialog.

How it works...

As described in the Vaadin API documentation, `AbstractJavaScriptComponent` is a base abstract class for `Components` with all the client-side logic implemented using JavaScript. When a new JavaScript component is initialized in the browser, the framework will look for a globally defined JavaScript function that will initialize the component. The name of the initialization function is formed by replacing it with the name of the server-side class. If no such function is defined, each super class is used in turn until a match is found.

JavaScript's `onbeforeunload` event cannot be cancelled, because of security reasons, but if an event handler function for the `onbeforeunload` event returns a string value, this text will be shown in a confirmation dialog box, where the user can confirm whether to stay on or leave the current page.

See also

More information about the `AbstractJavaScriptComponent` class can be found in the *Vaadin 7 Loves JavaScript Components* article at `https://vaadin.com/blog/-/blogs/vaadin-7-loves-javascript-components`.

API of `AbstractJavaScriptComponent` can be found at `https://vaadin.com/api/com/vaadin/ui/AbstractJavaScriptComponent.html`.

JavaScript's `onbeforeunload` event is described, for example, on the Dottoro web page at `http://help.dottoro.com/ljhtbtum.php`.

Index

E

F

G

H

I

J

L

M

V

W

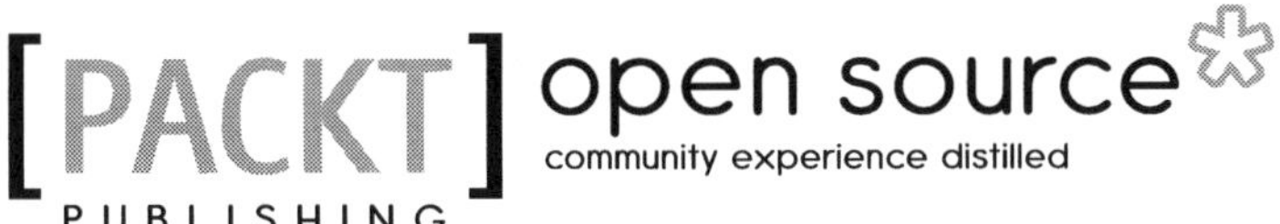

Thank you for buying
Vaadin 7 Cookbook

About Packt Publishing

Packt, pronounced 'packed', published its first book "*Mastering phpMyAdmin for Effective MySQL Management*" in April 2004 and subsequently continued to specialize in publishing highly focused books on specific technologies and solutions.

Our books and publications share the experiences of your fellow IT professionals in adapting and customizing today's systems, applications, and frameworks. Our solution based books give you the knowledge and power to customize the software and technologies you're using to get the job done. Packt books are more specific and less general than the IT books you have seen in the past. Our unique business model allows us to bring you more focused information, giving you more of what you need to know, and less of what you don't.

Packt is a modern, yet unique publishing company, which focuses on producing quality, cutting-edge books for communities of developers, administrators, and newbies alike. For more information, please visit our website: `www.packtpub.com`.

About Packt Open Source

In 2010, Packt launched two new brands, Packt Open Source and Packt Enterprise, in order to continue its focus on specialization. This book is part of the Packt Open Source brand, home to books published on software built around Open Source licences, and offering information to anybody from advanced developers to budding web designers. The Open Source brand also runs Packt's Open Source Royalty Scheme, by which Packt gives a royalty to each Open Source project about whose software a book is sold.

Writing for Packt

We welcome all inquiries from people who are interested in authoring. Book proposals should be sent to author@packtpub.com. If your book idea is still at an early stage and you would like to discuss it first before writing a formal book proposal, contact us; one of our commissioning editors will get in touch with you.

We're not just looking for published authors; if you have strong technical skills but no writing experience, our experienced editors can help you develop a writing career, or simply get some additional reward for your expertise.

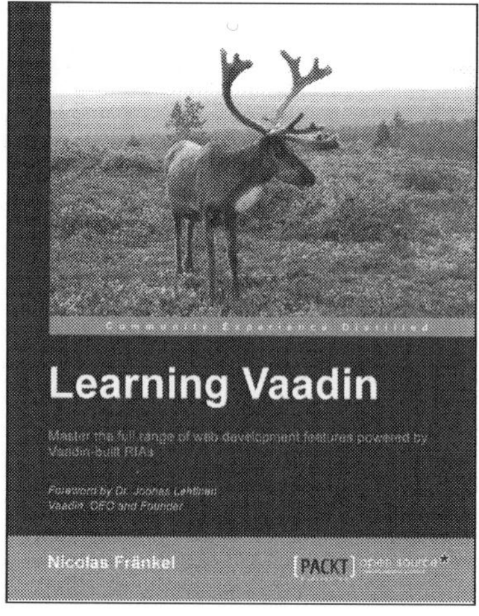

Learning Vaadin

ISBN: 978-1-849515-22-1 Paperback: 412 pages

Master the full range of web development features powered by Vaadin-built RIAs

1. Discover the Vaadin framework in a progressive and structured way
2. Learn about components, events, layouts, containers, and bindings
3. Create outstanding new components by yourself
4. Integrate with your existing frameworks and infrastructure
5. Pragmatic and no-nonsense approach

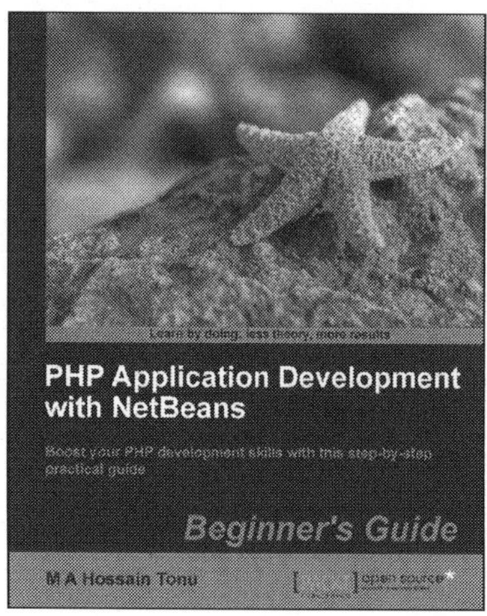

PHP Application Development with NetBeans: Beginner's Guide

ISBN: 978-1-849515-80-1 Paperback: 302 pages

Boost your PHP development skills with this step-by-step practical guide

1. Clear step-by-step instructions with lots of practical examples
2. Develop cutting-edge PHP applications like never before with the help of this popular IDE, through quick and simple techniques
3. Experience exciting features of PHP application development with real-life PHP projects

Please check **www.PacktPub.com** for information on our titles

Liferay Portal Systems Development

ISBN: 978-1-849515-98-6 Paperback: 546 pages

Build dynamic, content-rich, and social systems on top of Liferay

1. Use Liferay tools (CMS, WCM, collaborative API and social API) to create your own Web sites and WAP sites with hands-on examples
2. Customize Liferay portal using JSR-286 portlets, hooks, themes, layout templates, webs plugins, and diverse portlet bridges
3. Build your own websites with kernel features such as indexing, workflow, staging, scheduling, messaging, polling, tracking, auditing, reporting and more

---

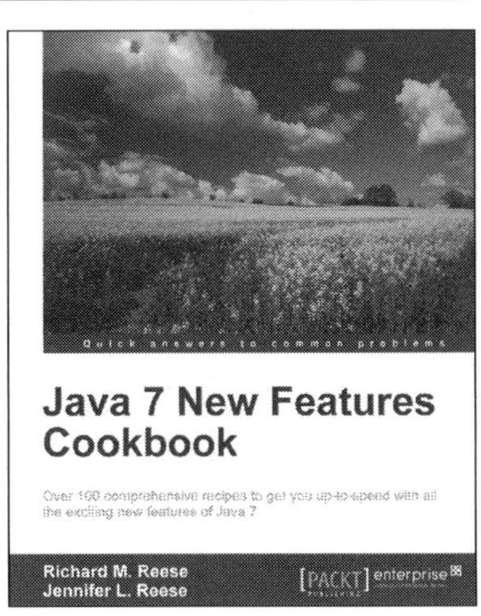

Java 7 New Features Cookbook

ISBN: 978-1-849685-62-7 Paperback: 384 pages

Over 100 comprehensive recipes to get you up-to-speed with all the exciting new features of Java 7

1. Comprehensive coverage of the new features of Java 7 organized around easy-to-follow recipes
2. Covers exciting features such as the try-with-resources block, the monitoring of directory events, asynchronous IO and new GUI enhancements, and more
3. A learn-by-example based approach that focuses on key concepts to provide the foundation to solve real world problems

Please check **www.PacktPub.com** for information on our titles

Printed in Germany
by Amazon Distribution
GmbH, Leipzig